Making Sense of American Liberalism

Making Sense of American Liberalism

Edited by
JONATHAN BELL
AND TIMOTHY STANLEY

UNIVERSITY OF ILLINOIS PRESS
Urbana, Chicago, and Springfield

First Illinois paperback, 2014
© 2012 by the Board of Trustees
of the University of Illinois
All rights reserved
Manufactured in the United States of America
1 2 3 4 5 C P 5 4 3 2 1
∞ This book is printed on acid-free paper.

The Library of Congress cataloged the cloth edition as follows:
Making sense of American liberalism / edited by Jonathan Bell
and Timothy Stanley.
p. cm.
Includes bibliographical references and index.
ISBN 978-0-252-03686-6 (hardback : alk. paper)
1. Liberalism—United States.
I. Bell, Jonathan, 1976– II. Stanley, Timothy.
JC574.2.U6M24   2012
320.51'30973—dc23   2011039814

PAPERBACK ISBN 978-0-252-08000-5

Contents

Introduction 1
Timothy Stanley and Jonathan Bell

Part I: Liberals and the Left

1. Partners for Progress? Liberals and Radicals in the Long Twentieth Century 17
   Doug Rossinow

2. From Popular Front to Liberalism: Redefining the Political in California in the Post–World War II Era 38
   Jonathan Bell

3. Going Beyond the New Deal: Socialists and the Democratic Party in the 1970s 62
   Timothy Stanley

4. From Friends to Foes: George McGovern, Hubert Humphrey, and the Fracture in American Liberalism 90
   Bruce Miroff

Part II: Liberals and Urban Policy

5. New York Liberalism and the Fight against Homelessness 113
   Ella Howard

6. Liberalism in the Postwar City: Public and Private Power in Urban Renewal   135
   Lizabeth Cohen

Part III: Coalitions

7. Albert Gore Sr., Liberalism and the South in the 1960s   159
   Tony Badger

8. Forgotten Architects of the Second Reconstruction: Republicans and Civil Rights, 1945–1972   181
   Timothy N. Thurber

9. Liberal Feminism and the Reshaping of the New Deal Order   202
   Susan M. Hartmann

10. Labor, Liberalism, and the Democratic Party: A Fruitful but Vexed Alliance   229
    Nelson Lichtenstein

    Contributors   249

    Index   253

Making Sense of
American Liberalism

Introduction

TIMOTHY STANLEY AND JONATHAN BELL

At the beginning of the twenty-first century, the future of American liberalism is uncertain. Liberals and their allies in social reform have much to celebrate, but plenty of challenges ahead. The difficult choices faced by the Obama administration are representative. On the one hand, the election of an African American president on a platform of activist government and health care reform was a stunning achievement. It fulfilled the promise of the civil rights revolution, while putting together an alliance of ethnic minorities, liberals, youth, labor, women, and the urban poor that promised a revival of the New Deal coalition. On the other hand, President Obama and the Democratic congress faced immediate and serious opposition from a revived conservative movement, big business, and the right-wing media. Many saw the credit crunch as an opportunity for social reform, but ballooning deficits reduced its appeal to Middle America. Nor did the Democratic majority always hold up under the weight of its own contradictions. Opportunities were missed and squandered by bad prioritizing and internal strife. There is a widespread feeling that, at the moment of their greatest opportunity since 1964, liberals might have blown it.

This book considers the challenges, setbacks, and accomplishments of American liberal reformers in the twentieth century. Covering themes such as gender, class, labor, race, urban development, and underlying ideology, ten experts in their given fields have identified ways in which liberal politics has helped shape the nation's political landscape over the last half century. All the writers are concerned with the work of mainstream liberals—officeholders, urban planners, social issue activists, trade unionists. They are situated mostly in the Democratic Party, although both parties have embraced progressive and reactionary policies at different times. The essays assess the motivations of social reformers, the conditions under which they operated, the tactics they employed, and the outcome of their endeavors. Some were heroes to the cause, some hurt it. All were genuine in their desire to transform America and expand equality of opportunity. The essays pay particular attention to the importance of grassroots coalition efforts to the functioning of "high politics" and policy making. Although all of these authors highlight the shortcomings of liberalism, they also acknowledge that it remains a vibrant movement full of potential.

The Historical Consensus

Making change happen in the twentieth century has been a difficult process, and the historiography reflects that. American politics has shifted to the right since the heyday of liberalism in the 1960s. Identification with the Democrats has declined and the Party has lost seven out of eleven presidential elections since 1968. Popular reaction to the social liberation and antiwar movements of the swinging sixties combined with antitax sentiment in the stagnating seventies to produce the Reagan Revolution in 1980. President Reagan's assault on taxes and spending tapped into an instinctive American antipathy toward big government. Fear that liberals were using state machinery to promote cultural revolution from above forged a powerful electoral alliance between social and fiscal conservatives that Democrats struggled to break.[1] Only when the Democratic Party rejected much of its liberal past did it win the presidency, in 1992. The economic and electoral success of Bill Clinton's administration fueled the popular suspicion that New Deal and Great Society liberalism is unpopular and anachronistic.[2] One might even suggest that the few moments of clear Democratic success have been thanks to Republican errors. Watergate, the recession of 1992, and the credit crunch of 2008 all certainly contributed to electing Democrats, who then struggled to sell government-driven reform to a skeptical public.

Several key liberal legislative goals have been frustrated. The 1930s and 1960s saw remarkable strides made in the right to form unions, business regulation, civil rights, and social welfare.[3] The record is more mixed from the late 1960s onward. Some important pieces of equalities legislation have either been defeated (the Equal Rights Amendment) or watered down after popular backlash (affirmative action).[4] The slow advance of gay rights is a case in point. Vacillating leadership from the Democratic Party has overseen delay in reform (allowing gays and lesbians to serve in the military) and significant defeats (the outlawing of gay marriage in California in 2008).[5] Public education remains underfunded and its syllabus controversial.[6] Health care reform has been piecemeal and unsatisfactory to many liberals. While Medicaid, Medicare, and the 2010 health care reform act have expanded coverage and funding, they fall short of the kind of comprehensive health care insurance of which Senator Edward Kennedy dreamed.[7]

There is an assumption in some quarters that these goals have failed because they are unpopular—even un-American. Liberalism is prone to nurse the appetites of special interest groups, often representing marginalized communities. While the Democratic Party's various causes are laudable, they are controversial and divisive.[8] Association with lifestyle campaigners like gays and feminists has alienated religious voters. Commitment to the black freedom struggle lost the South. The targeting of public moneys at poor and nonwhite communities has angered many middle-class taxpayers. Since 1964, no Democratic nominee has ever won a majority of the white vote.[9] A patchwork approach to the politics of identity has stripped liberalism of a universal, American narrative—presuming that one ever existed. There is a broad sense that the decline of a class-based discourse since the 1930s has splintered and paralyzed the Left. Coalitions are difficult to form between groups with divergent interests. Internal strife and widespread dislike of collectivism has prevented a serious social democratic discourse taking hold in American politics. The collapse of the New Deal order was inevitable, and labor's class-based appeals look more and more anachronistic.[10]

By contrast, recent work on conservatism has emphasized its popularity, innovation, and ability to exploit American mythology. The Goldwater implosion of 1964 is now widely regarded as a reorientation of the GOP away from elite, East Coast politics and toward the concerns of the expanding suburbs of the West and the South.[11] Manipulation of the issues of race, religion, and taxes helped effect Nixon's New Majority and Ronald Reagan's revolution. Arguably, Republican populism was still driven by the same old business interests, but it succeeded in convincing large numbers of middle-class voters that liberalism was the politics of tax-and-spend and social disorder.[12] Conservatism has on occasion divided and imploded—most notably in 1964, 1992, and 2008. But it is resilient. In the twenty-first century, the Right rebounded even in the wake of the credit crunch and the scandals that rocked the Republicans. The Tea Party movement was a prime example—spontaneous, media-savvy, a blend of racial and fiscal themes, populated by ordinary middle-class Americans, historically minded, and hugely popular.[13] As late as the mid-1960s, historians still wrote of U.S.

history as a Whiggish progression from barbarism to liberalism. The conservative movement was ideology-free, circumstantial, irrational, and too extreme to catch hold of the popular imagination. But in retrospect, the years of profound liberal reform (1932–1966) seem like the aberration and conservatism the norm.[14]

Few contemporary historians still share the "consensus" school's faith in American progressivism, yet things are not as bleak for liberalism as this catalog of problems suggests.[15] Indeed, these essays address a paradox—the continued advance of social reform in a conservative political context. Several historians have pointed out that even in the post–Great Society period the federal government has continued to expand; the bureaucracy has developed its own logic and momentum. Richard Nixon flirted with environmental protection, welfare reform, and affirmative action. Ronald Reagan was unable to abolish federal support for schools or privatize Social Security. And George Bush Jr. oversaw a massive increase in government regulation of education standards and health care spending.[16] Where liberal politicians have failed, the law courts have stepped in. The language of civil rights has been extended and defended via the courts into age discrimination, gay marriage, abortion, and equal access to public services.[17] Even where conservatives have succeeded in mounting popular opposition to social reform via referenda, the courts have typically upheld the consensus of the 1960s and overturned their decision. One of the most important public policy decisions that a president can make is in the appointment of Supreme Court justices—reflecting the power of legislation from the bench.[18]

Each of these essays enriches the narrative of twentieth-century American politics by reconsidering the experiences of reformers across different eras and in different fields. They analyze the stumbling blocks to reform (race, popular backlash, disunity, personality, economic recession), but also its triumphs—and what made them possible. American political history cannot be labeled uniformly conservative or liberal. Rather, there are conservative moments and liberal moments.[19] Throughout them, reform is possible if given the right leadership and political context. Liberal moments have included 1932, when the failure of the Hoover administration to alleviate the Great Depression put Roosevelt in the White House. In 1964, the assassination of John F. Kennedy, the moral impetus of the civil rights movement, and the implosion of the GOP gave the Democrats their last real presidential landslide. In 2008, war and recession created a profound liberal moment. Public desire for reform of the financial sector was brief but powerful. It is up to good presidential leaders to exploit those moments effectively. They have sometimes benefited from the Democratic domination of Congress and state governments during sustained, typically coincidental periods. Such success has even occurred in supposedly conservative epochs like the 1980s or conservative regions like the South during the same decade.[20]

Liberalism and Social Democracy

This collection of essays also revisits the difficult question of definitions that surrounds twentieth-century liberalism. Historians of the United States have provided rich narratives of the halting and tentative development of welfare systems since the early part of the century and have charted the relationship between government and the establishment of civil rights legislation since World War II.[21] But overarching histories of the relationship between ideology and policy making often suggest the United States never really participated in the social democratic experiment that proved so important in the political histories of many industrial democracies in the last hundred years, or if it did, that the United States departed radically from that path after 1945.[22] Many historians argue that the increased power of corporate capitalism after the war, together with the rise of private-sector pension and health programs, left Keynesianism and civil rights as the only real left-of-center policies in the federal government's arsenal. Any expansion of governmental involvement in areas such as health care and welfare was merely an extension of the existing Social Security system.[23]

Yet a number of the essays in this volume force us to define more rigorously the meaning of *liberal* and *left* in an American context in order better to understand U.S. political development over the last century. The ideology of social democracy turned upon questions of social and economic equality with the state as arbiter, using a range of redistributive economic policies together with civil rights legislation enforced through the courts to iron out some of the massive injustices in capitalist societies. Several of these essays demonstrate how labor unions, state governments and political activists, feminists, and presidential candidates engaged with this ideology, even if it proved less popular in the United States than elsewhere. Crucial battles over the future of the New Deal state between 1945 and the recent past, including those concerning "right to work" laws, minimum wages, working conditions, and a social safety net, have received detailed attention from historians of the Right. But closer consideration of those often termed "liberals" shows that these debates demonstrated an increased awareness of social democratic thought as the century wore on, as opposed to the gradual retreat from leftist nostrums after the New Deal often described in existing historiography.[24]

The collection identifies three analytical themes in the history of twentieth-century liberalism. Because of the importance of an enduring social democratic tradition, it begins by addressing the relationship between mainstream liberals, principally in the Democratic Party, and the wider American Left. Several of the essays in this volume question the idea that postwar liberalism was completely straitjacketed by private sector capitalism and cultural conservatism. Even the violent divisions of the 1960s testified as to how far American society had changed since the Progressive and New Deal eras had ushered questions of social reform and public policy onto the political stage. The thorny question of racial equality helped to defeat southern liberals and made a united front between liberalism and organized labor harder to realize. Yet the collapse of the awkward New Deal coalition between the urban North and the South was the inevitable consequence of the widening of the parameters of social democracy to embrace many who had fallen by the wayside prior to the 1960s.

Rather than viewing liberal politics through a teleological lens that emphasizes decline from a golden electoral age of the 1930s and 1940s, this collection focuses on the increased ideological and policy ambition of liberals in areas like urban renewal, welfare provision, and coalition building with movements striving for greater diversity of political representation. The themes of policy innovation and alliance complete the portrait of liberal politics in this volume. They suggest that the electoral challenges of contemporary left-of-center politics lie in many respects in the success of liberals in altering the social landscape of the United States in the last five decades, often prompting an angry backlash from those frightened by the pace of change. Liberalism has sometimes been a victim of its own success.

Part I explores the difficult but fruitful relationship between established Democratic and liberal politicians and the wider left in the twentieth century. In "Partners for Progress? Liberals and Radicals in the Long Twentieth Century," Doug Rossinow argues that from the Popular Front of the 1930s and 1940s through to the anti–Vietnam War movement and the "new politics" of the 1960s and 1970s, liberals and leftists worked together to strengthen individual political and social rights, to advance the interests of the industrial working class within the framework of liberal capitalist society, and to oppose war and empire. Although vestiges of the left-liberal tradition continued to exist after the 1940s and the onset of the post–World War II "red scare," it was greatly weakened by the 1950s and is little remembered today. Rossinow describes the left edge of the liberal political tradition across the broad sweep of industrial U.S. history, revealing both the way in which the radical left provided idealistic, sometimes utopian fuel for liberal reform projects and the broad influence of liberal ideas on the political left in the United States.

Jonathan Bell's "From Popular Front to Liberalism: Redefining the Political in California in the Post–World War II Era" situates the consumer boom and suburbanization of California in the twenty years after World War II in the context of the changing dynamics of liberal politics on the West Coast. The rise of the Democratic Party to power in California took place at a time in which a range of interest groups demanding greater racial, sexual, and economic equality began to gain political traction and found that the existing avenues of party political action were inadequate for their needs. Bell argues that the California Democratic Party in the 1950s acted as a meeting ground for a range of cross-class interests searching for political meaning in a suburbanized, consumerist political marketplace. The fact that the Democrats were so impotent in the early 1950s gave a new generation of political entrepreneurs on the liberal left an opportunity to recast liberal politics in a way that used the economic citizenship of the New Deal as a bridge to the social citizenship that characterized the politics of the 1960s. Creating the Democratic Party anew in the 1950s at a time of a sharp right turn in state Republican politics set the tone of political debate for the next generation, creating a sharp left-right binary in state politics over economic and social policy and individual rights in the wider community and forcing mainstream politicians to come to terms with the implications of social diversity in the nation's fastest growing state. Even if we accept the fact that a meaningful liberal-left coalition faded from view at the national level after the vicissitudes of the Popular Front era of the 1940s, this was certainly not the case at the state level, making us consider whether liberal politics is really best viewed at the federal level.

In any case, Tim Stanley's "Going Beyond the New Deal: Socialists and the Democratic Party in the 1970s" demonstrates the continued importance of a wide range of left politics as late as the 1970s in national politics. He shows how social democrats were able to infiltrate the Democratic Party in the post-Vietnam era and to move its domestic policy in a dramatically leftward direction. Operating in a period of fiscal restraint and rising conservatism, Stanley demonstrates that even members of the American Left were prepared to play up to conservative and mainstream ideas and images to sell their revolutionary policies. They borrowed the language of the tax revolt and the New Deal to appeal—not without some success—to the floating blue-collar voter. However, their attempt to introduce European-style party control over policy proved counterproductive. It split the Democratic Party and helped elect Ronald Reagan in 1980. Issue militancy can cost elections.

Bruce Miroff's "From Friends to Foes: George McGovern, Hubert Humphrey, and the Fracture in American Liberalism" shows how antagonism between different traditions of social reform can defeat their agenda. Far from being a coherent movement, postwar liberalism has been divided by class, generation, and philosophy. In the 1970s, the Democratic Party was torn apart by a conflict between New Dealers and their union allies on the one hand and New Politics people and their identity politics allies on the other. Their tragic failure to reconcile their differences led to a landslide defeat at the hands of Richard Nixon in 1972. Drawing allusions to contemporary politics, Miroff shows how personal conflicts (like the 2008 presidential primaries) can reflect significant disagreements between reform traditions. Whether those gulfs can be closed is one of the major questions of this book.

Part II examines specific policy innovations in a geographical space crucial to liberalism: the city. Beset by racial divide and internal divisions, another issue this collection examines is the challenge of making policy to help those without voice or power—a constituency that Jesse Jackson characterized as "the damned, the disinherited, the disrespected, and the despised." In "New York Liberalism and the Fight against Homelessness," Ella Howard uses the city as a case study of the challenges facing liberals as they struggled to tailor their social policies to a political culture often hostile to public aid to the indigent. She traces the interaction of liberal policy making and the fortunes of those on the margins of society over the second half of the twentieth century. She examines efforts to reform the behavior of the homeless as well as campaigns to renovate the areas in which they lived. New York liberalism shaped the development of urban renewal programs, substance abuse treatment programs, and mental health reform, and studying homelessness through that lens lends insight into our understanding of both liberal compassion and its limits.

Lizabeth Cohen's "Liberalism in the Postwar City: Public and Private Power in Urban Renewal" argues that it distorts the historical record to condemn all urban renewal efforts with one brushstroke. Rather, the reality was more complicated, and a major aspect of that complexity was the different balance in different places and moments of time between public and private power and resources. Although there was little escaping the necessity of involving private investment in urban redevelopment, the authority of the public realm over private sector activity varied and made a difference. This essay charts the evolution of the liberal city-building project over the postwar period, with particular attention to the shifting balance of power between the public and private realms, its implications, and, through this case, the historical evolution of postwar liberalism.

Part III examines the coalition-building that has defined and constrained liberal statecraft in the twentieth century, including both alliances with external activists and with party factions necessary for legislative change. The section begins with an example of political failure. In "Albert Gore Sr., Liberalism and the South in the 1960s," Tony Badger looks at the how race and war intersected in 1960s Tennessee to destroy the career of a relatively progressive southern senator. Postwar conservatives used coded racism to lure southerners from the Democratic column and to associate liberalism with African American special-interest-group politics. Gore failed to realize that his moderate position on civil rights alienated him from his white voters. No amount of Northern liberal support could save him as the Solid South began its defection to the GOP. His defeat represented a generational shift in liberalism. Never again would it be acceptable to rely on an ethical reputation or class envy to secure reelection—liberals would have to find new ways of talking to their constituents and building trust.

In "Forgotten Architects of the Second Reconstruction: Republicans and Civil Rights, 1945–1972" Timothy N. Thurber examines how the Republican Party responded to two central demands of the modern African American freedom struggle—economic opportunity and voting rights—from the 1940s through the early 1970s. He argues that scholars have underestimated the role of the Republican Party in shaping the Second Reconstruction. Liberal Democrats and civil rights organizations had to respond to what Republicans believed about the role of race in American life and the place of federal authority in racial matters as they struggled to get legislation through Congress and approved by the White House. Republican support, they correctly believed, was essential to what did become law. At the same time, a critical mass of the Republican Party was willing to support proposals that earlier generations of Republicans had overwhelmingly rejected. Their support was motivated by political concerns, a desire to fight communism abroad, and a sincere revulsion against some forms of racism. The legislative achievements of this period in the area of civil rights offer further evidence that, in hindsight, the 1945–1972 period stands out in the broader history of the twentieth century as the "liberal era."

Susan M. Hartmann's "Liberal Feminism and the Reshaping of the New Deal Order" addresses the view that liberals have failed to marry the demands of identity- and class-based politics. She argues that in the 1970s, liberals built a powerful alliance between feminists and New Deal–style economic reforms that expanded the Democratic coalition and continues to exert influence upon it today. Although feminists failed in many of their symbolic or legal goals (particularly in the ratification of the ERA or federal funding for abortion), they succeeded in passing legislation that vastly improved the lives of homemakers and women workers.

Finally, in "Labor, Liberalism, and the Democratic Party: A Fruitful but Vexed Alliance" Nelson Lichtenstein narrates the troubled relationship between liberals and union activists. Although the second half of the twentieth century has seen serious reversals in the fortunes of organized labor, the rise of labor politics between 1935 and the 1960s left a lasting legacy. In many respects labor unions in the New Deal era acted as the ideological lodestar of social democratic politics, pushing elected politicians to reconfigure the balance between management and labor in industrial relations policy and to establish a welfare system that provided some measure of economic security for working people. When unions became seduced by the lure of private-sector welfare packages as part of the collective bargaining process in the postwar years, government's capacity to shape the public-private relationship became blunted and the role of social democracy in American political life was severely circumscribed. Yet in more recent decades a newly galvanized public-sector and service-sector union movement has breathed new life into the labor wing of the Democratic Party and has provided strong grassroots muscle to the Obama administration's attempts to reform the nation's labor laws and to provide publicly funded health care to American citizens. If this relationship is to bear fruit, labor leaders have got to reach out for the ideological commitment to social democratic principles that guided their forebears in the Depression era.

In sum, these essays highlight liberals' failure to adjust to shifting constituencies and agendas, division between coalitional partners, and a confused reformist discourse. Lingering liberalism within the GOP was present in the civil rights revolution if the 1960s but was ultimately crushed by racism and the rise of the conservative movement. Yet this collection also shows that liberals and radicals have tried to overcome these problems by building local and national alliances of common self-interest. They have flirted with populist themes and images to win votes. As a result, reformers have established a long-term home in the Democratic Party and sometimes forced it to accept their agenda. Finally, liberals have scored successes on many fronts. They have furthered the interests of the working class, fostered the feminist revolution, and helped remake the urban landscape. Their potential for influence in the future remains great—so long as they can continue to adapt to a rapidly changing political context. America is as fertile a place for social reform as any other country in the West.

Notes

1. For the decline of the New Deal order, see Steve Fraser and Gary Gerstle, eds., *The Rise and Fall of the New Deal Order, 1930–1980* (Princeton: Princeton University Press, 1989); Steven M. Gillon, *Democrats' Dilemma: Walter F. Mondale and the Liberal Legacy* (New York: University of Columbia Press, 1992), 103–104; Alan Brinkley, *The End of Reform: New Deal Liberalism in Recession and War* (New York: Knopf, 1995); Bruce J. Schulman, *The Seventies: The Great Shift in American Culture, Society and Politics* (Cambridge, Mass.: Da Capo Press, 2002), 121–143. For Republican strategy and its success, see Donald T. Critchlow, *The Conservative Ascendancy: How the GOP Right Made Political History* (Cambridge: Harvard University Press, 2007), 128–137; Thomas J. Sugrue and John D. Skrentny, "The White Ethnic Strategy" in Bruce J. Schulman and Julian E. Zelizer, *Rightward Bound: Making America Conservative in the 1970s* (Cambridge: Harvard University Press, 2008), 29–51; Robert Mason, *Richard Nixon and the Quest for a New Majority* (Chapel Hill: University of North Carolina Press, 2004), 39; Matthew Lassiter, *The Silent Majority: Suburban Politics in the Sunbelt South* (Princeton: Princeton University Press, 2005), 4–5; Joseph Crespino, *In Search of Another Country: Mississippi and the Conservative Counterrevolution* (Princeton: Princeton University Press, 2005), 205.

2. Kenneth S. Baer, *Reinventing Democrats: The Politics of Liberalism from Reagan to Clinton* (Lawrence: University Press of Kansas, 2000), 22–35; William C. Berman, *America's Right Turn: From Nixon to Clinton* (Baltimore: Johns Hopkins University Press, 1998), 192; Iwan Morgan, *Beyond the Liberal Consensus: A Political History of the United States since 1965* (New York: C. Hurst and Co., 1994), 269.

3. For a positive reappraisal, see the essays in Sidney M. Milkis and Jerome M. Mileur, *The New Deal and the Triumph of Liberalism* (Boston: University of Massachusetts Press, 2002).

4. For the case of affirmative action, see John David Skrentny, *The Minority Rights Revolution* (Cambridge: Harvard University Press, 2002), 1–20.

5. Steven A. Shull, *American Civil Rights Policy from Truman to Clinton: The Role of Presidential Leadership* (New York: M. E. Sharpe Inc., 1999), 100–103.

6. Gareth Davies, *See Government Grow: Education Politics from Johnson to Reagan* (Lawrence: University of Kansas Press, 2007).

7. Jill S. Quadagno, *One Nation, Uninsured: Why the US Has No National Health Insurance* (New York: Oxford University Press, 2005), 201–214.

8. John A Farrell, *Tip O'Neill and the Democratic Century* (London: Little Brown, 2001), 525.

9. Thomas Edsall and Mary Edsall, *Chain Reaction: The Impact of Race, Rights and Taxes upon American Politics* (New York: Norton, 1991), 263; Dan T. Carter, *From George Wallace to Newt Gingrich: Race in the Conservative Counter Revolution, 1963–1994* (Baton Rouge: Louisiana State University Press, 1996), 43.

10. Gareth Davies, *From Opportunity to Entitlement: The Transformation and Decline of Great Society Liberalism* (Lawrence: University of Kansas Press, 1996), 3; Dominic Sandbrook, *Eugene McCarthy: The Rise and Fall of Postwar Liberalism* (New York: Alfred A Knopf, 2004), 219.

11. Lisa McGirr, *Suburban Warriors: The Origins of the New American Right* (Princeton: Princeton University Press, 2001), 111–146; Rick Perlstein, *Before the Storm: Barry Goldwater and the Unmaking of the American Consensus* (New York: Hill and Wang, 2001), 3–16.

12. Michael Kazin, *The Populist Persuasion: An American History* (Ithaca: Cornell University Press, 1998), 1, 245–268; Critchlow, *The Conservative Ascendancy*, 128–137.

13. John M. O'Hara, *A New American Tea Party: The Counter-Revolution against Bailouts, Handouts, Reckless Spending, and More Taxes* (Hoboken, N.J.: John Wiley and Sons Inc., 2010).

14. For examples of consensus school history, see William E. Leuchtenberg, *Franklin D. Roosevelt and the New Deal* (New York: Harper and Row, 1963); Richard Hofstader, *The Age of Reform: From Bryant to FDR* (New York: Knopf, 1956).

15. For the classic rebuttal to the consensus school, see James T. Patterson, *Congressional Conservatism and the New Deal* (Lexington: The University of Kentucky Press, 1967).

16. Cass R. Sunstein, *After the Rights Revolution: Reconceiving the Regulatory State* (Cambridge: Harvard University Press, 1990); Joan Hoff, *Nixon Reconsidered* (New York: Basic Books, 1995); Bill Press, *Train Wreck: The End of the Conservative Revolution (and Not a Moment Too Soon)* (Hoboken, N.J.: John Wiley and Sons Inc., 2008), 197.

17. John Skrentny, *The Minority Rights Revolution* (Cambridge: Harvard University Press, new edition, 2004); William J. Novak, "The Myth of the 'Weak' American State," *American Historical Review* 113:3 (June 2008): 752–772.

18. Paul Frymer, *Black and Blue: African Americans, the Labor Movement, and the Decline of the Democratic Party* (Princeton: Princeton University Press, 2008).

19. Timothy Stanley, *Kennedy vs. Carter: The 1980 Battle for the Democratic Party's Soul* (Lawrence: University Press of Kansas, 2010); Gary Donaldson, *Liberalism's Last Hurrah: The Presidential Campaign of 1964* (New York: M. E. Sharpe, 2003), 128–163.

20. James T. Patterson, *Restless Giant: The United States from Watergate to Bush v. Gore* (New York: Oxford University Press, 2005), 190.

21. Dawley, Alan, *Changing the World: American Progressives in War and Revolution* (Princeton: Princeton University Press, 2003); Linda Gordon, *Pitied but Not Entitled:*

Single Mothers and the History of Welfare, 1890–1935 (New York: Free Press, 1994); Gareth Davies, "The Unsuspected Radicalism of the Social Security Act," in Robert Garson and Stuart Kidd, eds., *The Roosevelt Years: New Perspectives on American History, 1933–1945* (Edinburgh: Edinburgh University Press, 1999), 56–71; Timothy Thurber, *The Politics of Equality: Hubert H. Humphrey and the African American Freedom Struggle* (New York: Columbia University Press, 1999); Michael Klarman, *From Jim Crow to Civil Rights: The Supreme Court and the Struggle for Racial Equality* (New York: Oxford University Press, 2009).

22. See Daniel Rodgers, *Atlantic Crossings: Social Politics in a Progressive Age* (Cambridge, Mass.: Belknap Press, 1998), ch. 11; Meg Jacobs, *Pocketbook Politics: Economic Citizenship in Twentieth-Century America* (Princeton: Princeton University Press, 2003); Seymour Martin Lipset, *American Exceptionalism: A Double-Edged Sword* (New York: Norton, 1997); Alan Brinkley, *The End of Reform: New Deal Liberalism in Recession and War* (New York: Knopf, 1995); Elizabeth Fones-Wolf, *Selling Free Enterprise: The Business Assault on Labor and Liberalism, 1945–1960* (Urbana: University of Illinois Press, 1994); Aaron Friedberg, *In the Shadow of the Garrison State: America's Anti-statism and Its Cold War Grand Strategy* (Princeton: Princeton University Press, 2000); Patrick Reagan, *Designing a New America: The Origins of New Deal Planning, 1890–1943* (Amherst: University of Massachusetts Press, 2000).

23. Alan Brinkley, *The End of Reform*; Alan Wolfe, *America's Impasse: The Rise and Fall of the Politics of Growth* (New York: Pantheon, 1981); Alonzo Hamby, *Beyond the New Deal: Harry S. Truman and American Liberalism* (New York: Columbia University Press, 1973); Jennifer Delton, *Making Minnesota Liberal: Civil Rights and the Transformation of the Democratic Party* (Minneapolis: University of Minnesota Press, 2002).

24. For a good recent treatment of these themes from a historian of conservatism, see Elizabeth Sandy Shermer, "Origins of the Conservative Ascendancy: Barry Goldwater's Early Senate Career and the De-legitimization of Organized Labor," *Journal of American History* 95:3 (December 2008): 678–709. For the retreat from the New Deal theme, see Jennifer Klein, *For All These Rights: Business, Labor, and the Shaping of America's Public-Private Welfare State* (Princeton: Princeton University Press, 2003); Jennifer Mittelstadt, *From Welfare to Workfare: The Unintended Consequences of Liberal Reform, 1945–1965* (Chapel Hill: University of North Carolina Press, 2005).

PART I

Liberals and the Left

1

Partners for Progress?

Liberals and Radicals in the Long Twentieth Century

DOUG ROSSINOW

Today's conservatives view the Left and liberalism as identical categories, while many on the left see these categories as separate and antagonistic. But neither of these views is adequate. Historically, left-wing radicalism and liberal reform often overlapped in U.S. political life. The inhabitants of this shared political territory formed a left-liberal tradition in U.S. politics, one that had its heyday in the years stretching from the 1880s to the 1940s and that withered in the years after 1950.

The kinship between many liberals and those on the left during the era between the 1880s and the 1940s was based in a broadly shared belief in a qualitative vision of progress, according to which American society was undergoing a fundamental transformation. Many who believed in this idea of progress deserve to be called *left-liberals*. They ranged from the evolutionary socialist Florence Kelley, who in 1888 consigned the "worn and rotten fabric of a perishing society" to history's dustbin, to the social democrat and philosophical pragmatist John Dewey, who averred in 1902 that he was "scientifically convinced of the transitional character of the existing capitalistic control of industrial affairs and its reflected influences upon political life," to the Communist Joseph Freeman, who remarked that in the mid-1920s he saw "a deep continuity between the great aspirations of the Renaissance, the French Revolution, the American Revolution, and the modern aspirations of socialism," to the famous writer Edmund Wilson, who embraced a Marxist version of this perception in the early 1930s when he noted that feudalism had been replaced long ago by "the modern bourgeois-governed world" and added, "now there is only one more step to go."[1] These figures illustrate the political range across which this belief in qualitative progress was dispersed during a long phase of U.S. history. But by the late 1940s, this animating belief in transformative change in American society had become embattled and fatally weakened. As went this belief in progress, so did the vitality of left-liberal politics. After the trauma of McCarthyism in the 1950s and the political conflicts over the Vietnam War in the 1960s, leftists and liberals seemed like strangers. Some concluded that this almost complete alienation was a structural condition of American politics, not realizing that it was a relatively recent phenomenon. Others, ironically, continued to view leftists and liberals as closely allied.

In the conversation of today's right, *left* and *liberal* are used as synonyms.[2] "It often seems as though the various conservative factions inside the Beltway would rather fight each other than take on the Left," wrote conservative political commentator Laura Ingraham in a book published in 2007. By "the Left" she meant Democratic Party liberals.[3] In his discussion of "the vast left-wing conspiracy against the CIA," popular radio and television host Sean Hannity included not only the authors of articles published in *Mother Jones* and the *Nation*, journals that are at least hospitable to radical left-wing views, but also "left-wing senator Frank Church," John Kerry, and Daniel Patrick Moynihan, U.S. senators who had little in common save their Democratic affiliation.[4] The index for Newt Gingrich's 2006 book, *Winning the Future*, contains no entries for "liberal" or "left," but rather combines them into a single entry for "Left-liberals."[5] Regarding the U.S. war in Iraq that began in 2003, Gingrich, the former Speaker of the U.S. House of Representatives, wrote, "The Left says that with better diplomacy, we could have France by our side in Iraq," even though most self-identified leftists criticized the U.S. government for fighting the war, not for fighting it with too few allies. Gingrich framed liberal church-state separationism in terms of "the secular Left's unending war against God in America's public life," and the threat posed to traditional American freedoms by "secular Left-liberal judges." He expressed concern about "a new and growing pattern among the Left-liberal establishment to view foreign opinion and international organizations as more reliable and more legitimate than American institutions." The only specific Americans Gingrich identified as representing this "new and growing pattern" of thought were three current or former U.S. Supreme Court justices (Sandra Day O'Connor, Ruth Bader Ginsburg, and Anthony Kennedy).[6]

Writers such as Ingraham, Hannity, and Gingrich generally described mainstream secular liberal figures and views when using the terms left or liberal. They routinely labeled moderate views radical. Other rightist authors offered a subtly different equation, expressing concern that liberalism is a Trojan horse inside of which lurks a revolutionary tradition, ready to assault fortress America from within. Michael Savage, a relatively controversial figure even within the conservative talk-radio environment, wrote, "The emergence of an international social liberalism, which is at its core soft-communism, is a very real threat to the sovereignty of our nation. . . . Euro-socialists and their American counterparts see a terrible beauty struggling to be born, a beauty that would like to sweep away our dying civilization and bring us into an unbrave new world."[7] A more widely respected figure, the former federal judge Robert Bork, in his 1996 work *Slouching towards Gomorrah: Modern Liberalism and American Decline*, argued, "The defining characteristics of modern liberalism are radical egalitarianism . . . and radical individualism." Bork conceded that this makes liberals a paradoxical breed, but in his view they are doubly dangerous for their simultaneous promotion of socialist policy and assault on bourgeois values. If they succeed, capitalism "will . . . be replaced with one or another variety of statism presiding over a degenerate society."[8] Although Savage identified the long heritage of European socialism as the wellspring of the American left's destructive secret program, Bork pointed instead to the "New Left" of the 1960s. Like many neoconservatives, Bork discerned an "adversary culture" flowering in 1960s radicalism and then dominating mainstream post-1960s liberalism.[9] He wrote that "the authentic voice of adolescent Sixties radicalism" was "impatient, destructive, nihilistic. Modern liberalism is its mature stage."[10]

Political historians might be forgiven their confusion. Individuals sympathetic to the values of the political left—the most basic and consistent of which have been the advocacy of social and political equality and antipathy toward capitalism as an economic and social system—may lament the absence of an organized left in the United States, at least one with any purchase on the U.S. political system. Moreover, many political historians of the United States, far from seeing liberal reform and left-wing radicalism as synonymous, have depicted them as separate, incompatible, and intrinsically hostile to one another in the American context.

Much of the responsibility for that perception may be laid at the feet of New Left historians and those they have influenced. New Left writings on U.S. history, which date from the dawn of the 1960s, in many respects remain deeply probing and superbly provocative reinterpretations of the American experience.[11] However, it is important to locate such interpretations within the broader framework of intellectual and political development in the "long twentieth century" in U.S. history that runs from the Gilded Age decades of the 1870s and 1880s until the present.[12] New Left history remains apposite where the history of U.S. foreign relations is concerned.[13] Its characteristic interpretations of domestic politics have worn less well. As it happens, New Left historians have shown more interest in the specific question of liberal-left relations than have most of their colleagues.

Typically, New Left historians have interpreted liberal reformers in the long twentieth century as effective agents of a conservative agenda, water-carriers for large business interests. In this view, liberals were uninterested in social justice in capitalist America. Instead they sought social stability. Establishmentarian liberals used strategies of both repression and cooptation in seeking to undermine efforts by disruptive out-groups and radicals who aimed to create egalitarian change. This interpretive scheme continues to influence some scholarly work. For example, one book published in the 1990s evaluated the New Deal reform efforts of Franklin Roosevelt's presidency as measures supported by big business concerns and reflecting the political and ideological hegemony of capital over labor in modern America.[14] In reality, Roosevelt and his supporters achieved the New Deal measures in the teeth of assertive business opposition, with scant support from corporate America. Another recent work detected in the birth of modern political liberalism during the Gilded Age and the Progressive Era a constitutionally conservative creed whose mission was to banish consideration of social class from U.S. politics.[15] However, statements by Progressive Era liberals themselves amply attested that they had class very much on their minds throughout their careers. The Socialist John Spargo's concern with "[t]he cruel and anomalous contrast of idle men and toiling children" was shared widely with less radical progressives, such as William Allen White, the Kansas editor who nonetheless distilled progressivism into the call for a "shift or redistribution of national income," to be "achieved by using government where necessary." The publicist Ray Stannard Baker wrote to Theodore Roosevelt in 1908 that "*class action is a condition now existent:* a mode of progress which cannot be at present dispensed with."[16] Progressives never achieved a consensus about class and politics, but they did not try to suppress issues of class.

During the Gilded Age and Progressive Era, a creative set of middle-class political actors—familiar figures such as Jane Addams, Henry Demarest Lloyd, and Florence Kelley prominent among them—founded a "new liberalism" in the United States, a creed whose two main ideological ingredients were laborism and Fabianism. These elements were laid atop preexisting elements in U.S. political life, such as producerism, Jacksonian individualism, and postmillennialist Protestant moral reform, which long had fueled insurgent and egalitarian movements. What was distinctive about the outlook of the new liberals was the way in which it combined these familiar elements and added to them new, more pronounced emphases on working-class advocacy and enlightened educated-class political leadership. In the 1880s and 1890s, figures led by L. T. Hobhouse and J. A. Hobson announced the formation of a "new liberalism" in Great Britain that would break sharply with the laissez-faire doctrine of that country's Liberal Party by embracing a gradualist, state-interventionist approach toward individual opportunity and decreased inequality.[17] Not until around 1910 did champions of new liberal politics in the United States start to call their doctrine liberalism. But the processes of revision followed parallel paths in the two countries. (Rarely had advocates of laissez-faire in the United States called themselves liberals in the nineteenth century. The first political group to use the term in any meaning were the Liberal Republicans in 1872—hardly welfare-state advocates. But classical liberals there were in abundance.)

The Fabian aspect of the new liberal identity, like the category of new liberalism, was a label native to Great Britain and not much used in the United States, but both terms well describe the politics of the American Gilded Age reformers who embraced the prospect of social transformation. Such reformers took an active role in the "social politics" that Daniel Rodgers discerned throughout the Atlantic world in the 1880s and 1890s.[18] In fact, they routinely signaled their political kinship with the Fabian Society, led by Sidney and Beatrice Webb. The Fabians termed themselves *evolutionary socialists*; the name they chose for themselves—after the Roman general Fabius, who supposedly used irregular tactics to achieve his strategic military objectives in slow, incremental fashion—built an emphatic embrace of gradualist politics into their very identity. They offered themselves as an administrative elite-in-waiting to a political party willing to embrace their program; while they were advocates of social equity and ended up allying themselves with the Labour Party, the Fabians voiced an overtly elitist vision of controlled social change. American new liberal admirers of the Fabians were less sure that they were destined to rule, but this did not stop them from identifying themselves as the Fabians' opposite numbers. Frederic Howe said, "The liberalism of the middle of the [nineteenth] century is being Fabianized," and his fellow American progressive Amos Pinchot admiringly called the Fabian Society "the foundation of the progressive movement in England."[19] In the 1920s, Beatrice Webb's autobiography was a fixture on the desk of one of the best known settlement house leaders of her day, Mary McDowell of Chicago's University Settlement.[20]

As laborites, the new liberals viewed themselves as advocates for working-class interests. They took as their point of political departure the urgent need to reorient American politics to address the new realities of socioeconomic class in meaningful ways—ways that would not merely ameliorate suffering but create a new, more unified and just social order. Kelley was unusual among the new liberals of the late Gilded Age in the influence of Marxism upon her thinking, but she was typical in her recognition of class injustice in America. Her Marxism simply got her to that recognition quicker. "In the great strife of classes . . . where do I belong?" she asked the New York Association of Collegiate Alumnae in 1887. "Shall I cast my lot with the oppressors . . . to piece and cobble at the worn and rotten fabric of a perishing society?" The question, posed thus, answered itself: of course not. Solidarity with wage earners and commitment to fundamental social change went together, and they formed the cause Kelley embraced. Yet Kelley made her mark institutionally as a pioneering factory inspector. Surely she remained an advocate of labor's interests, but to do so she enacted a Fabian role as a government bureaucrat. We need not conclude that she had changed her stripes; her divided political self, straddling the line between reform and radicalism and between the need for working-class empowerment and the growing reality of professional-class power, was characteristic of the new liberals. Jane Addams, hailing from a different ideological background than Kelley, followed a different trajectory and ended up in a similar place. She somewhat reluctantly embraced organized labor as a necessary and good instrument of change, initially preferring a stance of class mediation to one of class partisanship, but by the 1890s she offered Hull-House, her famous settlement in Chicago, as a base of operations to women wage earners' trade unions in particular. Once Addams took up this new, more partisan vantage point, she never gave it up, even as she maintained her Fabian confidence in her own fitness for moral authority. Unlike Kelley, Addams had no Old Testament–style denunciations of gradual change to live down, and she was bothered not at all by the ambiguities of the new liberalism.[21]

Activists and thinkers such as Lloyd and Addams expressed an aversion to Marxism, socialism, and class rule, but these antipathies should not divert our attention from their commitment to social change in an egalitarian direction and to partnership between working-class and middle-class forces in pursuit of that goal. These new liberals had conflicts with some to their left and cooperated with others. Their politics was not marked by hostility to the left as such. Lloyd, at his life's end in the early twentieth century, despaired of American socialists because of their Marxism, lamenting, "I cannot, for the life of me, see how the present social contest can be described as one between capitalists and the working class." He derided what he perceived as the socialist notion that "the working people alone are to be trusted." Instead he spoke for "the people," who were not restricted to any one economic class.[22] Two decades later, Walter Weyl of the *New Republic*, the progressive journal par excellence, echoed Lloyd, writing "We must not believe that wage-earners are noble merely because the attainment of many of the ends they strive for run parallel to the line of social development."[23] But, to repeat, it would be incorrect to infer hostility to the left *tout court* from the frequent progressive rejection of socialism and Marxism. Lloyd's 1888 speech delivered in Chicago, "The New Conscience, or the Religion of Labor," which expressed his enduring political vision, advocated social solidarity, rooted in Christian values, as against individualist ethics, and identified the labor movement as the moral core of a projected cross-class alliance for society's overhaul in an urban, industrial age. Lloyd, like Addams, stood near the center of the American version of "social politics," which in the European context we have no trouble identifying as the moderate wing of social democracy. In Europe advocates of politics similar to those of Lloyd and Addams were less leery of Marxism or a socialist identity.

The secondary basis for the sometime friendship between liberal reformers and radical leftists, after the shared belief in transformative social change, lay in the deep and pervasive liberal commitments of U.S. political culture, which imprinted American radicals just as they did reformers and conservatives. U.S. new liberals were unlikely to announce themselves as social democrats. Leftists, for their part, harshly criticized capitalism and went considerably further than liberals in their pursuit of equality. Yet, in addition to these distinctively leftist commitments, the "common sense" of most on the left in the long twentieth century also encompassed belief in the truth and goodness of individual freedom, natural rights, constitutional government, and the sovereignty of "the people."[24] While radicals' rhetoric—and their doubtless sincere beliefs—often positioned them as sharp critics of contemporary political liberals, in practice those on the left frequently did the work of liberalism, fighting for individual rights and lawful government as well as for the empowerment of "the people."

During the 1910s, the World War I years, and the "red scare" that immediately followed, the Industrial Workers of the World (IWW) staged repeated "free speech fights" that helped solidify First Amendment freedoms of speech and assembly, and leftists joined liberals in forming the American Civil Liberties Union (ACLU, founded in 1920) to struggle for the legal rights of dissenters during wartime and peacetime both. Roger Baldwin, the main leader of the ACLU for decades, was himself a jailed draft resister during the war and something of an anarchist as a young man. Some would question the sincerity of leftists in working for constitutional liberties; the charge of cynicism about "bourgeois" rights would prove a potent accusation in subsequent years against American Communists, including those, such as William Z. Foster, who served on the ACLU's national board. Yet radicals could wax positively sentimental about "traditional" American freedoms (sometimes framed as traditional Anglo-American liberties). The more important point is that, objectively speaking, the cause of liberalism sometimes relied on the activities of leftists. In the 1920s, conservatives circulated "spider-web charts" designed to reveal the dense network of contacts between reformers and radicals, expressing the Trojan-horse view of liberalism as the vehicle for revolution.[25] Liberals, then as now, might have been inclined to deny the charge of close affiliation with radicals, out of fear that the conspiratorial character of conservative accusations would license broad political repression. Yet, where the world of the 1910s and 1920s is concerned, the spider-web charts were far less than downright false. The links they depicted were generally real. It was the meaning of these links that was misconstrued, since they often revealed the liberal commitments of radicals at least as much as the hidden radical agenda of liberals.

World War I and the Bolshevik Revolution polarized the left half of the U.S. political spectrum, but much of this turned out to be temporary. Some leftists embraced revolutionary politics in the United States and spurned evolutionary socialists as well as liberals, and liberals themselves were split between pro- and antiwar camps, with antiwar liberals moving leftward. Yet in many cases these were passing strains in deeply rooted relationships rather than permanent ruptures. The journal the *Public* editorialized in 1918, "Liberals and radicals of all shades and degrees of opinion are finding a common ground," working for "that new social order of which we have dreamed...."[26] The ACLU continued to function during the 1920s as the leading united front organization of left-liberal politics. Radicals and liberals in this group worked for "bourgeois" liberties. Whatever its ambiguities, left-liberal politics survived the first red scare of the twentieth century. The era of the Great War and the 1920s did, however, give birth to what would become a standard leftist critique of liberal reformers, a critique that could be dusted off for any future occasion of disillusion.

This long-gestating critique of liberalism found new opportunities for ventilation with the onset of the Great Depression. When John Chamberlain wrote *Farewell to Reform* and Lincoln Steffens brought out his *Autobiography*, published respectively in 1932 and 1931, they were not voicing perspectives recently acquired, and they devoted forceful prose to the disheartening performance, as they saw it, of liberals, led by President Woodrow Wilson, during the Great War. Chamberlain and Steffens emphasized their view that liberals lacked courage and clarity. Chamberlain associated liberals with "failure," by which he meant most of all intellectual failure. He scored "the unwillingness of the liberal to continue with analysis once the process of analysis had become uncomfortable." He derided those who maintained, in his view, a sentimental attachment to an individualistic political economy. Yet Chamberlain's most pungent evidence in support of his indictment concerned the war. "LaFollette had been willing to continue with the analysis of the War; so had Bourne. But liberalism in general couldn't stand the gaff."[27] *The gaff* meant the obloquy heaped on those who had opposed the "war to end all wars" once war fever took hold in America in 1917. Robert LaFollette, U.S. senator from Wisconsin, remained an antimonopoly man until the end, and Chamberlain had no respect for that. But LaFollette and Randolph Bourne, the writer and avatar of the "lyrical left" of the 1910s, by standing fast against U.S. entry into the war, made themselves heroes alike to left-wing intellectuals who saw Wilson's war as a crusade to save British imperialism. Steffens, one of the original "muckraking" journalists of the 1890s, came to prefer the honest men (as he saw them) in the ward-heelers' clubhouses and the Kremlin to the sentimentality he associated with the liberals. He saw Wilson as a mere tactician, while he admired Vladimir Lenin as a strategist. "Lenin was a navigator, the other a mere sailor." He thought Wilson was inveigled into joining Britain's war because he had no north star to guide him. In contrast, Steffens valued in the American socialists he encountered "their vision, their imminent hope, of a better world," because he thought it made them "unpurchasable.... fanatics."[28] Standing on the cusp of a new era of bold liberal reform, Steffens and Chamberlain saw little evidence of the transformative vision that had formed a crucial part of American reform liberalism's ideological grounding.

The experiences of the 1930s and 1940s blunted and, eventually, virtually immobilized the left-liberal belief in transformative progress in America. Several factors contributed to this outcome. First, believers in this scenario always had seen organized labor as a crucial player in the drama, but the trade-union movement cast its lot with the reform politics of the New Deal and definitively rejected the path of political insurgency. Second, the global conflict with fascism led many reformers and radicals alike to revise upward their evaluation of American society and politics, and both antifascism and the attractions of the New Deal led self-defined "progressives" of this era to redefine progress as an expansion of existing wholesome aspects of American life. Supporters of the antifascist, pro-Soviet Popular Front of the 1935–1948 period pushed liberals to support a moderate racial egalitarianism, transforming the content of U.S. political liberalism. In the process, they grounded hope for positive change in America's racial regime in the assertion of a national creed and a proud mongrel national character, and they conceived of this aspect of progress more as the extension of liberal principle than as the supersession of liberalism. Third, the shifting terrain of an internationalized political environment facilitated a concerted attack by anticommunist liberals on both Communists and their liberal allies, fomenting a civil war among liberals that the anticommunists won. The defeat of the "progressives" in this civil war spelled the withering of any robust concept of historical progress within U.S. liberalism.

Ever since the 1880s, new liberals had viewed wage earners as central players in their projected vision of political and social transformation, not only advocating partial working-class empowerment in the nation's political economy but also betting heavily on the force of the organized working class as a motor of political change. Liberals who believed in transformation were eager to work with proletarian comrades in a shared cause, and in many individual and local instances they did so, frequently supporting labor struggles against employers and for economic rights. Yet the liberals usually came from middle-class backgrounds and their most ambitious political schemes tended to reap disappointing harvests of trade-union support. Unions were the most important agents of organized working-class political life, and liberals assumed they would work with unions. But the unions had their own agendas, characteristically focused on bread-and-butter demands. On a local basis the support of unions and union federations was up for grabs in the framework of partisan competition, and beginning in the early twentieth century the American Federation of Labor (AFL), led by Samuel Gompers, got involved in national politics; in the 1910s, in the era of Woodrow Wilson's presidency, the national Democratic Party and the AFL cemented a political alliance that would shape the trajectories of both partners in this relationship for many decades.[29] Trade unions became central to liberal politics but could be chary of left-liberal programs of political realignment.

This came clear in the 1930s, when left-liberals saw a big opportunity for third-party organizing that could shift the political system leftward. Such activities, focused in groups like the League for Independent Political Action and the Farmer-Labor Political Federation, came to naught, despite high initial expectations in some quarters. A large share of this failure stemmed from the lack of interest that organized labor showed in the effort. The New Deal era was a bad time to try to entice labor to give up on the mainstream political system, which suddenly seemed more responsive to labor's demands than ever. The year 1936 was the target for third-party organizers, and 1935's Wagner Act (despite Roosevelt's equivocal support of it) and other New Deal measures swung labor behind FDR's reelection bid like no presidential candidacy before it. Plenty of union activists were Popular Front supporters, and some were Communists. But in the Popular Front era the Communists supported Roosevelt and the New Deal. (Their slogan could have been ¡*Popular Front sí, third parties no!*). The Popular Front was not a vehicle of political insurgency; it was what the writer Max Lerner, in 1936, called the "liberalism of the progressive labor movements."[30] Labor's Non-Partisan League was a landmark vehicle for labor's financial involvement in presidential politics, and it proved the coup de grâce to third-party organizing in that year, in the words of left-liberal intellectual Alfred Bingham.[31] Labor's embrace of the Democratic Party in the 1930s spelled the death of national third-party organizing indefinitely into the future. With it went a core element in the vision of political transformation that long had animated left-liberal politics.

No development within liberal politics was more fateful or ironic than the ascendancy of racial liberalism, whose rise eventually displaced the cause of labor as the emotional heart of liberal politics in America. Racial liberalism came in large measure from the Left and helped to redefine American liberalism. Considering the history of U.S. liberalism from the 1940s until the early twenty-first century as a whole, the essential ingredients of this creed have been advocacy of civil rights and the pursuit of inclusive economic growth.[32] But the rising cry from the Left for racial justice transformed American radicalism as well, making a militant form of racial liberalism, along with an anti-imperialist and prorevolutionary stance in global affairs, the new bottom line for "radicals" during the Cold War and after.

For fifty years, racial justice was almost entirely absent as an issue in liberal politics. Some new liberals were involved in the formation of the National Association for the Advancement of Colored People in 1909, and educators and others advanced a movement for "intercultural" understanding in the 1920s as a way of pushing back against ethnocentrism and intolerance in the era of the second Ku Klux Klan. But liberals generally wished to have nothing to do with racial issues, and almost no one defined liberal politics as a creed of racial justice. The left, on the other hand, made a consistent point of protesting American racism and embracing the cause of African Americans from the era of World War I onward. Only in the mid-1930s, through the vehicle of the Popular Front, did leftists, black and white, import antiracism into American liberalism's mainstream.[33] In 1935 left-wing African American intellectuals convened the Joint Committee on National Recovery to bring public attention to the plight of African Americans, and this led to the formation of the National Negro Congress, an umbrella political organization with a Popular Front orientation. In the late 1930s and then more powerfully during World War II, which was justified in some quarters as a struggle against radical racism, Popular Front liberals succeeded in infiltrating advocacy of civil rights and opposition to the grossest forms of American racism, as well as an embrace of cultural pluralism, into the mainstream of U.S. liberalism. Leftists still felt free to deride liberals as insensitive to the evils of racism when they wished. But, increasingly, Popular Front liberals asserted that opposition to Jim Crow segregation and to racism in general was essential for those who wished to be true to liberal principles. When Roosevelt dropped Vice President Henry Wallace, who had emerged as a forceful spokesman for civil rights, from his ticket in 1944 in favor of Harry Truman, the African American historian Rayford Logan lamented the switch as a "tragic blow to the cause of liberalism and democracy."[34] By the late 1940s, anticommunist liberals felt compelled to compete with the Popular Front for the loyalties of those who felt passionately about issues of racial justice; the far-reaching civil rights program that Harry Truman offered in 1948, like Hubert Humphrey's famous Democratic convention speech of that year, symbolically completed the arrival of civil rights as a bedrock liberal commitment, even if some would express bitter disappointment in the future over compromises and equivocation.

From the 1940s forward, leftist criticism of liberals on race matters took two forms, neither of which did as much to clarify the differences between radicals and liberals as the radicals seemed to think. First, leftists criticized liberals for lacking commitment and courage, for placing a premium on social peace and for being unwilling to stare down defenders of racism and inequality. Such criticism echoed the Chamberlain/Steffens charge that liberals lacked principle and guts. These were criticisms more of personal character than of ideas or program. They suggested that liberals would be radicals if they just showed more grit. Second, liberals faced criticism from their left for lacking a sufficiently "structural" approach to tackling racism, for neglecting institutional racism and focusing too much on reforming individual attitudes. Radicals commenced such criticism of racial liberalism when *An American*

Dilemma, by Gunnar Myrdal, was published in 1944. Racial liberals, starting in the 1940s, hearkened to Myrdal's analysis as they advanced the need to reform "attitude," a social scientific concept then coming to the fore, through educational efforts.[35]

Such efforts were, indeed, easily divorced from attention to the economic and institutional structure of racial disadvantage that would prove so tenacious in American society. Yet leftists had denounced white attitudes and demanded individual reeducation long before liberals did. The concept of "white chauvinism" originated on the Left. Communists had staged mock "trials" of white members accused of harboring bad attitudes about race. Leftists characteristically criticized liberals for not confronting white prejudice directly and aggressively enough, a criticism that undermined complaints about focusing on racial attitudes; leftists thought their moral superiority over liberals inhered precisely in their more progressive attitudes. The rise of race as a concern for both liberals and radicals set the stage for a new era of U.S. political history. Liberals who did not believe in fundamental social change were positioned to dislodge left-liberals from the reform universe, partly because left-liberals themselves had pivoted toward a racial-justice agenda that nontransformative liberals were prepared to go far toward incorporating without compromising their basic outlook.[36]

Critics of the Popular Front had been vocal within the anti-Stalinist left and among anticommunist liberals since the 1930s, but the events of the 1939–1948 years—the Nazi-Soviet pact of 1939 most of all, but also the Communist commitment to a third-party challenge to Truman in 1948—created a more favorable ground for anticommunist efforts to purge the Popular Front from the ranks of respectable liberalism. Wallace, running as the Progressive Party candidate for president in 1948, found himself humiliated after a successful effort by Truman's camp to depict him as a Communist tool. The shock troops of the anti-Wallace effort, which was in truth a device for delegitimizing the Popular Front, were the members of Americans for Democratic Action (ADA). As John Roche of ADA wrote to the Socialist Party candidate Norman Thomas after the election, "We done our best—and kept the intellectuals away from Henry Wallace."[37] As Jonathan Bell explains, the onset of the Cold War shifted American politics rightward by emboldening antistatist themes that redounded negatively on domestic social democratic ambitions among liberals. Paul Douglas, in the mid-1930s a left-wing economist who disdained the New Deal as weak tea, exemplified this trend of the late 1940s, reemerging as a vital center Democrat who won election to the U.S. Senate from Illinois in 1948. Douglas not only attacked the Wallace campaign as

Communist-controlled; he trimmed his sails on domestic policy, arguing carefully that Americans should "conserve what we have and in a temperate fashion . . . push on for fresh progress." The social democrat Lewis Feuer lamented after the election that, in both domestic and foreign policy arenas, liberals seemed focused on "criticism of socialism" rather than on advancing a meaningful progressive program.[38]

If the intramural conflict between vital center liberals and Popular Front progressives banished left-liberals from the ranks of recognized liberal politics in the late 1940s, in the 1950s, the second red scare, popularly known as McCarthyism (after Senator Joseph McCarthy, a latecomer to the cause), drove the historical reality of left-liberal politics down America's collective memory hole. Liberals often endorsed the repression of leftist remnants, as with the Smith Act trials of Communist Party leaders, or with the proposed Communist Control Act of 1954, sponsored in the U.S. Senate by the quintessential northern Cold War liberal, Humphrey of Minnesota.[39] Liberals in the 1950s often protested only against right-wing measures that might capture non-"progressive" liberals in the net. Liberals felt pressed to separate themselves from even a deranged perception of any red tinge. In this they were really ratifying the stance that already had taken shape among anticommunist liberals, and that had led to their triumph within liberal precincts—for example, in the CIO, which expelled eleven left-led unions in 1949–1950 over their officers' refusal to file affidavits swearing they were not Communists.[40] The most profound impact of McCarthyism on left-liberal politics was not to extirpate it, since this had largely occurred by 1950. Rather it was that liberals became so strident in their anticommunism as to erase left-liberal politics from the nation's political lexicon, with the effect that young people growing up in the 1950s and 1960s often were unaware such a thing was possible. Young dissidents in the 1960s frequently thought they had to reinvent the Left and they saw Cold War liberalism as liberalism per se.

When a New Left appeared in the United States in the 1960s, its members quickly expressed their alienation from Cold War liberals. In 1962, Students for a Democratic Society (SDS), the most important New Left organization, held what would become a well-known conference at a camp in Port Huron, Michigan, owned by the United Automobile Workers. But such ties between liberal and labor groups and the young radicals proved tenuous and short-lived.[41] With the Cold War still raging, the New Left's neutral stance in the superpower conflict and its warm embrace of third world revolutionaries made them seem irresponsibly radical to most liberals. New left thinkers saw liberals as part of a conservative establishment, a view they encapsulated in the concept of "corporate liberalism."⁴² Here we come full circle to the origins of the New Left historians' interpretation of liberal-left relations. In its early years the New Left distinguished between corporate and populist forms of liberalism and offered itself as a partner for the latter; in 1963, an important SDS statement called for a revival of the "populist and progressive" heritage of American liberalism and lamented that too many liberals gravitated toward "cocktail parties and seminars" instead of trying to rock the boat in the name of the people.⁴³ As late as 1965, Carl Oglesby of SDS called for "humanist liberals" to break with President Lyndon Johnson's Vietnam War policy. But that was a last gasp of hope for such a cleavage in liberal ranks, and Oglesby seemed to be placing no bets on a positive outcome.⁴⁴

In the late 1960s, the alienation of young leftists from liberal politics accelerated, shadowing the growing scale of the war in Southeast Asia. In addition to the war, the disillusionment among young African American activists with the liberal Democratic Party establishment, symbolized in the contretemps over the seating of the Mississippi delegation at the Democrats' national convention in 1964, also pushed white radicals away from liberals.⁴⁵ SDS leaders soon derided what Todd Gitlin called "the sham of pluralism," a liberal political doctrine of dispersed power that New Left radicals viewed as a mask for corporate domination, and New Leftist Tom Hayden was reported by his comrades to view liberals as the "most dangerous enemy" of the Left.⁴⁶ By decade's end, titles such as *The End of Liberalism* were commonplace in left-leaning academic precincts.⁴⁷ The amalgam of issues that called forth such bitterness, a combination of foreign policy and domestic issues, while important, appears in retrospect as the occasion for the expression of deeply sown suspicions, born of a longer history. New left radicals generally showed little awareness of the internecine strife between vital center and progressive liberal camps that had marked domestic politics in the 1940s. But they grew up in the atmosphere of McCarthyism and they had reason to view liberals, from a left-wing stance, as untrustworthy prospective allies, fatally drawn to power. It is no wonder that historians shaped by the intellectual analysis of the New Left should have taken this historically specific understanding of liberal politics for the intrinsic character of U.S. liberalism.

Ironically, although leftists might be expected to bid liberals farewell because of differences over the prospect of social transformation, as New Left radicals gave up on liberalism, they themselves expressed little hope for such a transformation. This most recent vigorous left-wing movement in U.S. history reflected scant belief in progress to a new stage of social development. To be sure, some New Left radicals avowed their socialist commitments in the late 1960s and early 1970s, but even when they did, one has to say that theirs was a none-too-optimistic brand of socialism; it was a matter of values, not of expectations. The pessimistic radicals of that era, although they pressed their support for insurgencies by the oppressed that could win important concessions from the power elite, saw before them a rather barren vista. The vision of qualitative progress, which had had a home for many decades among both liberals and leftists in America's long twentieth century, ran aground, and finally found few champions even among the radicals who might have been expected to rally to it.

Despite the acrimony that marked left-liberal relations during the Vietnam War era, in the 1970s, 1980s, and afterward, radicals and reformers collaborated in numerous specific political efforts in American life, whether these focused on feminist demands, U.S. foreign policy (with many liberals reconsidering their Cold War commitments starting in the later phase of the Vietnam conflict), or other areas.[48] Activists around the United States paid more attention to the willingness of fellow Americans to commit themselves to particular aims than to declarations by nationally known intellectuals that liberals and leftists had nothing in common. However, this post-1960s left-liberal cooperation has been mainly defensive and piecemeal, working for very limited victories in beating back the tide of a conservative era. Recent left-liberal politics, like the broader political tendencies from which it has borrowed, has reflected little faith that it forms the vanguard of a new age—with feminist organizing, at least in some cases, a notable exception.

Conservatives in the twenty-first century confront a liberalism shorn of any connections to more radical politics or ideology. Their concept of left-liberalism is far more apt for a description of reform politics in the period from the 1880s to the 1940s than it is for any substantial force in U.S. politics in recent years. On the other hand, scholars influenced by New Left interpretations make the opposite error, projecting backward throughout the long twentieth century a picture of left-liberal conflict more descriptive of the specific conditions of the Cold War era. Leftist radicalism and liberal reform do retain a common ancestry embodied in the Enlightenment tenets of a universal human destiny, a universal human nature, and the prospect of social transformation which, even if wrenching, will create a better world. However, these beliefs in general exist now only in a highly attenuated form and, when expressed openly, invite severe rebukes from intellectuals with both liberal and radical political affiliations.[49] In particular, the belief in qualitative progress is rarely voiced in America and would seem alien to many who call themselves progressive. Even a more modest, incremental concept of progress sounds only in muted form. The term *progressive* has returned to contemporary political discussion largely as a matter of convenience. Progress itself appears a fugitive belief, and in its absence, any contemporary or future left-liberal politics must be quite different in outlook than that which once animated U.S. politics.

Notes

1. Kathryn Kish Sklar, *Florence Kelley and the Nation's Work: The Rise of Women's Political Culture, 1830–1900* (New Haven: Yale University Press, 1995), 132; John Dewey, quoted in Robert B. Westbrook, *John Dewey and American Democracy* (Ithaca: Cornell University Press, 1991), 92; Joseph Freeman, *An American Testament: A Narrative of Rebels and Romantics* (New York: Farrar and Rinehart, 1936), 667; Edmund Wilson, *The American Jitters: A Year of the Slump* (1932; New York: Books for Libraries/Arno Press, 1980), 312–313.

For an explication of similar expectations of social change as they were expressed on a theoretical level, the work of Howard Brick is without peer. See his book, *Transcending Capitalism: Visions of a New Society in Modern American Thought* (Ithaca: Cornell University Press, 2006).

2. It might be objected that I use the terms *conservatism* and *the right* interchangeably in discussing the contemporary political scene, while I question the conservative equation of liberalism with the Left. However, in my view the recent political development of the United States has been characterized by a process of asymmetric polarization, featuring a relatively high level of ideological coherence on the right side of the political spectrum and within the Republican Party. For relevant discussion, see Jacob S. Hacker and Paul Pierson, *Off Center: The Republican Revolution and the Erosion of American Democracy* (New Haven: Yale University Press, 2005) and several of the essays in *The Transformation of American Politics: Activist Government and the Rise of Conservatism*, eds. Paul Pierson and Theda Skocpol (Princeton: Princeton University Press, 2007).

3. Laura Ingraham, *Power to the People* (Washington, D.C.: Regnery Publishing, 2007), 6.

4. Sean Hannity, *Let Freedom Ring: Winning the War of Liberty over Liberalism* (New York: ReganBooks, 2002), 28–36; q. on 28.

5. Newt Gingrich, *Winning the Future: A 21st Century Contract with America* (Washington, D.C.: Regnery Publishing, 2006), 266. The book was originally published in 2005 but the 2006 version is "Revised and updated," according to the copyright page.

6. Gingrich, *Winning the Future*, 14, 43, 58, 72.

7. Michael Savage, *Liberalism Is a Mental Disorder: Savage Solutions* (Nashville, Tenn.: Nelson Current, 2005), xiii.

8. Robert H. Bork, *Slouching towards Gomorrah: Modern Liberalism and American Decline* (New York: ReganBooks, 1996), 5, 7.

9. For a basic statement of this thesis, see Irving Kristol, "The Adversary Culture

of Intellectuals" (1979), in Irving Kristol, *Neoconservatism: The Autobiography of an Idea* (Chicago: Ivan R. Dee, 1999), 106–122.

10. Bork, *Slouching towards Gomorrah*, 34. Bork's interpretation of the 1960s is a rehash of the view offered earlier in Allan Bloom, *The Closing of the American Mind* (New York: Simon and Schuster, 1988).

11. Founding works of this interpretive school include William Appleman Williams, *The Tragedy of American Diplomacy* (Cleveland: World Publishing, 1959) and Gabriel Kolko, *The Triumph of Conservatism: A Re-interpretation of American History, 1900–1916* (New York: Free Press of Glencoe, 1963).

12. This is not necessarily the way historians think about the twentieth century. For example, see E. J. Hobsbawm, *The Age of Extremes: A History of the World, 1914–1991* (New York: Vintage, 1996), the subtitle of whose British edition is *The Short Twentieth Century, 1914–1991*.

13. For a vigorous and compelling statement, see Robert Buzzanco, "Whatever Happened to the New Left? Toward a Radical Reading of American Foreign Relations," *Diplomatic History* 23 (Fall 1999): 575–607.

14. Colin Gordon, *New Deals: Business, Labor, and Politics in America, 1920–1935* (Cambridge: Cambridge University Press, 1994). See the persuasive critique by Howell John Harris in his review essay, "Interwar American Histories: Left, Right, and Wrong," *Historical Journal* 42:1 (1999): 293–308.

15. Shelton Stromquist, *Reinventing "The People": The Progressive Movement, the Class Problem, and the Origins of Modern Liberalism* (Urbana: University of Illinois Press, 2006).

16. John A. Thompson, *Reformers and War: American Progressive Publicists and the First World War* (Cambridge: Cambridge University Press, 1987), 41, 43, 78.

17. Among other works, see Stefan Collini, *Liberalism and Sociology: L. T. Hobhouse and Political Argument in England, 1880–1915* (Cambridge: Cambridge University Press, 1979) and Peter Weiler, *The New Liberalism: Liberal Social Theory in Great Britain, 1884–1914* (New York: Garland Publishing, 1982).

18. Daniel T. Rodgers, *Atlantic Crossings: Social Politics in a Progressive Age* (Cambridge, Mass.: Belknap Press of Harvard University Press, 1998).

19. Thompson, *Reformers and War*, 75, 76.

20. Rodgers, *Atlantic Crossings*, 64–65.

21. Worthwhile recent works on Addams include Victoria Bissell Brown, *The Education of Jane Addams* (Philadelphia: University of Pennsylvania Press, 2004) and Louise W. Knight, *Citizen: Jane Addams and the Struggle for Democracy* (Chicago: University of Chicago Press, 2005).

22. John L. Thomas, *Alternative America: Henry George, Edward Bellamy, Henry Demarest Lloyd and the Adversary Tradition in America* (Cambridge, Mass.: Belknap Press of Harvard University Press, 1983), 349. On Lloyd, see also Chester M. Destler, *Henry Demarest Lloyd and the Empire of Reform* (Philadelphia: University of Pennsylvania Press, 1963).

23. Thompson, *Reformers and War*, 252.

24. The classic description of this deep liberal creed is Louis Hartz, *The Liberal Tradition in America: An Interpretation of American Political Thought since the Revolution* (New York: Harcourt, Brace, 1955). Important discussions of the background of liberal thought also include Guido de Ruggiero, *The History of European Liberalism*, trans. R. G. Collingwood (1927; Boston: Beacon Press, 1959); Dorothy Ross, "Liberalism," in *Encyclopedia of American Political History: Studies of the Principal Movements and Ideas*, ed. Jack P. Greene (New York: Charles Scribner's Sons, 1984), 750–763; James T. Kloppenberg, "The Virtues of Liberalism: Christianity, Republicanism, and Ethics in Early American Political Discourse," *Journal of American History* 74:1 (June 1987): 9–33; Joyce O. Appleby, *Liberalism and Republicanism in the Historical Imagination* (Cambridge: Harvard University Press, 1992); and John Gray, *Liberalism*, 2nd ed. (Minneapolis: University of Minnesota Press, 1995).

25. On the red-baiting of the first half of the 1920s, see Nancy F. Cott, *The Grounding of Modern Feminism* (New Haven: Yale University Press, 1987). A key document in the campaign was *Revolutionary Radicalism: Its History, Purpose and Tactics, with an Exposition and Discussion of the Steps Being Taken and Required to Curb It* (a Report of the Joint Legislative Committee Investigating Seditious Activities, Filed April 24, 1920, in the Senate of the State of New York) (Albany: J. B. Lyon Co., 1920), especially *Part 1: Revolutionary and Subversive Movements Abroad and at Home*. This was generally known as the Lusk Committee report, named for the relevant legislative committee in Albany.

26. Thompson, *Reformers and War*, 231.

27. John Chamberlain, *A Farewell to Reform: The Rise, Life and Decay of the Progressive Mind in America* (1932; Gloucester, Mass.: Peter Smith, 1958), 304–305.

28. Lincoln Steffens, *The Autobiography of Lincoln Steffens* (New York: Harcourt, Brace and World, 1931), 525, 798.

29. See Julie Greene, *Pure and Simple Politics: The American Federation of Labor and Political Activism, 1881–1917* (Cambridge: Cambridge University Press, 1998).

30. Sanford Lakoff, *Max Lerner: Pilgrim in the Promised Land* (Chicago: University of Chicago Press, 1998), 100.

31. Donald L. Miller, *The New American Radicalism: Alfred M. Bingham and Non-Marxian Insurgency in the New Deal Era* (Port Washington, N.Y.: Kennikat Press, 1979), 133.

32. Other commitments were highly important as well for liberals during discrete segments of this sixty-year period. For about the first twenty years after 1948, an expressly antirevolutionary foreign policy was also a basic element in liberal politics; during the 1948–1968 years the Cold War liberals established a consensus stance concerning U.S. relations with the world for the first and only time in the history of U.S. liberalism. Disagreement would return to liberal foreign policy discussion starting in the later years of the Vietnam War. At around the same time, taking off in the 1970s, feminism started quickly to make inroads among liberal reformers. But

neither a consistent foreign policy stance nor a consistent feminism stretches across the entire length of U.S. liberalism's posttransformational phase.

33. See Glenda Elizabeth Gilmore, *Defying Dixie: The Radical Roots of Civil Rights, 1919–1950* (New York: W. W. Norton and Co., 2008) for a forceful exposition of this view.

34. Patricia Sullivan, *Days of Hope: Race and Democracy in the New Deal Era* (Chapel Hill: University of North Carolina Press, 1996), 186. On the complexities of left-liberal thought and politics during the war years, see the discerning discussion in Frank A. Warren, *Noble Abstractions: American Liberal Intellectuals and World War II* (Columbus: Ohio State University Press, 1999).

35. Gunnar Myrdal, *An American Dilemma: The Negro Problem and American Democracy* (New York: Harper and Brothers, 1944). See Walter A. Jackson, *Gunnar Myrdal and America's Conscience: Social Engineering and Racial Liberalism, 1938–1987* (Chapel Hill: University of North Carolina Press, 1990).

36. On the rise of "vital center" liberalism and its racial commitments, see Steven M. Gillon, *Politics and Vision: The ADA and American Liberalism, 1947–1985* (New York: Oxford University Press, 1987) and Jennifer A. Delton, *Making Minnesota Liberal: Civil Rights and the Transformation of the Democratic Party* (Minneapolis: University of Minnesota Press, 2002).

37. Norman D. Markowitz, *The Rise and Fall of the People's Century: Henry A. Wallace and American Liberalism, 1941–1948* (New York: The Free Press, 1973), 296.

38. Jonathan Bell, *The Liberal State on Trial: The Cold War and American Politics in the Truman Years* (New York: Columbia University Press, 2004), 144, 159.

39. See William W. Keller, *The Liberals and J. Edgar Hoover: Rise and Fall of a Domestic Intelligence State* (Princeton: Princeton University Press, 1989).

40. See Ronald L. Filipelli and Mark McCulloch, *Cold War in the Working Class: The Rise and Decline of the United Electrical Workers* (Albany: State University of New York Press, 1995) and Steven Rosswurm, ed., *The CIO's Left-Led Unions* (New Brunswick: Rutgers University Press, 1992), as well as Ellen Schrecker, *Many Are the Crimes: McCarthyism in America* (Boston: Little, Brown, 1998).

41. For a revisionist view, see Peter B. Levy, *The New Left and Labor in the 1960s* (Urbana: University of Illinois Press, 1994).

42. The journal *Studies on the Left*, based at the University of Wisconsin in Madison, under the primary influence of the historian William Appleman Williams, advanced this concept forcefully. See Kevin Mattson, "Between Despair and Hope: Revisiting *Studies on the Left*," in *The New Left Revisited*, eds. John McMillian and Paul Buhle (Philadelphia: Temple University Press, 2003), 28–47.

43. "America and the New Era" (1963), in *The New Left: A Documentary History*, ed. Massimo Teodori (Indianapolis: Bobbs-Merrill, 1969), 177.

44. Carl Oglesby, "Trapped in a System" (1965), in *The New Left*, ed. Teodori, 182.

45. See Clayborne Carson, *In Struggle: SNCC and the Black Awakening of the 1960s* (Cambridge: Harvard University Press, 1981), ch. 9, 12, and Carol Polsgrove, *Divided*

Minds: Intellectuals and the Civil Rights Movement (New York: W. W. Norton and Co., 2001).

46. Todd Gitlin, "Power and the Myth of Progress" (1966), in *The New Left*, ed. Teodori, 189; the characterization of Hayden's view was from Paul Potter, quoted in Todd Gitlin, *The Sixties: Years of Hope, Days of Rage* (New York: Bantam, 1987), 166.

47. Theodore J. Lowi, *The End of Liberalism: Ideology, Policy, and the Crisis of Public Authority* (New York: W. W. Norton and Co., 1969).

48. For illustrations, see, among other works, Barbara Epstein, *Political Protest and Cultural Revolution: Nonviolent Direct Action in the 1970s and 1980s* (Berkeley: University of California Press, 1991); several essays in Van Gosse and Richard Moser, eds., *The World the Sixties Made: Politics and Culture in Recent America* (Philadelphia: Temple University Press, 2003), including Sara M. Evans, "Beyond Declension: Feminist Radicalism in the 1970s and 1980s" (52–66) and Van Gosse, "Unpacking the Vietnam Syndrome: The Coup in Chile and the Rise of Popular Anti-Interventionism" (100–113); and Cynthia A. Brown, *Soul Power: Culture, Radicalism, and the Making of a U.S. Third World Left* (Durham: Duke University Press, 2006).

49. For a provocative analysis, see several recent works by John Gray, including *Enlightenment's Wake: Politics and Culture at the Close of the Modern Age* (London: Routledge, 1995) and *Black Mass: Apocalyptic Religion and the Death of Utopia* (New York: Farrar, Straus and Giroux, 2007), especially ch. 2. See Oliver Bennett, *Cultural Pessimism: Narratives of Decline in the Postmodern World* (Edinburgh: Edinburgh University Press, 2001) for a survey of the subject.

2

From Popular Front to Liberalism

Redefining the Political in California in the Post–World War II Era

JONATHAN BELL

In January 1952 a *New Republic* article argued that "one can see at least the wedge of the mixed economy, in the recent legislation in, say, California on the various trade-union and other 'private' insurance schemes at least the first sign of the Welfare State." The 1950s would, the author argued, throw up new problems and challenges that would conceivably herald a major step toward social democracy configured for a prosperous world: "In the vast American scene, the approach toward the Welfare State will probably not come through any dramatic political shift, but in a variety of ways: by the growth of trade union and other social-insurance schemes, by an increasing practice of including such schemes in employer-employee contracts, by greater federal planning, by the capture of this or that local political machine by progressive forces, by greater economic equality for the Negro community, or by the general spread of the Welfare State outlook as is already happening." A crucial question, and one that frames my work, was "the cultural one. 'After the leveling, after the British National Health Service or the American owner-occupied home, what next?'"[1]

California missed out on the far-reaching political realignment of the New Deal era. In the late 1940s the state Democratic Party was a factionalized, chaotic mess, a curious amalgam of Popular Front communists and fellow travelers, old-style political bosses, special interests, and a handful of New Deal liberals. Ten years later the Party had captured power at all levels and, under Governor Pat Brown and a Democratic legislature, went on to enact one of the biggest state government programs of public power, college expansion, welfare state building, and civil rights law in state history. At the same time, California became the largest state in the union and one of the fastest growing economies in the United States, a standout example of the consumer boom and developing muscle of American corporate power that took shape in the postwar years. This paper aims to situate the consumer boom and suburbanization of California in the twenty years after World War II in the context of the changing dynamics of liberal politics on the West Coast. The rise of the Democratic Party to power in California took place at a time in which a range of interest groups demanding greater racial, sexual, and economic equality began to gain political traction and found that the existing avenues of party political action were inadequate for their needs. These interests, including homophile organizations and civil rights groups pushing for fair housing and fair employment laws, framed their demands around an idea of social citizenship that demanded access to economic resources and to equal rights in society. At the same time, a Democratic Party that had to find an ideological raison d'être in a consumer age was forced to adapt its message and electoral appeal to reconcile the legacy of the New Deal with the idea of civil rights for the socially marginalized that was rapidly becoming an important strain of social democratic politics across the industrialized world. I argue here that the California Democratic Party in the 1950s acted as a meeting ground for a range of cross-class interests searching for political meaning in a suburbanized, consumerist political marketplace. The fact that the Democrats were so impotent in the early 1950s gave a new generation of political entrepreneurs on the liberal left an opportunity to recast liberal politics in a way that used the economic citizenship of the New Deal as a bridge to the social citizenship that characterized the politics of the 1960s.

Although there is an increasingly rich historiography on the subject of the revitalization of corporate capitalism in the postwar decades and the concomitant rise of a powerful Republican Party, the concept of left-of-center interests as political entrepreneurs in this period remains only partially understood.[2] An international dialogue on the left expanded the parameters of how intellectuals and politicians understood and conceptualized social inclusion, equality of opportunity, and individual rights, with significant implications for how we chart the development of a rights discourse in the United States in the second half of the twentieth century. Historians have ably framed this debate on the left through recourse to intellectual history, demonstrating how vibrant arguments in left-wing journals, liberal and left organizations, and university departments reshaped the relationship between highbrow political thought and grassroots social movements.[3] There is also a growing historiography on the ways in which consumerism and the rise of a suburbanized middle class had important political implications for the nation's economic, racial, and community structures.[4] Unlike their counterparts that examine the New Right, these studies about consumer politics and intellectual liberalism and leftism rarely dovetail with party political history, perhaps because although the relationship between a radical antistatist business community and the Republican Party is easy to discern, the trajectory of Democratic Party identity is more confusing and seemingly has less political authority over the long term than its right-wing rival.[5] Nonetheless, an analysis of the ways in which new political interests and liberal entrepreneurs gave the California Democratic Party an expanded political language through which to formulate a legislative program in the 1950s and 1960s helps us to understand why the Party gained such a level of power in state politics despite its humble fortunes in the 1940s.

A party political framework also explains how the rise of Democratic Party activism through a network of clubs across the state gave those searching for meaning after the collapse of the Popular Front a new outlet for their political organizing, which in California acted as a form of social networking in urban and suburban communities. There are plenty of studies of conservative politics as community organizing, often using Orange County as an example, and some on the way in which Popular Front politics before 1945 acted as a way of anchoring people in an otherwise alienating and sprawling metropolis like Los Angeles.[6] The idea that urban and suburban community politics could have meaning for so-called "liberals" in the period between the collapse of the Popular Front and the rise of the New Right in the 1960s is worthy of closer investigation: it will be argued here that creating the Democratic Party anew in the 1950s at a time of a sharp right turn in state Republican politics set the tone of political debate for the next generation, creating a sharp left-right binary in state politics over economic and social policy and individual rights in the wider community and forcing mainstream politicians to come to terms with the implications of social diversity in the nation's fastest growing state.

Political Culture in California at Midcentury

The social and economic changes of the Depression and World War II had affected California at least as manifestly as anywhere else in the Union. Whether we think of the mass of displaced Okies in the 1930s or the millions who descended on the Golden State to seek employment in war industries in the 1940s, there was no question that California was undergoing rapid and significant social changes that required collective solutions. The state's population had swollen in the 1940s alone from a little under 7 million to 10,586,223. The African American population had rocketed from 124,000 in 1940 to over 462,000 ten years later.[7] Between 1941 and 1944 California's manufacturing employment rose an extraordinary 201 percent, compared to the national average of 51 percent. The state government had become responsible for coordinating one of the nation's largest war economies, a network of plants and factories that had sprung up almost overnight and required new roads, water supplies, and public power.[8] Undergirding this picture of change was a history of political progressivism and radicalism that had found expression with the gubernatorial campaign of Upton Sinclair in 1934 and the pension campaigns of Francis Townsend and George McLain through the 1930s, together with the rise of a powerful Communist movement in the state that was among the largest in the nation. The Party had by the outbreak of war infiltrated the left wing of the Democratic Party and most of the CIO unions on the West Coast, and was involved in any number of civil rights and civil liberties organizations that formed the lynchpin of mass political engagement in these years.[9] California was the home of the progressive wing of the Republican Party, symbolized by Senator Hiram Johnson and Congressman Richard Welch of San Francisco, and also home of stalwart supporters of the New Deal such as Democratic congressmen Jerry Voorhis of LA and George Outland of Santa Barbara. Though the state's citizens had elected a Democrat to the governorship only once since 1888—Culbert Olson in 1938—they were comfortable with Republicans such as Earl Warren who, having defeated Olson's chaotic administration after just one term, would oversee the largest expansion in state government capacities in state history up to that time. If Warren's phrase that war had "caused us to actually jump into our future" had meaning, a casual observer could be forgiven for thinking that the postwar settlement would involve a progressive pact between government, social movements, and private enterprise that would invigorate the liberal spirit of the New Deal age.[10]

In fact, California politics at the midpoint of the twentieth century was a world unusually unsuited to the demands of a modern industrialized state. The reforms of Hiram Johnson's administration in the 1910s that had been designed to break the power of organized factions and lobbyists over the state's political system had the opposite effect by the 1930s, and had calcified political activity into an organized chaos of individual candidacies, one-party dominance over the legislature and local government, and a lack of serious mainstream public debate about the ideological direction of the state and the country. Political scientists such as David Mayhew and James Q. Wilson have described this phenomenon, leading Mayhew to go so far as to assert that there is "no point dwelling" on California's political system insofar as it is "the last place anybody would look to find traditional party organizations."[11] Yet it is important to lay out the dynamics of late 1940s California politics to show what was missing from public discourse and political organizing in these years and how that lack of a serious engagement with left-wing ideas in postwar party politics would shape the formation of a new age of political activism in later years.

Recent studies of political movements associated with the Left that have focused on California have inevitably focused on local studies of neighborhoods, local civil rights efforts, and nonparty campaigns of civil and economic rights centered in specific communities, whether they be the bohemian enclave of Edendale in Los Angeles or African American sections of West Oakland.[12] Yet as Ellen Reese has pointed out, these localized examples of political pressure usually met with successful opposition so long as conservative economic and political interests controlled politics at the state level, as in the case of the repeal of a welfare rights proposition by powerful antiwelfare interests in 1949.[13] The Republican Party's control of the legislature and most local governments, due in part to a tradition of Republicanism in the state and in part to the effects of California's peculiar cross-filing law, severely restricted the political options open to Californians between the 1920s and 1950s and helped to reinforce a strong rightward turn in the state's politics in these years.

It could be argued that Earl Warren's governorship demonstrated the futility of attempting to analyze California politics through the prism of party. In many respects, however, Warren's occupation of the governor's mansion in Sacramento marked the high point of progressive ascendancy within the state's Republican Party. For one thing, the limited ideological reach of political discourse among state Republicans meant their solutions to social problems could never keep pace with demand. For another, probusiness, bitterly antigovernment interests in the Party were, after 1945, making a serious challenge to the broker state being delicately established under Warren, and they were determined to sweep aside any political consensus in a bid to establish private sector control over the economy. Warren's short-lived attempt to establish some kind of state health insurance system was a major casualty of the growing political clout of antistatist Republican legislators and their powerful financial backers in the California Medical Association and Chamber of Commerce. Days after Warren's announcement of his Social Security–based insurance scheme in January 1945, the CMA met in Los Angeles and, in Warren's words, "all but declared the plan to be the work of the Devil." In a propaganda campaign that formed part of a wider national campaign against government-administered health care in the 1940s, the CMA "stormed the legislature with their invective," and Warren's bill "was not even accorded a decent burial."[14] The *New Republic*'s verdict that when Warren "discovered the hornet's nest that he had uncovered, he began to run for cover and had it conveniently killed in committee" is perhaps unfair, but its broader accusation that the vigorous actions of conservative interests in rolling back social welfare entitlements in the years after the war, and the generous funding of Republican candidates by antistatist interests, demonstrated the limits of progressive political activity in Sacramento in these years is hard to refute. It is also true that Warren "owed a great debt to [Joseph] Knowland, northern California's most powerful political figure, to Norman Chandler of the *Los Angeles Times* and to the Hearst interests. He appointed Knowland's son William to the U.S. Senate. Contributions to his campaigns have come from many of the most powerful reactionary forces in the state."[15] As the forces of capitalism began to gear up for a full-on assault on the regulatory power of the state, an attack that would culminate in an attempt to reintroduce the open shop to labor contracts in the late 1950s, it was not at all clear that progressive Republicanism possessed either the political strength or the ideological conviction with which to stem the antistatist tide.

Before the renaissance of the 1950s, Democratic Party organization was rendered ineffective by its internal divisions and inability to combat Republican power. For every account of a political house party, public meeting, or Young Democrat group was a story that told a very different tale: a Democratic Party in Alameda County, which contained over 200,000 registered Democrats in the late 1940s and could not get a quorum at its meetings; county committees that never met; bitter infighting among members of the state central committee over some members' links to communists and supporters of the Progressive Citizens of America and other fellow-traveler groups.[16] Fresh from his comprehensive drubbing at the hands of a conservative Republican in the 7th congressional district in Oakland in 1946, Democratic candidate and prominent Alameda businessman Patrick McDonough put the blame for the Party's electoral disaster squarely on the dissident left-wing elements in the Party who had been using it as a Popular Front vehicle since the 1930s. "The election did not come out as perhaps we all wished," he wrote a business associate, "but as for myself, I do not regret the outcome. The political situation here in California for us Democrats is very much confused. This defeat permits all of us to take a stand and begin inviting those whose views and actions do not harmonize with the best interests of the Democratic Party and our form of government to disassociate themselves from our party, and perhaps the best thing would be to form a party of their own. With this group we are always in danger of losing with their help."[17] Despite the fact that fellow-traveler organizations such as the Hollywood branch of the Independent Citizens' Committee of the Arts, Sciences, and Professions (ICCASP) had participated in voter registration drives and get-out-the-vote campaigns, authored an FEPC ballot initiative, and endorsed favored liberal candidates publicly to their membership, they had not been able to prevent the Republican tide, nor had they been able to convince enough registered Democrats that their gubernatorial candidate, soon to be Wallaceite Robert Kenny, was a preferable candidate to Earl Warren, nor that congressman Ellis Patterson, a known fellow traveler, should win the Party's Senate nomination.[18] After the 1946 political massacre, it was not hard to see why liberal but establishment figures like McDonough saw the Popular Front hue of the California Democratic Party as fatal to the Party's political fortunes. Though President Truman would carry California narrowly in his 1948 reelection effort, no Democrat would win an election for statewide office other than for the post of attorney general until 1958.

The unhappy marriage of the state's principal labor organizations and the GOP also set the scene for a Democratic renaissance that would be based around suburban activism rather than a labor alliance. Hope Mendoza Schechter, a leading figure in the garment workers' union and Democratic activist in a predominantly Latino part of southeastern LA, recalled with frustration the political ambivalence of the AFL in her neighborhood and statewide: "CIO—you could almost bank on Democratic endorsements—but not AFL. That was touch and go and a lot of politicking and a lot of work, in order to swing meaningful endorsements for Democrats." She was determined to build up a liberal Democratic movement in her overwhelmingly working-class district, but found her union leadership unwilling to ruffle the feathers of Republican contacts in Sacramento, including corrupt Attorney General Fred Howser, who lost to Democrat Pat Brown in 1950 despite the AFL's continued backing of Howser: "In the nineteenth congressional district, I maintained a totally Democratic headquarters. I was in charge of the whole nineteenth congressional district.... I remember going to a Central Labor Council meeting ... and [IGLWU Director of Public Relations and Education Sigmund Arywitz] hadn't told me in advance, and to my horror, found out that he'd bounced me off ... because I had worked for Pat Brown.

The irony is that Pat Brown later appointed him Commissioner of Labor." Schechter argued that labor's reluctance to be more daring in its efforts to shape state politics frustrated ambitious and hard-working activists like her. The leadership "were being opportunistic. They knew [a Republican] was going to win anyway, and so they might just as well—there was no sense in fighting it. He's going to win. I just took the position that they could have gone for no endorsement and that way, leave those of us who want to retain a few ideals, a little flexibility. This other way . . . your hands were tied."[19] The AFL endorsement process often did refuse to endorse Republicans if they were antilabor or had overwhelmingly conservative records, but in many cases the conventions in the early 1950s were plagued by disputes between delegates over whether or not to endorse both Republican and Democratic candidates in a district where both were friendly to labor, or whether to withhold endorsement in cases where insufficient information about candidates had been made available.[20] CLLPE Secretary C. J. Haggerty even confessed in his speech to the 1952 convention to being "almost nauseated" by the choice of endorsements for the state legislature. Comments from the floor were more categorical: "I have looked through these endorsements," said one delegate, "and I think in very few instances are we going to be at battle with the Chamber of Commerce or the Merchants and Manufacturers. In many instances I think we are going to be in the same corner with them. . . . It seems to me that we have reached not the basic fundamentals of 'rewarding our friends and defeating our enemies,' but a placating of the powers-that-be in the spirit of 'we will be nice to you if you will be nice to us.'" The delegate noted that Earl Warren, praised in the League's political newsletter, had signed the reapportionment bill, and that reapportionment in 1952 along GOP-approved lines "is going to do us more harm than any acts that the Legislature passed during the 1951 session."[21] It was certainly true that the absence of a natural alliance between organized labor and a New Deal–dominated political establishment made the prospects of an amicable settlement of industrial relations questions particularly unlikely in California as the 1950s wore on.

The Club Movement and the Rise of the Democratic Party

An atmosphere of excitement and anticipation filled the conference hall as hundreds of left-leaning activists, fresh from the disastrous 1952 campaign, met to work out where to go from their recent defeat. The meeting, held in

Asilomar, near Monterey, in January 1953, was advertised as a forum where party activists could reflect on the lessons of the 1952 electoral debacle and decide how best to enthuse voters into going to the polls and voting Democratic. The conference program was entitled "How to End the Republican Stranglehold in California," and laid out a blueprint for a new organization, the California Democratic Council, which would mobilize members behind a specific candidate in party primaries to prevent damaging free-for-alls in contests for public office. In the final report of the meeting, liberal congressman George Miller Jr. argued that the "test of a political party" should be its capacity to "rally the people to the ideals and principles for which it stands," and the emphasis of the agenda was on developing a coherent political identity for California Democrats.[22] The Stevenson campaign of 1952 had encouraged a wave of enthusiasm across California and the setting up of Stevenson clubs, and the assembled activists at Asilomar wanted to maintain the momentum of the preceding year and formalize the club structure. Stewart Udall, influential Democratic congressman from Arizona who later became JFK's secretary of the interior, claimed in a 1958 article that "Stevenson acted as a fulcrum for the upsurge of his party in several of the states. It was hardly accidental that many of the Stevenson strongholds of 1956—California, Oregon and Pennsylvania, to name a few—were the states where Stevenson's 1952 campaign set in motion new forces and personalities. In many instances it was this fresh corps of amateurs and egghead recruits who provided the extra drive that revitalized weak party organizations."[23]

The delegates consisted of an impressive cross-section of the party membership, from elected office holders like George Miller and Pat Brown to party grandees such as State Committeeman Roger Kent to neophyte campaigners like Phil Burton and Alan Cranston. The assembled throng also represented a cross-section of society. Burton was a scruffy city boy from San Francisco who never owned his own home and who had little time for the niceties of San Francisco society. "He didn't own any place to live," recalled political ally Willie Brown. "Maybe he had one or two suits and didn't care about those kind of things."[24] Cranston and Kent, on the other hand, were representatives of a Bay Area moneyed aristocracy that dominated the social world of Marin and the lower Peninsula. Cranston, the first chairman of the CDC who would play a crucial role in developing an ideological conscience for the Party, had grown up in a wealthy Palo Alto family and had been a journalist watching the march of Fascism in Europe before working for the Office of War Information during the war. A champion sprinter, he embodied the easy charm and political enthusiasm that a privileged background conferred.

Kent was a household name in Marin county: his father had been a prominent progressive Republican in the Hiram Johnson era, and the family home at Kentfield was a well-known landmark in a neighborhood where discreet but obvious wealth was hardly unusual. As he later recalled, Democrats in staunch Republican Marin were a rare but dedicated bunch as "they had to be pretty tough to survive, and they had to be pretty dedicated. I think this is a pattern that you'd see in other parts of the country, where an affluent—and oftentimes, it's a campus-type group, this not being one of those—community will generate very strong Democratic leadership. This may be because they have time enough or money enough to do some work that the poor working man would love to do if he were able to."[25]

Delegates from Southern California represented the same powerful mixture of labor Democrats from blue-collar LA suburbs and wealthy suburban activists. Steve Zetterberg, who had taken on Nixon in his congressional district in 1948 and who was a major player in Democratic politics in Claremont and Pomona, represented the type of well-connected suburban professional who would form the backbone of the CDC and shape left-of-center activism in the 1950s and 1960s. The Asilomar meeting, he recalled "was just bubbling over with excitement and interest and application of a lot of people to the Democratic issues. By issues, I mean not issue-issues but also program, finance, and so on. It was not just all in one big auditorium. It was a lot of separate meetings where there was a lot of participation."[26] From the same district came Carmen Warschaw, an uncompromising, straight-talking party strategist and leader who would later run for the chair of the state party and who was one of the most important women in California Democratic politics. She was no idealist neophyte, having formed a Democratic organization in Los Feliz in the 1940s, worked on Jerry Voorhis's campaigns, and who would play a key role in getting people like Jesse Unruh, the future Speaker, elected to the assembly. "We all were in Asilomar at that time," she later remembered.[27] James Q. Wilson in his 1966 study of club politics stressed the middle-class, privileged background of CDC activists: "Over half were under 40 years of age, over 60 percent had a college education or better, most were in professional occupations, and practically no one was Catholic while nearly half were Jewish in their religious background." He emphasized the change in style of California politics that club activism would bring, bringing a greater emphasis on fighting for principle than power and a heightened sense of amateur activism over precinct organization. The Asilomar meeting, however, demonstrated that the CDC, at least in its early days, was a mixture of party regulars and new activists, of working class and middle class, and that the mixture of idealism and the practicalities of gaining power defined how party politics worked in California.[28] The meeting set up the CDC as an umbrella group to charter Democratic clubs as local activist cells that would revitalize party political activity across the State.

There was no doubt, however, that the majority of successful clubs that were chartered after the Asilomar meeting were in wealthy and middle-class white areas of places like West LA, home to several clubs of several hundred active members each, or suburbs where community organizing provided a social outlet for politically aware citizens. The Democratic Club of Claremont in the rapidly growing Southland drew up a constitution that contained the following statement: "In order to promote the principles and activism of the Democratic Party, and to provide for all people the highest degree of justice and social welfare, we associate ourselves together to establish the Democratic Club of Claremont." Club chairman Steve Zetterberg wanted to replace the second clause with "to stimulate an active interest in public affairs," seemingly because the statement as originally written suggested that the club itself would be the agent of justice and social welfare, whereas in truth clubs existed to get public opinion behind party candidates who would then make policy in the state legislature.[29] Nonetheless, the statement of intent differed in tone and emphasis from previous Democratic Party statements like that of the Alameda club of 1949, which pledged merely to support the Party.[30] The new emphasis was on supporting a political stance—social justice—and on supporting the Democratic Party insofar as it was the agent of that political worldview. The Constitution of the Club pledged "to give as many registered Democrats as possible . . . an effective voice in the affairs of the Democratic Party in this District and in the State," and meetings of the local club regularly attracted dozens of well-connected citizens to discuss questions such as capital punishment and conditions in women's prisons. When issues upon which the club had taken a stand came up for discussion in the state legislature, club members would be called into action to write and put pressure on legislators to vote the right way. "We who are the working Democrats now have an obligation and responsibility to keep ourselves informed on the issues, and to support that program," argued the legislative chairwoman of the Claremont area club in April 1959.[31] The growth of these clubs across the Southland dovetailed with the increasing clout in the 1960s of African American and Latino political activism that formed the basis for a rainbow coalition of interests that began to shift the center of gravity in LA politics away from the racist conservatism of Mayor Sam Yorty.[32]

The West Beverly Club in the Fairfax area of West LA, one of the most active and successful in the state, heavily Jewish and home to many who had cut their teeth in communist struggles in LA in the New Deal era, had its own political action chairman who organized get-out-the-vote campaigns, brought in political speakers to address the club, and made it the mission of the organization to "help elect the type of candidates that believe in the same things we do."[33] Issues that united these activist volunteers included bitter opposition to the House Un-American Activities Committee, support for organized labor, support for universal health insurance and an expanded welfare state, and civil rights.

The club movement thrived in the late 1950s because it reflected the importance Californians attached to joining groups as a way of making sense of their position in a sprawling, rapidly changing social milieu, and it also reflected the desperate need many Californians felt for political engagement in a state in which political debate since 1952 had become a trendsetter on both left and right.[34] Clubs acted very much like Communist cells that had proven so popular in California in the 1930s, or like local groups of Mattachine homophile activists who had come out of the Communist movement in Los Angeles, or like local committees dedicated to the passage of FEPC.

The link between the political message and the social involvement that made local clubs successful can be observed by comparing clubs with local chapters of Americans for Democratic Action in the 1950s. By the mid-1950s the California ADA was in crisis. Chapters in LA and San Francisco had collapsed, despite several attempts to resurrect them. National ADA leader Sheldon Pollack concluded in July 1956 that the fact that ADA policy was being made in Washington and disseminated to local chapters just did not work in Southern California, and that local Democratic clubs "absorbed all of the political interests of people who had been active in the [ADA] chapter." CDC clubs made their own policy, participated in the drawing up of a political agenda at annual conventions, and had a direct stake in the election of a California Democratic Party to power, rather than a generalized commitment to liberalism espoused by a distant ADA high command three thousand miles away. Just as importantly, the very ideology that formed the core raison d'être of ADA was out of step with the California scene. Pollack suggested that the reason for ADA weakness was that "the initial enthusiasm generated by a new organization and the turmoil of the postwar world has subsided, and the issues we support, while apparently important, do not seem as vital, nor of such immediate consequence.... Liberals are willing to support them but not so willing to actively work on their behalf." This defeatist statement contrasted starkly with the vigor with which California Democrats were organizing and growing in the 1950s. Nor did Pollack understand the power that the link to the Party gave clubs as they recruited members: the advance of the Democratic Party gave the membership a goal, a more tangible direction than Pollack's criticism that the club movement had become so enmeshed with the Party that there might be "more room for an independent organization that would keep the party people mindful of issues."[35] Later events would prove that too close a connection between party and club movement could lead to schisms and disillusionment, but it also made a popular commitment to political participation more concrete, and the divisions between parties over policy more clear-cut and important.

Some ADA observers of the California scene were more aware of the importance of what was going on there in the 1950s. "Continuous defeat in state and local politics in the past made difficult the growth of responsible state-wide party organization," reported Paul Seabury, a Berkeley political science professor involved in the local ADA chapter, "but it has made it possible for the newly emergent Democratic organization in the state to be far more responsive to the forces of 'modernity' within the party.... By and large it is something new in American politics: a broad movement of well-educated liberals whose political cohesiveness derives not from ethnic, or narrowly based economic interest, but from a deep 'concern' with political issues transcending the 'self-interest' of the movement itself. The 'great issues' of American politics and international affairs for them have been overriding." Seabury noted the insularity of the club movement, which did not have much traction outside the state, but felt that perhaps ADA could provide the bridge from state to national politics: "Perhaps the very 'freshness' of our Western political milieu may produce here part of the vigor and intellectual initiative so greatly needed in national politics."[36]

This was unlikely to happen so long as the East Coast ADA leadership remained obsessed with communism and the Cold War at a time when clubs like the West Beverly club were prompting a reappraisal of the entire basis of Cold War liberalism. Indeed, the origins of the Democratic renaissance in California lay in its Popular Front past and a widespread revulsion at the impact of domestic anticommunism on California politics. Many members of clubs in Southern California had fellow traveler and communist pasts, and were moving into mainstream politics on the basis that the issues-oriented clubs were shifting the parameters of California party politics leftward. Sheldon Pollack wanted to use ADA to "counteract the infiltration of the Democratic clubs" and characterized activists at the CDC Issues conferences as "commies and fuzzies," but he simply missed the point of where the strength of the clubs originated.[37] ADA national organizer Nathalie Panek in 1954 put her finger on the answer even as she was condemning the fact that "fuzziness among decent liberals out here seems almost endemic," the term "fuzzy" apparently meaning less than hysterically anticommunist. She had been told "by sane and respectable people that the Democratic Party here is really a united front outfit—old style—and that some of the blossoming Democratic clubs have been or are in the process of being taken over by the CP. To round out the picture I should tell you that in the two months I have been here I have had more stupid pre–ADA-type of arguments on whether we can work with Communists than I have had in the last five years. And I don't think one of the arguers was a knowing fellow traveler."[38] Most in the club movement, including CDC leader Alan Cranston, had never been communists or fellow travelers, and others, like Saul Reider, had exchanged communism for Democratic activism: all were united in disgust at the California Republican Party's sacrifice of Helen Douglas and Jimmy Roosevelt at the altar of anticommunism in 1950, and all were dedicated to the establishment of the Democratic Party on the basis of issues of relevance to Californians in the 1950s, not the dark years of the late 1940s when Cold War liberalism had conspired with the Right to all but destroy not only the remnant of Popular Front politics but the entire structural basis of liberalism in California.

The 1956 Election and the Crystallizing of the Democratic Message

The way in which local party strategists directed Adlai Stevenson's 1956 campaign in California highlights how the particular contours of state politics created a bridge from the Popular Front schisms of the 1940s to the rights discourse of the 1960s. California was a symbol of modernity that was directing Democratic Party politics in new directions, a fact that would impact significantly upon Stevenson's campaign. In just one year between 1951 and 1952 the official population of California had grown from 11,100,000 to around 11,550,000. The areas of fastest job creation were in commercial and service sector industries, and the pressures on public services, including water, transportation, and public power, were major issues that transcended party political divisions and made the articulation of a political message challenging. A CDC brochure entitled "The Consumer in the Modern Market Place" argued that the "potential market for all types of goods and services is so great in California because average income is higher than the average national income (one-fourth higher); population expansion is in the group heavily dominated by active buyers, i.e., eighteen- to forty-five-year-olds; employment is high; business climate is good in the sense that the demand for housing, for highways, for other services and goods is expanding." The overriding question of the brochure asked how "can the Democratic clubs and Democratic Party assist in the fight to protect the consumer interest?"[39] A California AFL-CIO leaflet produced in late 1956 and later revised and reprinted was headed "Consumer, Beware! A Guide to Installment Buying," which attempted to advise California workers how to cope with rapidly burgeoning levels of available credit and debt in the nation's fastest growing economy, by 1960 one of the world's ten largest.[40] Historians have in recent years crafted detailed studies of the emergence of this "consumers' republic" in the United States both in terms of the political import of consumption to consumers and workers themselves and in terms of the development of a militantly probusiness, antiregulatory movement that it encouraged in places where rapid population and economic growth offered opportunities for business elites to dominate the political process.[41]

In California, economic concerns predicated upon consumer interests and rapidly growing pressures on public services pushed the Stevenson campaign and the Democratic Party in the opposite direction to the antistatist dynamic at work in Sunbelt states. A confidential report compiled by a PR company working for Stevenson in California before the crucial primary clash against Estes Kefauver stated that

> the issues of credit, jobs and inflation should in some way be underlined. . . . An informant in the consumer credit business explained that the average indebtedness in Los Angeles and other rapidly growing parts of California is far higher than the nation as a whole. These communities of small new homes, depending on the automobile for transportation and oriented towards California style easy living are overhung by the shadow of monthly payments and mortgages. . . . Perhaps this is the time for a new New Deal focus on a tremendous increase in productivity and the leisure that goes with it (Perhaps talk about the goal of a 35-hour week but do not use the word Automation). One of the manifestations of the pressure on living standards here is a widespread pattern of two jobs per man in the hope of meeting mortgages and payments. A psychiatrist told us that his patients here show far more than the usual anxiety about earning enough to keep up in the rat race.

The report urged Stevenson to "show the voters that he cares for the things they care about by describing in concrete and emotionally charged language the problems from which they are suffering." There was not as much popular interest in health insurance or the injustices of Taft-Hartley as might have been expected, stated the report, but the "New Deal–Fair Deal as a whole has not lost its glamour. A New Deal program is what the Democratic voters want, and other forms of welfare legislation are popular.... There are other things... such as job stabilization, consumer debt, and above all, a rapid increase of living standards." The report concluded: "What this adds up to is a kind of New Deal package. Aside from pointing out a few issues which should be de-emphasized most all that is said above adds up to noting a widespread groping for a vigorous restatement of a New Deal approach on bread-and-butter matters, coupled with foreign affairs, civil rights and an occasional unifying pep talk to the active Democrats. The bread-and-butter package should appeal to the rapidly growing lower middle-class suburbs and might include such items as schools, water, taxes, and consumer debt."[42]

This conclusion found support in responses by local Democrats to a questionnaire sent out by Stevenson's campaign team in order to build up a statewide picture of issues that mattered to Californians. One question asked respondents for evidence of the status of local schools, housing, hospitals, and welfare. The response of the San Francisco party was that "our schools are excellent; housing is growing old, needs redevelopment; hospitals good but getting old; general health, good; social security, fair. We have thousands of old, lonely men and women living a meager existence in cheap apartments and hotels on skid road [sic], South of Market. Better provision for them would be a boon to the community as well as themselves. Governor Stevenson should tour our Howard Street flophouses and point up the human misery.... He should visit our Hunter's Point 'temporary' housing where negroes live because they can't get good private housing at rates they can pay. He should dramatize his interest in these problems." Another question read: "what do you consider to be the key issues in your city and area in 1956? At what points is the Republican record strongest or most vulnerable to attack and at what point do you believe the Democratic position is strongest or weakest?" The response: "Governor Stevenson must show our people that the farm depression is a terrible danger to all America, that it and the unemployment in various areas in the United States are tell-tale signs of the gravest importance showing that the Republicans have failed and will fail to protect our people against another depression.... On the other hand, in four years Governor Stevenson can consolidate and *advance* the Democratic gains in social and old-age security, health preservation ... health insurance (this need not touch the doctor-patient relationship but can cover all the costly incidentals of catastrophic illness such as hospital, laboratory, drugs, nurses, technical therapies), farm security, housing, SEC."[43] The San Francisco case is revealing as the Party there acted as a meeting ground for party regulars and club activists, all of whom shared a headquarters at 212 Sutter Street, demonstrating the fluid boundaries between party and volunteer club.⁴⁴

A correspondent in Los Angeles sent Stevenson a "copy of a health-education-welfare draft for Los Angeles. . . . I hope that it is also a start, although a puny one, toward developing a theme for the Age of Abundance. . . . I would cite health-education-welfare high on the list, with particular emphasis on the old folks. Small business is another."⁴⁵ Gerald O'Gara, a veteran of San Francisco Democratic politics, argued in April that "Governor Stevenson to win must punch harder. As of now, the contrast between him and Eisenhower is too pale, too vaguely defined. Governor Stevenson must put on the mantle of Wilson, Roosevelt, and Truman and wear it boldly and proudly. . . . If he is not the apostle of the Democracy that crusades for labor (by which I mean all work for wages), for the small farmer, for the old, the sick, and the jobless, for children, for Negroes, for peace, for the small businessman, for a better life for all Americans (especially the little fellow) without a ceiling, either permanent or temporary, and a vigorous, unremitting fighter for the better life—then he is nothing as a Democratic candidate in 1956."⁴⁶

The social democratic edge to Democratic Party thinking in California in part reflected the increasing influence of club activists and left-of-center thinkers in the Party's affairs; it also formed a reaction to the increasing anti-regulatory business control over Republican Party strategy. Central, however, to the left turn in Democratic politics during the 1956 presidential primary contest was the place of civil rights in party discourse, made vitally important not only by the growing pressure for a state FEPC but also because Estes Kefauver made race an underlying rationale behind his run for President. Even after Kefauver withdrew from the race in July 1956, Stevenson's team remained concerned that his political enemies nationwide "will seek to cut down his lead and ultimately defeat his candidacy primarily by attacking his alleged position on civil rights. They will contend and argue that he has equivocated on the civil rights issue, that he seeks to accommodate the southern wing of the Party and that he will not be a liberal president who will forthrightly face the issues in this critical area of our national life."⁴⁷ Stevenson had made serious mistakes during the primary season, asserting in Minneapolis in March that northern states had to put their own house in order before "we cast a stone at Alabama." A New York supporter called this speech "sheer political ineptitude," and Walter Reuther at a press conference tactfully replied to a question about Stevenson and civil rights that "I think that maybe if I were making speeches, I would say things differently than perhaps Mr. Stevenson says them."⁴⁸ In California, Stevenson's PR advisers were categorical: "Any new boners on the civil rights and desegregation issues—that is, any further actions on which Stevenson sounds indecisive, unindignant, or cool about the whole thing could be catastrophic for the Negro vote."[49] Not only that, civil rights was increasingly forming the new central issue for left-wing elements in the Democratic coalition, white as well as black. "Kefauver has benefited in California from a misunderstanding of the 'moderation' point and from his relatively more vigorous positions on such issues as natural gas and civil rights," wrote one Stevenson informant after having met with prominent state Democrats, including Roger Kent, Paul Ziffren, Richard Richards, and Peter Odegard.[50] The far left element of the California Democratic Party was increasingly latching on to civil rights as a principal cause after the collapse of communism in the United States: "A large part of the energy behind the Kefauver campaign comes from pinks and fellow travelers, not to mention out and out Communists," claimed Stevenson's public relations consultants in California.[51] Stevenson's speech to the CDC convention at Fresno in February, at which he followed Kefauver and gave a lackluster speech, was widely seen as a major setback to his campaign. John Bartlow Martin later referred to Stevenson's speech as "the Fresno fiasco," and an observer wrote that he had "noted the letdown his loyal supporters experienced at the Fresno convention of the California Council of Democratic Clubs—when he followed Kefauver and gave a scholarly, high-minded address." This correspondent begged Stevenson to make his speeches "inspired, provide definite benefits, frightened by black and definite evils and dangers—not gray shadows of possible disadvantages."[52] The increasing power of civil rights as a theme in California politics—and San Francisco passed a citywide fair employment practices ordinance in 1956—added a social citizenship dimension to the Party's agenda and forced those running for office to take much more forthright stands on issues than was often the case elsewhere.

Stevenson could not carry California in 1956, but the impact of his campaign on state politics was significant. "There isn't any question in my mind," Roger Kent asserted some years later, "but that we would have carried California if it hadn't have been for the Suez crisis. We were running a very good campaign. The campaign was enthusiastic for Stevenson. The people were for Stevenson. It was going our way."[53] It is impossible to factor in such imponderables, but the signs in California were suggestive. Democrats won enough seats in the State Senate to produce a tie with the Republicans; they were just three seats short of gaining the Assembly. Phil Burton won his Assembly seat in San Francisco with a strongly left-wing campaign against a popular incumbent Republican.[54] More importantly, a coalition of economic and social rights advocates that encompassed labor, civil rights groups, and those pushing for a consumer-oriented social democratic politics was gradually coalescing into a major political force, with the Democratic Party as its lynchpin. Though this phenomenon had a particularly Californian flavor thanks to the growth of the clubs and the legacy of Popular Front influence that made civil rights and economic rights together especially potent on the Party's left wing, there were signs elsewhere that new Democratic strength was building in areas where the contours of 1950s social problems were influential. An example was South Dakota, where George McGovern used worry over farm income and concern that the Cold War was leading the United States toward a real conflict to breathe life into a moribund Democratic Party. "Farmers' share of the consumer's food dollar has shrunk more than 10 cents since 1947," he reported to his constituents in January 1956. "The spread between farm and retail prices widens. Yet farmers do not have the conviction that their city cousins on mainstreet are prospering."[55] Former Connecticut Democratic congresswoman Chase Going Woodhouse argued in 1957 that the "Democrats need a new line. . . . I have tried out the idea of 'conformity,' of the need for 'angry young men' such as were around Roosevelt. . . . The changes in American life towards conformity and 'tranquillizers,' the attitude of the Eisenhower administration in not telling the public anything that might disturb them etc has troubled people. Few were courageous enough to speak out when McCarthy et al were strong but now they would like to be associated with people who did."[56]

The landmark elections of 1958 would change the political landscape of both California and the nation dramatically, demonstrating the extent to which a new political order was on the horizon, with enormous consequences for the economic and civil rights of California citizens. There is no space here to detail the self-immolating right turn of the state Republican Party on the question of labor rights and the union shop that finally pushed organized labor into the Democratic camp in California, nor to examine the raft of civil rights and welfare state legislation enacted under the Brown administration between 1959 and 1963.[57] It is important to recognize, too, that the marriage of convenience between club activists, regular Democrats, labor unions, and civil rights interest groups quickly came under severe pressure when challenged by a coalition of homeowners, business groups, and Republicans hungry for a return to political hegemony. The key issue here is to note the origins of the rights revolution of the 1960s in California in the building of a new Democratic Party in the 1950s that bridged the divide between grassroots organizing and party politics and set the stage for the association of Democratic politicians with the espousal of an ideology of social inclusion. I do not argue that the strong presence of suburban rights activists in the Democratic renaissance was in itself an advantage, and do not deny the inability of liberalism to become totally dominant in the state as a whole. The bourgeois tenor of Democratic statecraft inevitably privileged legal rights over the erasure of class divisions and became caught between the articulation of principle and the day-to-day machinations of a regime in power dedicated to the solving of questions of water provision, infrastructure-building, and economic growth that required a rather uncertain commitment to economic justice. The optimism and freshness of West Coast liberalism in the 1950s did, however, make it comparatively easy for groups committed to racial and sexual equality to integrate themselves into Democratic policy elites earlier than in many other states, and explains also the damage Cold War foreign policy caused the state party far earlier than elsewhere. California "liberalism," an uneasy synthesis of redistributive social policy, managed economic growth, and social citizenship through equal protection legislation, came into being due to the particular political circumstances of postwar California, but it had implications for the future of the American Left that extended far beyond the state's boundaries in the last decades of the twentieth century.

Notes

1. J. R. Feyrel, "Thoughts on the Welfare State," *New Republic* January 28, 1952, 11–13.

2. See Thomas W. Evans, *The Education of Ronald Reagan: The General Electric Years and the Untold Story of His Conversion to Conservatism* (New York: Columbia University Press, 2006); Elizabeth Fones-Wolf, *Selling Free Enterprise: The Business Assault on Labor and Liberalism* (Urbana: University of Illinois Press, 1994); Kimberly Phillips-Fein, "American Counterrevolutionary: Lemuel Ricketts Boulware and General Electric, 1950–1960," in Nelson Lichtenstein, ed., *American Capitalism: Social Thought and Political Economy in the Twentieth Century* (Philadelphia: University of Pennsylvania Press, 2006), 249–270; Elizabeth Tandy Shermer, "Origins of the Conservative Ascendancy: Barry Goldwater's Early Senate Career and the De-legitimization of Organized Labor," *Journal of American History* 95:3 (December 2008): 678–709; Lisa McGirr, *Suburban Warriors: The Origins of the New American Right* (Princeton: Princeton University Press, 2001).

3. Howard Brick, *Transcending Capitalism: Visions of the New Society in Modern American Thought* (Ithaca: Cornell University Press, 2006); Daniel Geary, "'Becoming International Again': C. Wright Mills and the Emergence of a Global New Left,

1956–1962," *Journal of American History* 95:3 (December 2008): 710–736; Kevin Mattson, *When America Was Great: The Fighting Faith of Postwar Liberalism* (New York: Routledge, 2004).

4. Lizabeth Cohen, *A Consumer's Republic: The Politics of Mass Consumption in Postwar America* (New York: Vintage, 2004); Meg Jacobs, *Pocketbook Politics: Economic Citizenship in Twentieth-Century America* (Princeton: Princeton University Press, 2004); Daniel Scroop, "The Anti-chain Store Movement and the Politics of Consumption," *American Quarterly* 60:4 (December 2008): 925–949; Matthew Lassiter, *The Silent Majority: Suburban Politics in the Sunbelt South* (Princeton: Princeton University Press, 2006).

5. A good example is the controversy following publication of Bruce Miroff's *The Liberals' Moment: The McGovern Insurgency and the Identity Crisis of the Democratic Party* (Lawrence: University Press of Kansas, 2007), in the sense that Miroff sees the McGovern movement as a product of the politics of 1968 (a McGovernite insurgency was in place in all but name in California by the end of the 1950s) and in the sense that critics of this book fail to see the significance of a left-liberal movement that arguably collapsed before it had even coalesced in 1972. See Kenneth S. Baer, "Glory Days: A Review of Bruce Miroff's *The Liberals' Moment*," *The Forum* 5:4 (2008): article 9.

6. The following are just a handful of examples: McGirr, *Suburban Warriors*; Kevin Schuparra, *Triumph of the Right: The Rise of the California Conservative Movement, 1945–1966* (Armonk: M. E. Sharpe, 1998); Daniel Hurewitz, *Bohemian Los Angeles and the Making of Modern Politics* (Berkeley: University of California Press, 2007); Fraser Ottanelli, *The Communist Party of the United States: From the Depression to World War Two* (New Brunswick: Rutgers University Press, 1991).

7. See *Statistical Abstracts of the United States* (U.S. Dept. of Commerce, 78th annual edition, 1957), 30, table 27.

8. John Aubrey Douglass, "Earl Warren's New Deal: Economic Transition, Public Planning, and Higher Education in California," *Journal of Policy History* 12:4 (2000): 473ff.

9. See Hurewitz, *Bohemian Los Angeles*; Robert O. Self, *American Babylon: Race and the Struggle for Postwar Oakland* (Princeton: Princeton University Press, 2003); Ottanelli, *The Communist Party of the United States*, 118–119; Harvey Klehr, *The Heyday of American Communism: The Depression Decade* (New York: Basic Books, 1984), especially 173–176.

10. Douglass, "Earl Warren's New Deal," 473.

11. David R. Mayhew, *Placing Parties in American Politics: Organization, Electoral Settings, and Government Activity in the Twentieth Century* (Princeton: Princeton University Press, 1986), 185; see also James Q. Wilson, *The Amateur Democrat: Club Politics in Three Cities* (Chicago: University of Chicago Press, 1966), 96–109; John R. Owens, Edmond Constantini, and Louis F. Weschler, *California Politics and Parties* (New York: Macmillan, 1970).

12. See Hurewitz, *Bohemian Los Angeles*; Self, *American Babylon*; Josh Sides, *LA*

City Limits: African American Los Angeles from the Great Depression to the Present (Berkeley: University of California Press, 2003).

13. Ellen Reese, *Backlash against Welfare Mothers: Past and Present* (Berkeley: University of California Press, 2005), ch. 6, especially 87.

14. Warren, *The Memoirs of Earl Warren*, 187–188. For detailed analysis of the AMA's successful campaigns against federal health insurance, see Alan Derickson, *Health Security for All: Dreams of Universal Health Care in America* (Baltimore: Johns Hopkins University Press, 2005); Colin Gordon, *Dead on Arrival: The Politics of Health Care in Twentieth-Century America* (Princeton: Princeton University Press, 2003); Jonathan Bell, *The Liberal State on Trial: The Cold War and American Politics in the Truman Years* (New York: Columbia University Press, 2004).

15. "Warren, the Myth and the Record," *New Republic*, June 23, 1952, 11–13.

16. For the Alameda case, see Francis Dunn, assemblyman from the 13th district, to Patrick McDonough, congressional candidate in the 7th district in Alameda, October 8, 1945, McDonough MSS, Bancroft Library, Box 1, Democratic Party County Central Committees file.

17. McDonough to Edward Heller, January 20, 1947, McDonough MSS, Box 1, outgoing letters 1946–1947 file.

18. See minutes of the ICCASP campaign committee, Hollywood branch, January 30, 1946, James Roosevelt MSS, Box 192, ICCASP C file; Malcolm Hash, Roosevelt's secretary, to Lela Bullock, April 4, 1946, on Patterson endorsement, ibid., B file.

19. Hope Mendoza Schechter, "Activist in the Labor Movement, the Democratic Party, and the Mexican American Community," interview conducted by Malca Schall, 1977–1978, Women in Politics Oral History Project, Bancroft Library, University of California, Berkeley, 42–46.

20. See proceeding of the 1952 preprimary convention of the California LLPE, April 7, 1952, 65–76: these 11 pages of the transcript report a debate over whether to endorse liberal Republican Milton Marks for state assembly as well as his Democratic opponent, an act that would require a change to the endorsement rules. In the end, only the Democrat was endorsed, though numerous incumbent Republicans still gained AFL endorsement in 1952.

21. Ibid., 105, 114–116.

22. Final report of the Workshop Conference at Asilomar, February 1953, Cranston MSS, Box 11, Asilomar file.

23. Stewart L. Udall, "Why Adlai Stevenson Haunts the Democrats," *New Republic*, May 19, 1958.

24. Willie Brown oral history, 39.

25. Roger Kent oral history, 35. Wealthy liberal activism in Marin was indeed an impressive force as the county became increasingly liberal and Democratic as the century went on, even though its socioeconomic composition changed little.

26. Stephen Zetterberg oral interview, State Government Oral History program, California State Archives, Sacramento, 75.

27. Carmen Warschaw oral interview, "A Southern Californian Perspective on Democratic Party Politics," Bancroft oral history project, 120, 147.

28. Wilson, *The Amateur Democrat*, 16.

29. Draft of constitution of Claremont Democratic Club, Zetterberg MSS, Box 1, Democratic bylaws 1953 file.

30. Alameda County Democratic Council Revised By-Laws, C. L. Dellums MSS, Box 25, Alameda County Democratic Council file.

31. Constitution of the 21st Congressional District Democratic Council, Zetterberg MSS, Box 1; Memo from Cricket Levering to club legislative organizers, April 29, 1959, Zetterberg MSS, Box 2, CDC 1959–1960 file.

32. For a detailed exposition of this argument, see Raphael J. Sonenshein, *Politics in Black and White: Race and Power in Los Angeles* (Princeton: Princeton University Press, 1993).

33. President of West Beverly Club, *West Beverly Bray* newsletter, June 1958, CDC MSS, Southern California Library for Social Studies and Research, Los Angeles, Box 25, File 12.

34. For studies of the right-wing equivalent of grassroots organizations that encouraged people to become "joiners" on the basis of political enthusiasm, see McGirr, *Suburban Warriors;* Schuparra, *Triumph of the Right.*

35. Sheldon Pollack to Marvin Rosenberg, July 18, 1956; Pollack to ADA organizing committee, June 12, 1957; Pollack to Rosenberg, February 28, 1958, ADA MSS, reel 57, no. 5.

36. Paul Seabury to Sam Beer, national chairman of ADA, nd, late 1950s, ADA MSS, ibid.

37. Sheldon Pollack to Paul Seabury, December 18, 1959, ADA MSS, ibid.; Pollack to Violet Gunther, March 6, 1961, ADA MSS, reel 58, no. 5.

38. Nathalie Panek to David Williams, ADA Director of Education, May 20, 1954, ADA MSS, reel 58, no. 7.

39. "The Consumer in the Modern Market-place," CDC issues brochure, February 1960, California Democratic Party MSS, Box 1, consumers file.

40. "Consumer Beware!" leaflet, California Democratic Party MSS, Box 1, consumers file; "California: A Survey," *The Banker* (November 1968): 992–995. This British journal noted the importance of California to the world economy, stating on page 992 that "California's statistics are more akin to a country than a state."

41. See Cohen, *A Consumer's Republic*; Jacobs, *Pocketbook Politics*; Fones-Wolf, *Selling Free Enterprise*; Evans, *The Education of Ronald Reagan*; Elizabeth Tandy Shermer, "Counter-organizing the Sunbelt: Right-to-Work Campaigns and Anti-union Conservatism, 1943–1958," *Pacific Historical Review* (February 2009).

42. "The Stevenson Campaign in California—A Research Report from Edward L. Greenfield and Company," Stevenson MSS, Box 299, Folder 5, and Box 249, Folder 1.

43. San Francisco party reply to Stevenson campaign questionnaire, Stevenson MSS, Box 248, Folder 7. Emphasis original.

44. Roger Kent oral interview, Bancroft Library, UC Berkeley, 29–30, 43.

45. Harry Ashmore to Stevenson, May 4, 1956, Stevenson MSS, Box 248, File 7.

46. Gerald O'Gara to Ken Hechler of Stevenson campaign staff, April 26, 1956, Stevenson MSS, Box 248, File 7.

47. L. Howard Bennett to James A. Finnegan, July 27, 1956, Stevenson MSS, Box 248, File 1.

48. Harry Harris to Edward Greenfield, March 6, 1956, Stevenson MSS, Box 268, File 4; Walter Reuther press conference, April 26, 1956, Stevenson MSS, Box 268, File 9. See also Jennifer Delton, *Making Minnesota Liberal: Civil Rights and the Transformation of the Democratic Party* (Minneapolis: University of Minnesota Press, 2002).

49. Stevenson campaign research report, Stevenson MSS, Box 299, Folder 5.

50. Letter from unnamed Stevenson informant to Stevenson, January 17, 1956, Stevenson MSS, Box 303, File 6.

51. Stevenson campaign research report, Edward L. Greenfield and Company, Stevenson MSS, Box 299, Folder 5.

52. John Bartlow Martin quoted in Porter McKeever, *Adlai Stevenson: His Life and Legacy* (New York: Morrow, 1989), 366; Gerald O'Hara to Ken Hechler, April 26, 1956, Stevenson MSS, Box 248, File 7.

53. Roger Kent oral interview, 136.

54. I have discussed this election and the importance of Burton in California politics in Jonathan Bell, "Social Democracy and the Rise of the Democratic Party in California, 1950–1964," *Historical Journal* 49:2 (June 2006): 497–524. See also John Jacobs, *A Rage for Justice: The Passion and Politics of Phillip Burton* (Berkeley: University of California Press, 1995).

55. George McGovern Press Release, January 17, 1956, "Cost of Living Investigation Is Proposed: Your Congressman's Notebook," McGovern MSS, Princeton University, Box 657, File 1. McGovern had won his House seat in a staunchly Republican farm state in 1954.

56. Chase Woodhouse to William Benton, September 30, 1957, Benton MSS, University of Chicago, special collections, Box 282, Folder 5.

57. See Jonathan Bell, *California Crucible: The Forging of Modern American Liberalism* (Philadelphia: University of Pennsylvania Press, 2012), ch. 6 and 7, and this book provides a fuller treatment of the ideas in this chapter; Ethan Rarick, *California Rising: The Life and Times of Pat Brown* (Berkeley: University of California Press, 2005).

3

Going Beyond the New Deal

Socialists and the Democratic Party in the 1970s

TIMOTHY STANLEY

The 1970s are widely regarded as a turning point in the American political evolution from Great Society liberalism to Reaganomics. As such, many political historians are dismissive of or even uninterested in the experiences of liberal and leftwing activists in this period. Often they are portrayed as excessively militant, fractured, and injurious to good, popular Democratic government.[1] At best they were naive and incidental. At worst they contributed to the defeat of a moderate but well-intentioned Democratic president.[2] To be sure, this consensus is not wholly inaccurate. However it is sweeping and, by confirming a rigid orthodox story of Democratic decline, tends to lock liberals out of their own history. It presumes total, catastrophic failure and incompetence at all levels. As such it overlooks evidence of rationality, coalition building, and limited policy success. Few groups have been more unfairly excluded from the mainstream political history of the decade than U.S. socialists.

The purpose of this essay is not to validate the socialist interpretation of the 1970s. It is simply to reconsider what socialists did, why, and with what success. Socialists have not entirely escaped serious academic attention. Andrew Battista's work on labor radicalism in the 1970s and 1980s goes some way to identifying the influence they enjoyed within trade unions.[3] Maurice Isserman's research has given new life to appreciations of the intellectual ingenuity of socialists in the postwar period (Michael Harrington in particular).[4] But a balanced reappraisal of their role in the rapidly changing Democratic Party of the 1970s has yet to be written. This is a tragedy, for not only did they play a big part in the evolution of the Party from an organization dominated by the machine to one dominated by ordinary activists, but their clever manipulation of this process provides a model for how other left-leaning activist groups might do the same.

This essay examines how the Democratic Socialist Organizing Committee (DSOC) emerged from a fractured socialist movement as a tight, unified, youngish group that successfully infiltrated mainstream Democratic politics. It exploited a revival of New Deal thinking in the context of recession and, despite its low numbers, enjoyed some influence upon its policy-making process. During the Carter administration it was, arguably, the focal point for liberal opposition to the president's policies. As such, it gained a degree of respectability for U.S. socialism that had not been enjoyed since the 1930s. In truth, it only did so by disguising much of its radicalism, but this accomplishment should not be dismissed out of hand. Finally, the essay considers why DSOC fell apart and what this has to say about the potential and limits of socialist activism within mainstream U.S. politics. The DSOC experiment happened at the wrong time. Inflation made its emphasis upon unemployment seem anachronistic, and mainstream Democrats recognized this. The moderate policies of the Carter presidency and the election of Ronald Reagan suggest that socialists sailed against a rightward wind. Labor's declining influence reduced the impact of a restored alliance between unions and ideologues. Socialists hoped to inject a new populism into the Democratic Party. The radicalism and disunity that they spawned probably contributed to its defeat.

Nevertheless, DSOC punched well above its weight and it is worth considering how. In 1976, DSOC told delegates at the Democratic Party's nominating convention that it needed to go "Beyond the New Deal" in order to tackle the complex problems of the 1970s. It was a subtle phrase that appealed to the liberal heritage of mainstream Democrats while simultaneously tapping into the fear that they were running out of ideas. DSOC's success lay in its ability to appear comfortably, even boringly, liberal while also offering new ideas and energy. Even if they failed to affect a revolution in federal policy making and did more harm than good, this strategy gave them a hitherto underappreciated influence.[5]

Socialist Biographies

The origins of DSOC provide a fascinating insight into the long-term relationship between liberals and socialists, as well the fratricidal tendencies of the American Left. In the postwar, anticommunist era, the U.S. socialist movement crumbled. Not even its broad opposition to the "bureaucratic collectivism" of the U.S.S.R. could save it. In 1956, Eugene Debs's Socialist Party polled fewer than 3,000 votes in the presidential election. Pockets of support remained with the labor movement and isolated socialists were active in organizations like the Americans for Democratic Action, but the 1950s were not a fertile era for U.S. leftists.[6]

Things improved in the 1960s. The Cuban revolution, the dynamism of the Kennedy administration, civil rights, and a burgeoning student movement leant energy and credibility to a revived American Left. Socialist ideas permeated the Port Huron Statement, Black Power, and antiimperialist critiques of the Vietnam War.[7] The publication of academic Michael Harrington's seminal study of U.S. poverty, *The Other America*, marked a turning point in the newfound respectability of socialist thought. In an era when moderate politicians of right and left were committed to using state power to improve people's lives, socialism's "can do" attitude and material promise attracted a whole new audience.[8]

Yet the 1960s did not mark socialism's entrance into the political mainstream. The reasons for this are complex and diverse. The peace and Civil Rights movements diverted energy from the Left, and redirected it into either the Democratic Party or community organization and activism. Moreover, in a pattern that would become fairly typical, socialists responded to success by turning on each other.[9] A benign political climate was no guarantee of pragmatism or good leadership. In the wake of Vietnam, pro and anti war socialists went their separate ways. When the Socialist Party disintegrated in 1972–1973, the Social Democrats USA emerged as America's leading anticommunist leftist organization.[10] It enjoyed significant support within the ranks of the AFL-CIO, which sat out the 1972 presidential election to protest at the Democratic Party's antiwar platform.[11] Throughout the 1970s it would attract the support of men often associated with New Deal liberalism—frequent speakers included Henry Jackson and Hubert Humphrey and even "neoconservatives" such as Ben Wattenberg and the Coalition for a Democratic Majority.[12] A core of independent-minded socialists stuck with the existing structure of the old Socialist Party to form the Socialist Party USA. Although insignificant on a national level, it enjoyed significant support in statewide elections in Wisconsin, Iowa, and Rhode Island into the twenty-first century.[13]

Antiwar socialists joined Michael Harrington in forming the Democratic Socialist Organizing Committee. Michael Harrington was a lapsed-Catholic, intellectual, pacifistic socialist who had once been described by Arthur

Schlesinger Jr. as "the only responsible radical" in America.[14] Harrington was impressed with George McGovern's 1972 campaign for the presidency—admiring not only its substance but its ability to mobilize a diverse coalition of young people, minorities, feminists, and radical trade unionists to capture control of the Democratic machinery and swing the Party leftward.[15] Indeed, for all its many faults the McGovern insurgency had found a permanent role to play for previously excluded sixties radicals.[16] Harrington began to wonder whether the new party—with its reformed convention arrangements, open primaries and commitment to diversity—might have room for socialists too.

DSOC was then an exercise in entryism. Its goal was to "influence the Democratic Party in a socialist manner, to adapt its policies and to make them work better in our interests."[17] The group acted as a caucus, attending Democratic Party meetings, filing delegates for conventions, and helping to author election platforms. Importantly, it also sought to act as "a bridge between progressive labor and the Democratic Party." Much of its earliest support came from the United Auto Workers union—especially its Vice President Douglas Fraser, who would prove an important ally when he became president of the UAW in 1977. The group's organizational strength was in California and New York.[18] The Socialist Party had always enjoyed significant support among the Jewish environs of New York City and the cosmopolitan, radical politics of the region played into DSOC's hands. In Los Angeles, dissolute communists and peace activists made up the core of the organization, although as a rule it should be noted that ex-communists resisted DSOC's overtures. Bella Abzug, though a participant in the later Democratic Agenda, was not friendly toward DSOC because of her earlier affiliation with Sovietism. Bitter memories of the anticommunism of the Socialist Party remained.[19]

Although DSOC was guided by two middle-aged public intellectuals—Michael Harrington and the literary critic Irving Howe—what really marked its membership from Social Democrats and the Socialist Party USA was its relative youth. None of its staff was over forty and most cut their teeth in the peace and civil rights movements of the 1960s.[20] Importantly, few had family ties to the old Socialist Party and many more came from traditionally Democratic backgrounds. Maxine Phillips was a good example. Phillips was born into a solidly Democratic, middle-class family in Pennsylvania. Although her social worker father had voted socialist as a youth and she knew so-called "red diaper babies," her upbringing was mainstream in its liberalism. So conservative and apolitical was her hometown that she caused a minor scandal when she wore a Kennedy pin to school in 1960.

Politicized by the Vietnam War, Phillips came to New York in the summer of 1968 at the age of twenty and worked as a paid activist in future mayor Ed Koch's first campaign. Koch was running in the silk-socking district and Phillips became embroiled in machine politics, working alongside working-class Jewish, Irish, and Italian activists. She even ran for a position on her local Democratic Committee in the early 1970s. Phillips worked as a publicity officer for a child welfare group and was active in the National Welfare Rights Organization.[21] The NWRO was committed to reforming the provision of welfare in the United States, increasing benefits and limiting social workers' powers.[22] Through her activism in this, Phillips was confronted with police brutality, the indifference of federal bureaucracies, and the shocking conditions of the welfare poor—all of which compelled her to challenge the economic and political status quo.

Two seminal events transformed this mainstream Democrat into a Democratic Socialist. The first was in 1974 when she was canvassed by Michael Harrington, who was running for a delegate seat at that year's midterm convention.[23] Many DSOC activists attest to the fact that Harrington was a remarkably charismatic person and perhaps one of the twentieth-century left's finest orators.[24] Phillips was similarly impressed and intrigued. The second turning point came when her local church ran a workshop on corporate capitalism. After the parishioners listened to a speaker attack the vagaries of the free market, Phillips's future husband suggested that what America really needed was socialism. During the discussion that followed, Phillips concurred but argued that third-party campaigns were doomed to failure. Her husband-to-be told her that Michael Harrington was coordinating a group that wanted to infiltrate socialist ideas and activists into the Democratic Party. The next day Phillips looked DSOC up in the phone book, rang up their New York office, and asked whether she could join. What is so interesting about Phillips's story is not just her roundabout way of entering socialist politics (which had little to do with either her family or college education), but also the role that Christianity played within it. The U.S. socialist movement was almost exclusively secular—yet Phillips came into contact with DSOC via a small gathering at an evangelical church.[25] She eventually became a coordinator of the Religion and Socialism Commission, which tried, in direct response to the Moral Majority's growing influence upon the GOP, to inject the language of Christianity into mainstream liberalism and reclaim evangelicalism for the Left.[26]

Phillips volunteered to work in the New York office but avoided attending actual grassroots DSOC meetings for as long as possible. Experience of the antiwar movement taught her that leftist organizations tend to be anarchic and confrontational, in short dull and ugly. Yet when she finally went to a local DSOC event she was pleasantly surprised. The chair was a "machine orientated" Catholic woman who had worked for years in New York Democratic politics. She knew exactly how to control and becalm a meeting of militant activists and it was this level of discipline that encouraged Phillips to believe that DSOC might actually be a viable political project. Overnight she went from sympathetic volunteer to committed activist. Phillips was appointed editor of the group's magazine *Democratic Left*. As is true of many DSOC activists, the movement became her life. She "downsized" her job and pay to work part-time for Harrington and even delayed her honeymoon to attend DSOC's annual conference.[27]

Building a Democratic (Socialist) Agenda

One of the great tragedies for sixties radicals is that they only gained real political and policy influence in the 1970s—an era of social and economic reaction.[28] Americans were reacting in part to the cultural revolution that had come before. Large numbers of white middle-class Americans fled the troubled inner cities for the sprawling suburbs, evangelical Christianity flourished, blue-collar workers clashed with antiwar protesters, and "profamily" activists launched campaigns to outlaw rights won by gays and lesbians in a handful of states.[29] The enlargement of the Democratic coalition to include the civil rights, feminist, antiwar, environmentalist, and gay movements catalyzed a loss of support among working-class voters.[30]

Things were just as bad on the economic front. Higher oil prices sparked an inflationary spiral, and wages and prices rose again and again to keep up with each other. Inflation exaggerated imbalances and imperfections in the domestic economy and rising costs led to closures and unemployment. The era of stagflation was born—a bizarre and fearful combination of high inflation and high unemployment.[31] Stagflation seemed to confound liberal orthodoxy on economics, which would normally fight unemployment with spending and inflation with cuts.[32] If an economy was experiencing both inflation and unemployment, it was unclear precisely what to do.[33] Unemployment peaked at 8.5 percent in 1975, while inflation hovered at 10 percent.[34] Middle America was less keen to bail out ailing sectors of the economy, because inflation had already caused personal taxes to spiral. Government spending, which had once been something that gave aid to the middle class, became a drain on their personal finances.[35] A new consensus emerged that saw big government as being not only authoritarian but inflationary, too. Policy makers began to argue that they faced a choice between raising or cutting spending, tackling unemployment, or reducing inflation. The spending that was necessary to create jobs programs or raise welfare payments would cause the incomes of those in employment to decline. Politicians had to decide where the votes were—helping those out of work or those already in it.[36] With unemployment up and manufacturing in decline, organized labor lost money, manpower, and influence.[37]

Paradoxically, as the general public edged rightward, some in the Democratic Party swung decisively leftward.[38] Watergate undermined the psychological and literal power of moderate elites and the new cadre of single-issue, "process-orientated" white-collar activists forced the Party to adhere to a set of policy positions that put it firmly on the left of the culture war.[39] Moreover, many liberals responded to the Crisis of Capitalism not with compromise but with a return to first principles. They believed that not only did government have a moral duty to prioritize the reduction of unemployment over inflation, but also that by so doing inflation could be reduced through economic planning and price/wage controls.[40] Senator Hubert Humphrey was, for instance, convinced that "the government of the United States requires an effective planning mechanism," and sought to create one through a full employment bill that mandated government to provide jobs for those who needed them. An heir to the New Deal emphasis upon work as an almost redemptive process, Humphrey-Hawkins (HR50) hoped to overcome the complex divisions of the 1970s: to "restore the New Deal coalition by concentrating on economic policies, such as full employment, that would apply to both whites and blacks alike." Liberals like Humphrey, "favored the politics of class over the politics of race."[41]

The broad support that HR50 enjoyed in the Democratic Party testified to its leftward drift. In 1976, monetarist guru Milton Friedman complained that "Support for that bill has become the litmus test of the true-blue Democratic faith of every candidate from Jimmy Carter to the aspirant for dogcatcher." With identity politics increasingly a cultural sine qua non in Democratic circles, Vietnam resolved, and both parties committed to détente, all the crises that once divided socialists from liberals (and socialists from socialists) had passed.[42] Less concerned about the taint of communism, liberals were happy to work behind the scenes with socialists. Some interesting new coalitions were produced as a result.[43] Michael Harrington set up a group called Environmentalists for Full Employment that tried, with some success, to unite the nascent green movement and big labor around the issue of Humphrey-Hawkins.[44] At its first conference, its newsletter reported,

People from different interest groups began to listen, and to acknowledge to one another the importance and legitimacy of one another's goals and strategies... representatives of each constituency described to others the mechanics of their organizations.... These sessions were an important link in the demythification of "foreign" groups, and in the process of getting acquainted.[45]

This was one example, among many, of socialists coming in from the cold.

Finally, socialists benefited from the revolution in the rules that governed the Democratic Party machinery. The McGovern-Fraser Commission determined that the primaries, rather than a brokered convention, should select the presidential candidate—expanding the influence of community and special interest organizers.[46] It enlarged the role of caucuses and primaries, using quotas to ensure that the delegations represented their state's racial, gender, and generational makeup.[47] As a result the power of labor and state parties over delegate selection declined.[48] Finally, the 1972 convention mandated a biannual midterm convention. Its goal was to assess the achievements and failures of Democratic officeholders—somewhat akin to a British-style party conference. In spirit, if not in fact, the platform became more akin to a manifesto commitment. It was this last innovation that DSOC would manipulate most skillfully.[49]

DSOC capitalized upon all of these changes. In the fall of 1975, DSOC moved away from independent lobbying and toward infiltrating the Democratic Party.[50] Aiming to challenge "a growing sense that problems like poverty were becoming intractable," DSOC sensed that it needed "an ideological fight back program" and that it could gain influence among liberals at the same time by using the 1976 Democratic Party platform as a vehicle for its philosophical offensive. To this effect it lobbied for adoption of three policies: the passage of Humphrey-Hawkins, tax reform, and "greater democratic control of investment decisions," which amounted to increased regulation of the free market.[51]

DSOC was surprisingly sensitive to the conservative economic climate. It stressed that all three of its goals were antiinflationary, and that its tax reform package was designed to capitalize upon the growing tax revolt. When Massachusetts voters passed Proposition 2.5 (which placed a ceiling on property tax increases), DSOC expressed sympathy with the measure. Rather than calling for its reversal, as many public sector unions did, it suggested "local aid formula reform to reflect the unequal impact of Prop 2.5 on communities" and measures such as "a revision of current sales tax exemptions to generate more revenue" and "a tax on computer software and services."[52] DSOC's involvement in tax reform demonstrated that liberals were conscious of its salience as an issue and, rather than avoiding it, attempted to appropriate it.[53] In spring 1979, a group called Tax Justice was founded. Its organizers believed that "the need for progressive tax reform is all the more urgent since conservative organizations have taken the initiative in the debate on tax reform to the detriment of consumers, workers, and taxpayers." It was designed to write alternative proposals for tax reform and to create "as broad based a coalition of labor, citizen, and local tax reform groups as possible." Coordinated by the AFL-CIO, its membership included the NAACP, ADA, Urban League, UAW, NOW, and the public sector union AFSCME.[54]

For socialists, each of their major pledges amounted to a "transitional demand" and was part of a wider "very clear and very conscious" strategy of avoiding overt association with economic socialism in order to appeal to mainstream liberals.[55] In order to create a momentum behind these proposals and construct an alliance to lobby for them, DSOC coordinated a preconvention conference entitled "Democracy '76." It was at this conference that the "big three" unions that would provide funding and personnel for the Democratic Agenda first worked together: UAW, AFSCME, and the Machinists.[56] In 1977 the Machinists' presidency fell to William Winpisinger, a socialist who lobbied the AFL-CIO to campaign "for broad social goals, like national health insurance, rather than concentrate on parochial measures like the common-situs picketing bill."[57] Both Douglas Fraser and Jerry Wurth (president of AFSCME) were vocal socialists too. Although they were members as private citizens, Winpisinger, Fraser, and Wurth could not affiliate their unions directly to DSOC. Thus Democracy '76 became a method of unofficially integrating labor machinery into organized left-wing activism, an opportunity "for education and ideological formation for [their] cadre."[58] It also tapped into growing militancy within unions.[59]

Democracy '76's ambition was the construction of a liberal Democratic convention platform and the establishment of a lobby that would work to ensure that the presidential ticket fulfill it. To quote one activist, at Democracy '76:

> The concept there was to bring together many groups of liberals, left activists who had traditionally worked together on issues . . . particularly through the civil rights movement, anti war movement, feminist movement, but not necessarily within the Democratic Party. We made an effort to bring together pressure on the Democratic Party to have a more progressive agenda in terms of the platform. . . . We were somewhat naïve, but effective nonetheless, in

pushing forward the idea that it should have merit, it should have weight and that the presidential campaign should campaign on ideas that have meaning.[60]

Democracy '76 proved a success. Over 1,000 delegates attended and it achieved its objectives of gaining national attention and creating an embryonic activist coalition. The convention agreed upon support for DSOC's three-point program and coordinated attendance at platform hearings and their submission to the DNC.

However, to everyone's surprise, the Left wasn't the only faction to benefit from party rule changes. Moderate Georgia governor Jimmy Carter exploited the new role of primaries and caucuses to secure the Democratic nomination in 1976. He rarely won a majority in any contest, but while a slew of left-leaning candidates divided up liberal votes, he secured pluralities among moderates, conservatives, small-town dwellers, and southerners. Carter was a centrist—a fiscal conservative and a social moderate. His post-Watergate critique of big government and his heralding of a new "age of limits" marked a departure from traditional liberalism. His nomination reflected the caution that even registered Democrats felt about further social reform.[61]

But the party machinery—particular labor and liberal groups—did not share that caution. In order to sew up the nomination and get their money, Carter was forced to accept perhaps the most liberal party platform to that point.[62] Present on that platform were DSOC's demands for full employment and tax reform. The degree of freedom of action at the convention (including its very public and noted presence at platform hearings) that DSOC enjoyed reflected Carter's unwillingness to challenge liberals within the Party as he tried to secure the nomination.[63]

Jimmy Carter was elected by a tiny majority in 1976, and opinions varied as to why. Carter believed that its narrowness was due to the unpopularity of the platform. He only won because of his unique appeal to rural dwellers and southerners.[64] DSOC and labor believed the problem lay with the ticket. They argued that the platform had encouraged blue-collar workers, women, minorities, and the workless poor to return in large numbers to the Democratic coalition. The New Deal had been resurrected, the number of people identifying as Republican was at a historic low, and several openly liberal candidates ran well ahead of Carter in state contests. DSOC believed that because he had publicly endorsed it, and because it had elected him, Jimmy Carter had an obligation to fulfill the party platform.[65] Whoever was right, these contrasting interpretations of what happened in November 1976 are key to understanding what happened next.

Jimmy Carter: Public Enemy Number One

After a year of vaguely liberal fiscalism and frustrated attempts at social reform on the Hill, President Jimmy Carter reversed his governmental strategy. As inflation spiraled out of control, he tried to apply the brakes by cutting federal spending, deregulating the economy, and reducing the size of government. At the same time he sought to renew America's aging military by investment in a new generation of weapons systems.[66] This volatile mix of meanness and militarism horrified liberals.[67] When Carter withheld administration support for Humphrey-Hawkins, rewrote it as a toothless bill that analyzed rather than regulated the economy, pushed it through Congress, and then ignored almost all of its provisions, a one-time labor ally called the president's endorsement of a liberal platform in 1976, a "cruel hoax."[68]

But what could liberals do? The American party system offers little role in policy making to grassroots activists. There is, ordinarily, only one convention every four years and only through the painstaking process of finding a liberal candidate, writing him a platform, and forcing it through the convention could he be made to deliver a more liberal outcome. This was a daunting task in and of itself, but it was made all the more complex by the incumbency.[69] Moreover, the history of rebellion against party officials within the Democratic Party was an inglorious one. The debates of the 1960s had torn the Party apart because there was no accord between activists groups. Nobody wanted a repeat of the bloody battles of 1968.

However, by the late 1970s the Left was far more united. Also, it had a mechanism by which to discipline the president that would be used effectively only once in the history of American politics: the midterm convention.[70] Perhaps unique among all liberal groups, DSOC recognized the potential power of the convention and began organizing early. DSOC's actions were informed by an almost European sensibility toward party organization and responsibility. Its members regarded the 1976 platform not only as a statement of principle, but as a set of concrete promises. It was a contract between Carter and the activists who elected him. Therefore, the midterm convention was an opportunity for those activists to collect their debt.[71]

Democracy '76 created a new umbrella organization called the Democratic Agenda. The Agenda was dedicated to holding "the Democratic Party accountable" to the promises it made in 1976.[72] "When the new administration failed to live up to those promises, the Democratic Agenda provided a meeting place and a strategy for action." Its coalition represented "the disenchanted who had done the most to elect the Carter/Mondale ticket: trade unionists, minority leaders, community action groups, feminists, senior citizens, and, perhaps for the first time, environmentalists and religious activists."[73] This coalition charged the Carter/Mondale ticket with ignoring its manifesto and felt a general sense of "dismay . . . you had a huge Democratic majority. But it's this new generation of Democrats who are more in to process than in to substance and much more into process than any kind of expansion of the welfare state . . . Carter's fiscal conservatism . . . really [dismayed] us. This was the genesis of where the Democratic Agenda originated from and became the main focus of opposition to Carter within the party."[74]

The Democratic Agenda employed a full-time director and three part-time organizers out of its office in Washington. It balanced a $61,500 budget, mostly sustained by annual donations of $10,000 each from the UAW, Machinists, and AFSCME.[75] It ran conferences every year in Washington, organized on a "state by state basis" with the primary ambition of "getting people excited about taking part at the Memphis convention." The effort in individual states meant that the Agenda was able to generate a degree of representation at the midterm convention that far outweighed its actual numerical strength.[76] In the afternoon session of the January 1978 conference, the delegates marched to the offices of the DNC to protest the administration's policies.[77]

The Agenda managed to include figures that would not have felt comfortable with DSOC, such as the Amalgamated Clothing Workers Union (AGWU) president Murray Finley, a passionate supporter of Social Democrats USA but a cofounder of the Democratic Agenda.[78] Indeed, as the Environmentalists for Full Employment had sought to unite labor and the ecology movement, so the Democratic Agenda hoped to unite a broader contingent of New Deal and New Politics Democrats. In a private letter to Fraser, Ruth Jordan reported of the 1979 Agenda conference that "More that 80 unions, industrial councils, and building trades councils were represented. The excitement generated by their contact with students, environmentalists, retirees, and others was electric."[79] The broad range of the Agenda was demonstrated by the 1979 conference, at which were discussed such issues as "the tenant's movement," "organizing working women," and "union busting and beyond."[80]

The Agenda's major organizational project was the 1978 midterm convention, at which it was "the only national effort to put issues discussion on the floor."[81] Its rationale was thus:

> Political pundits and ordinary people will watch the conference and will draw political conclusions from it. They may see a carefully orchestrated event in praise of Carter and the Congress. If they do, the conclusion will be obvious:

the upsurge and tumult in the Democratic Party, which began with the civil rights movement, is over. Former civil rights and anti-war activists have settled down to the "pragmatic" politics of the late 1970s and are accommodating themselves to [fiscal] conservatism. Or, if our efforts are successful, people will see a live and lively Party discussing and debating the future of our country. ... The conclusion will again be obvious: there is a broad and massive constituency which wants and will fight for social progress and economic justice, and that constituency is a force to reckon with in the politics of the 1980s.[82]

The midterm convention was therefore crucial for both ensuring the survival of 1960s activism within the Democratic Party and setting an agenda for the 1980s.[83]

Throughout 1978 the Agenda ran workshops and conferences across the country designed to enthuse sympathizers to run as delegates to the convention.[84] It wanted to encourage the Party to be "militant, tough. ... We want the Democrats in the White House and Congress to shape up. The party asks for and gets support from the constituencies we represent.... We want a real discussion at next year's mini-convention."[85] The Agenda benefited from low interest in the convention, allowing it to "steal a march on the administration" by fielding delegates in uncontested seats. The Agenda believed that gaining delegate strength could allow it to demonstrate its influence, but also hoped that it might force the administration to seek a compromise on policy.[86] Depending upon the influence of the "big three" unions, some states sent elected delegations that were almost entirely Agenda-supporting. The Michigan delegation, where the state party was orchestrated by the UAW and a self-declared socialist had run a respectable second in the 1978 gubernatorial Democratic primary, was dominated by the Agenda. So too was the Minnesota delegation, as the Agenda enjoyed considerable support among the Democratic Farmer-Labor Party, despite the DFL's historic links with the Social Democrats USA.[87] The Agenda delegates were also selected from traditionally conservative states, such as Alabama.[88] The Agenda monitored its delegates and was able to control 40 percent of those eventually elected.[89]

DSOC's invasion of the midterm convention via the Democratic Agenda proved to be a substantive disappointment but a psychological success. The administration approached the meeting with dread.[90] Rumors were circulating that liberal senator Edward M. Kennedy was considering a bid to take the presidential nomination away from Carter in 1980 and that he might make his move at the convention. The increasing likelihood of a Kennedy candidacy provided a focal point for opposition and an eloquent spokesman for discontent.[91]

The DNC tried to bend the rules to avoid conflict.[92] As *Time* explained, DNC Chair John White and administration/party liaison Tim Kraft, "tried to turn the miniconvention into an exercise in intraparty public relations, a sort of half-time pep rally. . . . White rigged the rules in an attempt to minimize debates on resolutions critical of Carter. But on the eve of the convention he made concessions to liberal groups, led by lame duck Minnesota Congressman Don Fraser and UAW President Douglas Fraser, to allow several dissident resolutions to get a full airing on Sunday." The Agenda won this concession by threatening to stage a walkout during Carter's speech "and flock instead to Senator Kennedy's session on national health insurance."[93]

The convention consisted of a day of speeches, a day of workshops and a day of debate.[94] There were twenty-four workshops, with subject matter spanning "defense policy and arms control," "energy," "welfare reform," and "the Democratic Party and the independent voter."[95] The resolutions sent by state parties were contradictory and parochial. The Democratic Agenda was considerably savvier. Throughout 1978 it had "worked with Democratic Party activists to develop a series of resolutions, almost all of them based on the 1976 Democratic Party platform and asserting either implicitly or explicitly the proposition that party platforms must be taken seriously."[96] In this regard, the Agenda's resolutions were an exercise in accountability and activist power. Each resolution began with the phrase "the Democratic Party reaffirms the following statements . . . in the 1976 Democratic Party Platform." They reminded Carter of his commitment to health insurance, Humphrey-Hawkins, and regulation of oil and gas.[97] They also pointed to the central point of activist concern regarding Carter's economic policies. "The problems which confronted this nation in 1976" they suggested, "have not yet been solved, yet it appears that the FY '80 budget will cut many social programs below 'current services' levels, while allowing the military budget to grow."[98] The Democratic Agenda easily gained the 25 percent of signatures required for consideration, which meant that on the last day of the conference they were considered as alternative wordings to the resolutions submitted by the administration.[99]

President Carter came to Memphis on Friday, December 8, 1978.[100] He was greeted by angry pickets.[101] One Michigan Congressman warned Carter that "we elected him and we can de-elect him."[102] More troubling was the disquiet among black officials awaiting massive cuts in aid to cities. One hundred black delegates voted to demand a face-to-face meeting with the president and John Conyers predicted that cuts would "flatly result in [Carter's] defeat in 1980."[103] Vernon Jordan had led a coalition of urban black leaders to the Oval

Office the previous week to signal disapproval.[104] They had been joined by Detroit Mayor Coleman Young, an important black Carter ally, who openly urged the convention to vote against the administration's urban spending plans.[105] A postconvention administration report noted that there had been "intense pressure on black delegates" to support the Democratic Agenda. It also noted that those delegates committed to supporting the administration did so despite "guaranteed grief about it back home."[106]

Carter's speech went well and the first day ran smoothly for the administration.[107] But the next afternoon, Kennedy delivered a barnstorming speech that signaled his intention to run for the presidency. He solemnly warned that "the party that tore itself apart over Vietnam in the 1960s cannot afford to tear itself apart today over budget cuts in basic social programs."[108] Evidence suggests that his decision to run was influenced by the groundswell of support he received from Agenda activists.[109] There was no doubt in the Democratic Agenda's collective mind that "the idea of a Kennedy candidacy came out of that speech and came out of that convention."[110]

The resolutions debate the next day proved equally embarrassing for Carter. When it came to talking about full employment, the UAW and the Democratic Agenda wanted the Party to adopt language that would commit the administration to achieving an ambitiously low level of joblessness of 3 percent. On the evening before the debate, Doug Fraser and his staff met privately with Eizenstat to negotiate compromise language. The administration, which had decided to alter its definition of an acceptable rate of unemployment, hoped to split the UAW off from the Agenda. This would embarrass militant supporters of Humphrey-Hawkins and also diffuse a "draft Kennedy" movement. It was trying to avoid "a headline in the *New York Times* that read that rank-and-file Democrats had rejected the President." Infuriated with Carter's position, Fraser "stormed out" of the meeting and left his staff to speak for him. The meeting quickly reached an impasse, with both sides recognizing that any settlement that involved conceding ground would be regarded as a political victory.

Failing to reach a compromise, a floor fight was held the next day. Both the Agenda and the administration operated a whip, the administration's effort orchestrated by Hillary Clinton. The UAW hoped to avoid a vote altogether because it had no desire to embarrass Carter and thus weaken its influence within the administration. However *Don* Fraser put forward a motion for a roll-call vote. The Chair misread the motion to refer to *Doug* Fraser and announced erroneously that the UAW had requested the vote rather than the mayor of Minneapolis. Forced to choose between a loss of face among unionists and antagonizing the administration, Douglas Fraser acknowledged the motion as being by his hand and whipped for its passage. He lost the vote, but the administration was alarmed by the narrow margin of defeat.[111]

To be sure, the Agenda did not carry the midterm convention. It rarely hit above its 40 percent delegates in votes and lost every resolution fight. But it won a psychological victory.[112] Scooping attention from a media desperate for a story, the Agenda showed "the broader anger of Democrats" toward the administration. "It turned in to a moment when our side took on Carter and was perceived to have won, even though we lost numerically.... It laid the seeds for ultimately turning our back on Carter and backing Teddy Kennedy."[113] It was the Agenda that had marshaled the opposition and been on the floor when Kennedy first signaled his intentions.[114] Various liberal and labor groups poured their resources into the Democratic Agenda as a proven bridgehead into the Democratic Party.[115]

What impressed the national media most about DSOC's triumph was its new alliance with the once virulently anticommunist labor movement.[116] "The unions have been Democratic stalwarts since the New Deal," began one typical postconvention analysis, "and until this year, they tended to oppose the militant minorities in the Party. In Memphis however, the dissidents were led by Douglas Fraser of the UAW. The attitude to George Meany, head of the AFL-CIO, on economic issues is 'right on.'" The potential for labor to undermine the antiinflation program with wage increases was significant. "Unless the president can make some changes soon, his effort to hold the line on inflation could quickly transform his relations with labor in to a state of costly and unnecessary and perhaps self-defeating war."[117] This was an accurate interpretation of the growing militancy within labor. In October 1978 an internal UAW memo suggested that administration reticence was forcing labor to "use our economic power to win political concessions."[118] The wider implication of Memphis was that liberals intended "not to defeat or embarrass the president, but to send him the message that their support cannot be taken for granted." Their "improvised coalition" had successfully sparked debate and garnered national attention. At the heart of that coalition was DSOC—an organization that never enjoyed more than 3,000 members.[119]

Business Week warned its largely corporate readership that "socialism is no longer a dirty word to labor." It noted with anxiety that all seventeen building unions, traditionally "considered the most conservative element of organized labor," had placed a $700 advert in DSOC's newsletter. "The ad 'proudly salutes' DSOC... for its firm and militant support of the American labor movement." *Business Week* blamed anger at the Democratic Congress for the failure to pass prolabor reforms and DSOC's strategy of developing apparently innocuous alliances such as the Democratic Agenda for the leftward swing. The magazine ominously stated that DSOC enjoyed a weight of influence within the Democratic Party comparable with the Moral Majority within the Republican Party, even though it could muster but a fraction of its numerical support.[120] This open and growing critique of free market capitalism was not limited to DSOC-supporting unions, but was also typical among those aligned with the Social Democrats USA.[121]

The Kennedy Disappointment

The midterm convention was a high-water mark for DSOC's influence. After that, the organization fell apart—although not before taking the Democratic Party down with it.

The problem was that while DSOC was adept at platform writing and activist organization, it was inept at mature electoral politics.[122] Kennedy's candidacy inevitably diverted attention and resources from the organization, and eventually tore it apart. Not everyone supported it or even liked the senator.[123] Michael Harrington was a fan, describing Kennedy as "the odds-on-best man"—a view generally held within DSOC.[124] However some constituent groups within the Agenda (such as Tom Hayden's Campaign for Economic Democracy) remained neutral, while others (such as Finley's AGWU) campaigned for the President because they saw the race as divisive.[125] Ultimately the Agenda chose to stay out of the contest, with DSOC voting to endorse Kennedy and run members as delegates to the Convention.[126] With the return of high politics, activist organizations became quickly subsumed within personality-driven campaigns. Their time and energy diverted, DSOC began to flag. "In the context of a direct Kennedy-Carter struggle . . . [i]t was difficult," conceded one activist, "for Democratic Agenda to be as prominent in 1980 Democratic politics as it was in 1978." DSOC's attempt to exert European-style grassroots party discipline within a personalized system could not be made to work.[127]

Worse still, the socialists returned to old, bad habits. An acrimonious internal split tore DSOC over primary tactics.[128] Before Kennedy had declared and buoyed by their recent publicity, many members urged Harrington to enter the primaries as a protest candidate.[129] The movement had reached a crossroads, with many activists firm in their belief that the economic crisis augured well for a socialist candidate. Many more were determined to avoid splitting the Agenda project and planned instead to build upon their new network.[130] Although the debate was resolved by Harrington's endorsement of Kennedy, it bitterly ruptured DSOC and it never regained its momentum or the impressive degree of unity it had built among the Left.[131] Some quit to join the Citizen's Party, a vainglorious populist movement that barely scraped 0.3 percent in the 1980 presidential election.[132]

This is not to imply that DSOC immediately imploded in the aftermath of the 1978 midterm convention. Far from it. The Agenda played a key role in the 1979 Draft Kennedy movement, which was spontaneous in the sense that it sprung up without guidance or money from the candidate himself.[133] They created a coalition titled the National Call for Kennedy.[134] The National Call was motivated in part by anger with "a government that is hopelessly paralyzed" but it also publicized Kennedy's alternative record as a liberal, a broad record that appealed to various constituencies.[135]

Arguably, such organizational success only contributed to the eventual defeat of Jimmy Carter and the election of Ronald Reagan. The 1980 Democratic primaries split the Party and weakened Carter as a candidate. In late 1979, Kennedy beat Carter in most polls by margins of 2–1. He enjoyed an identical lead over likely Republican nominee Ronald Reagan. This suggested that the socialist backing of Kennedy and a return to populist, liberal appeals was a good idea. However, history intervened.[136] In November 1979, hostages were taken at the American embassy in Tehran. In December, the U.S.S.R. invaded Afghanistan. Both crises gave Carter a chance to impress the public with his leadership.[137] Meanwhile, Harrington's description of Kennedy as the "best candidate" proved naive. Kennedy performed poorly on the stump and media discussion of his involvement in the death of an intern at Chappaquiddick in 1969 hampered his message. Carter stormed the early primaries.[138]

But the Left refused to give up. When unemployment jumped in March 1980, Kennedy snatched a couple of comeback victories. Running on a platform of ideas largely borrowed from the Agenda and its liberal allies, he won states as diverse as New York, California, Michigan, South Dakota, and New Mexico.[139] As Kennedy gained delegates, a contested convention seemed more likely. The Agenda testified at the platform hearings. Although the Senator lost the nomination, he delivered the speech of his career and secured the passage of a platform even more liberal than that which had been touted in 1976.[140] Among its promises were the Democratic Agenda's goals of tax reform, full employment, and increased regulation—although its direct influence was slight. Rightly or wrongly, the Agenda regarded the platform fight as a litmus test of its strength within the Party and left the convention well pleased with itself.[141]

Kennedy's swan song performance and the liberal platform were bittersweet victories. Polls confirmed that both were very popular with the public.[142] But, far from the helping the actual nominee, they confused Carter's moderate message and exposed the bitter disappointment of his own party. Some hoped that victory on the Kennedy platform would result in an administration committed to the labor-alliance and social reform. In practice, Kennedy only wounded the incumbent further and contributed to the election of a real conservative in November.[143]

As soon as the Democratic Party lost power, DSOC's influence proved meaningless. Ronald Reagan's landslide victory in 1980 killed socialism. It seemed to confirm that the wider public wanted nothing to do with it (although in polls it regularly expressed sympathy for its policy positions) and the Democrats' loss of office removed DSOC's bargaining power. Without the threat of embarrassing a sitting president and undermining his reelection they had no leverage or political importance.[144]

More importantly, the Democratic Party of the 1980s was less open to socialist ideas and activists than it had been in the previous decade. To be sure, there were the socialistic campaigns of Jesse Jackson in 1984 and 1988. But as a rule, the Democratic Party began to slowly reject its tax-and-spend liberalism in favor of balanced budgets, social moderation, and business-friendly policies.[145] This was reflected in a tightening of its rules in an effort to squeeze out special interest groups and outsider presidential candidates. In 1981 the Hunt Commission revised convention rules to emasculate the midterm and introduce "superdelegates" into the 1984 primaries that would weaken the chances of outsiders taking the nomination. Eventually, the midterm was abolished altogether.[146]

DSOC ceased to exist in 1982. It split in two: one half joined with the New Left's New American Movement and the other, more anticommunist half formed the poorly named Committee Against the NAM Merger (CATNAM). The split reflected the fragility of a movement that was so easily influenced by personality and faction. The New American Movement became the Democratic Socialists of America (DSA) and backed Jesse Jackson in 1988.[147] CATNAM preferred more mainstream candidates such as Walter Mondale. Michael Harrington stuck with the DSA until his death in 1989. In 2007, the DSA endorsed Barack Obama for the presidency.[148]

Radicals in a Conservative Age

The story of DSOC's rise and fall has several things to say about the condition of postwar American liberalism. First, it proves the point of historians

Jonathan Bell and Timothy Thurber that social democratic ideas continued to enjoy surprising levels of support within the Democratic Party long after the New Deal ended.[149] While commentators like Alan Brinkley have argued that Democratic radicalism spluttered and died in the face of anticommunism, broad support for ideas like the Humphrey-Hawkins full employment bill or national health insurance suggest that this is not the whole story.[150] DSOC's achievements might have been short-lived, but its degree of influence was (for a recent leftist American movement) remarkable. The relatively easy fraternization of men like Humphrey, Winpisinger, Wurf, Fraser, and Harrington suggests that mainstream liberals and labor leaders were far more open to socialist ideas than is widely understood.

Second, a dose of recession is bad for America but good for American liberals. In the 1970s unemployment not only concentrated Democratic minds on the economy (where less division existed over policy priorities) but also facilitated coalition building between previously antagonistic groups. Experiments like the Democratic Agenda were made possible by the challenge of mass unemployment. As was shown in 1992 and 2008, liberals tend to express greater energy, imagination, and unity when pushing economic ideas. Similarly, they also tend to get a fairer hearing by mainstream party leaders looking for populist themes on which to get elected. Although the historical orthodoxy remains that the 1970s was a politically conservative decade, for the bulk of the Democratic Party it was actually a period of radicalization. New ideas and strategies were thrown up that defy the historiographic orthodoxy of collapse and retreat into moderation. DSOC's response to Proposition 2.5 was not unusual—while many liberals regarded the tax-cutting ethos of the era with regret, many also saw it as a challenge that required a renewal of liberal activism and ideas.[151]

Third, discipline is everything. Perhaps no message comes out of the 1970s more strongly than the need for unity and focus. DSOC was itself the product of faction, and its collapse in the wake of the 1980 election reflected a cycle of achievement, hubris, and self-destruction. This is an ironic tragedy considering the relative degree if harmony of purpose and action that it brought to liberals in the 1970s.

The benefits of socialist-liberal alliance-making for the Democratic Party are less obvious. Socialists felt that a period of economic stagnation called for a more radical agenda—a new New Deal. They tied that to a seventies sensibility of greater openness and participation, producing a democratic revolt against an incumbent president that tried to remind him of the commitments he had made to the electorate. This is all logical and the sporadic moments of popularity enjoyed by Senator Kennedy suggests that it was far from fanciful.

There were moments of real potential for the America left in the 1970s—but they were fleeting and dependent on the leadership of flawed men.

However, DSOC failed to recognize the declining power of organized labor. In turn, labor failed to realize that its agenda had become that of a special interest group. Neither spoke anymore for Middle America as a whole. Without Kennedy's personality to sell them (and his personality was controversial, too), the ideas that the socialist-labor alliance touted had only limited appeal. Unions blamed Carter for the defeat of labor reform legislation, but it was a Democratic Congress that voted it down. The Democratic mainstream understood that voters were more concerned with quality of life issues than workers' rights and social justice. Perhaps if DSOC had been founded in the 1960s, when inflation was low and tax returns high, its agenda might have gained better traction.[152]

The DSOC story illustrates the risks Democratic administrations run of promising one thing and then doing another. Many historians are right that Jimmy Carter was ahead of his time in trying to fashion a post–New Deal centrist agenda that could appeal to a more prosperous nation. But he antagonized many elements of his coalition unduly and made many commitments rashly (particularly to implement Humphrey-Hawkins and deliver National Health Insurance). Democratic presidents ignore their base at their peril. But, vice versa, the base must recognize the limits that history places upon friendly presidents. Inflation and deficits make selling social reform to the public an uphill struggle. Policy radicalization is a good thing for the grassroots, but it can alienate the wider public and undermine the party leadership's ability to sell a coherent message. This happened in Britain, where militancy and internal division crippled the British Labour Party and kept it in opposition for 18 years.[153] Arguably, it helped put Reagan in the White House in 1980. It also gave Democratic Party conservatives the rationale to end the experiment in grassroots democracy that began in 1968 and embrace policies that would appall the average Seventies liberal.

Notes

1. For representative work on the political and cultural state of liberalism in the 1970s, see Peter N. Carroll, *It Seemed like Nothing Happened: American in the 1970s* (New Brunswick: Rutgers University Press, 1990), 348; William C. Berman, *America's Right Turn: From Nixon to Bush* (Baltimore: John Hopkins University Press, 1994), 58–59; Bruce J. Schulman, *The Seventies: The Great Shift in American Culture, Society and Politics* (Cambridge, Mass.: Da Capo Press, 2002), 121–143; Edward D. Berkowitz, *Something Happened: A Political and Cultural Overview of the Seventies* (New York:

Columbia University Press, 2006), 227; David Frum, *How We Got Here: The Decade That Brought You Modern Life—For Better or Worse* (New York: Basic Books, 2000), 12; Michael Barone, *Our Country: The Shaping of America from Roosevelt to Reagan* (London: Collier MacMillan, 1990), 572.

2. Introduction in David Brian Robertson, *Loss of Confidence: Politics and Policy in the 1970s (Issues in Policy History, No 8)* (University Park: Pennsylvania State University Press, 1998). This structuralist interpretation is supported by administration memoirs: Jimmy Carter, *Keeping Faith: Memoirs of a President* (New York: Bantam, 1983), 99; Hamilton Jordan, *Crisis: The Last Year of the Carter Presidency* (New York: Putnam Adult, 1982), 363–365.

3. Andrew Battista, *The Revival of Labor Liberalism* (Chicago: University of Illinois Press, 2008), 83–102.

4. Maurice Isserman, *The Other American: The Life of Michael Harrington* (New York: Public Affairs, 2000), 303–337.

5. Interview with Jack Clark, September 25, 2006.

6. Isserman, *Other American*, 105–139.

7. Robert A. Gorman, *Michael Harrington: Speaking American* (New York: Routledge, 1996), xv–xxii; interview with Heather Booth, September 19, 2006.

8. Isserman, *Other American*, 216–217.

9. Ibid., 256–302.

10. "Socialist Party Now the Social Democrats, USA," *New York Times*, December 31, 1972, 30.

11. Bruce Miroff, *The Liberals' Moment: The McGovern Insurgency and the Identity Crisis of the Democratic Party* (Lawrence: University Press of Kansas, 2007), 239.

12. Sydney Blumenthal, *The Rise of the Counter-Establishment: The Conservative Ascent to Political Power* (New York: Union Square Press, 2008), 115–116.

13. "Inside Socialist Party Headquarters," *New York Times*, October 20, 2008, A22.

14. "Author Will Head New Socialist Unit," *New York Times*, October 15, 1973, 41.

15. Isserman, *Other American*, 296–302.

16. Jonah Raskin, *For the Hell of It: The Life and Times of Abbie Hoffman* (London: University of California Press, 1996), 226.

17. Interview with Jack Clark.

18. Interview with Harold Meyerson, September 22, 2006; transcript of interview for *Democratic Left*, September 20, 1980, Mandler Papers.

19. Interview with Harold Meyerson.

20. Interview with Jack Clark.

21. Interview with Maxine Phillips, September 26, 2006.

22. Premilla Nadasen, *Welfare Warriors: The Welfare Rights Movement in the United States* (New York: Routledge. 2005), 3.

23. Interview with Maxine Phillips.

24. Interview with Harold Meyerson.

25. Interview with Maxine Phillips.

26. Private Notes on Religion and Socialism Commission, undated, Maxine Phillips Papers; interview with Jim Wallace, September 24, 2006.

27. Interview with Maxine Phillips.

28. Introduction in Steve Fraser and Gary Gerstle, eds., *The Rise and Fall of the New Deal Order, 1930–1980* (Princeton: Princeton University Press, 1990); James L. Sundquist, *Dynamics of the Party System: Alignment and Realignment of Political Parties in the United States* (Washington D.C.: Brookings, 1983), 437; Everett Carll Ladd, "The Brittle Mandate: Electoral Dealignment and the 1980 Presidential Election," *Political Science Quarterly* 96:1–25; Stanley B. Greenberg, *Middle Class Dreams: The Politics and Power of the New American Majority* (New York: Random House, 1997), 141.

29. Schulman, *The Seventies*, 1–20.

30. Richard Scammon and Ben Wattenberg, *The Real Majority* (New York: Coward-McCann, 1970), 35–45.

31. Iwan Morgan, *Deficit Government: Taxing and Spending in Modern America* (Chicago: Ivan R. Dee, 1995), 116–117.

32. Alonzo Hamby, *Beyond the New Deal: Harry S. Truman and American Liberalism* (New York: Columbia University Press, 1973), 297–303; form letter, Hawkins and Reuss to House Sponsors, January 9, 1975, Hawkins Papers, Box 82.

33. Berkowitz, *Something Happened*, 166.

34. "Economic Policy," *Congressional Almanac*, 1975, 91.

35. Barone, *Our Country*, 572; "Mutiny in California," *New Republic*, June 3, 1978, 5; "Massachusetts," *New Republic*, November 4, 1978, 20; interview with Mike Dukakis, September 14, 2006.

36. Gary M. Fink and Hugh David Graham, *The Carter Presidency: Policy Choices in the Post-New Deal Era* (Chapel Hill: North Carolina University Press, 2001), 95–117.

37. Michael Goldfield, *The Decline of Organized Labor in the United States* (Chicago: University of Chicago Press, 1989), 3–25.

38. John W. Sloan, *The Reagan Effect: Economics and Presidential Leadership* (Lawrence: University of Kansas, 1999), 45.

39. John A. Farrell, *Tip O'Neill and the Democratic Century* (London: Little Brown, 2001), 442.

40. Letter, Humphrey to Sar A. Levitan, July 20, 1977, Case Files, Humphrey Papers, Box 2; Press Release, "Humphrey on Welfare," 1972, Humphrey Papers, Box 150.K.9.3(B).

41. Timothy Nels Thurber, *The Politics of Equality: Hubert H. Humphrey and the African American Freedom Struggle* (New York: Columbia University Press, 1999), 9.

42. David Garrow, *Privacy and Sexuality: The Right to Privacy in Roe vs. Wade* (New York: Macmillan, 1994), 473–599.

43. "Fact Sheet: Coalition of Labor Union Women," undated, Papers of the National Organization of Women, 1958–2002, Schlesinger Library, Radcliffe Institute, Harvard University, Boston, Box 89.

44. "Environmentalists for Full Employment: Jobs and Energy," newsletter, 1976,

Hawkins Papers, Box 87; "Environmentalists for Full Employment," spring newsletter, 1977, Hawkins Papers, Box 35.

45. "Environmentalists for Full Employment," fall newsletter, 1976, Hawkins Papers, Box 35.

46. "Reforms within Democratic Party," *New York Times*, March 7, 1972, 38.

47. Letter, Karen DeCrow to NOW Politics Taskforce, December 5, 1972, NOW Papers, Box 48.

48. Thomas H. Hammon, "Another Look at the Rules in the 1972 Democratic Presidential Primaries," *Western Political Quarterly* 33:1 (March): 50–72.

49. "Missouri Compromise," *New York Times*, December 10, 1974, 45.

50. Norman Binbaum article, "Building of an Opposition," unsourced in Papers of AFL-CIO President, Lane Kirkland (unprocessed), George Meany Library, National Labor College, Washington D.C., Box 52.

51. Interview with Jack Clark.

52. "Progressive Caucus Amendments at 1981 Massachusetts Democratic Issues Convention," April 11, 1981, Mandler Papers; *Yankee Radical*, May 1981, Mandler Papers; see also the activities of the Mass. Tax Reform Association, in *Yankee Radical*, March 1981, Mandler Papers; Minutes, Cambridge, Mass., branch of DSOC meeting, December 2, 1980, Mandler Papers.

53. Letter, Fraser to Carter, November 8, 1977, Fraser Papers, Box 15.

54. Tax Justice report by VP Hardy, May 8, 1979, Executive Minutes, Meany Library.

55. Interview with Clark.

56. Letter, Harrington to DSOC key contacts, August 15, 1978, Fraser Papers, Box 4; letter, Harrington to Fraser, undated, Fraser Papers, Box 4.

57. "Wimpy Takes Command," *Time*, July 11, 1977.

58. Interview with Jack Clark.

59. In a typical speech in 1978 Winpisinger told the Chicago Chapter of DSOC that "in the tradition of Gene Debs and Norman Thomas, we are going to raise enough hell that sooner or later the American people are going to wake up." Calling for industrial action to protest administration policies, he proclaimed, "I'm fed up with the idea that the trade union movement has to prove its respectability by accepting and endorsing the ground rules of big business." "Wimpy on the Attack," *Herling Letter*, May 19, 1980.

60. Interview with Ruth Jordan.

61. "The Well Planned Enigma of Jimmy Carter," *New York Times*, June 6, 1976, 195.

62. Interview with Stuart Eizenstat, September 21, 2006; Carter later expressed the view that it was this period of negotiation that weakened both his presidential candidacy and his administration—tying him to promises he could not fulfill. Interview with Jimmy Carter, November 29, 1982, *Miller Center, University of Virginia, Jimmy Carter Presidential Oral History Project*, 43.

63. "Detractors and Supporters Agree His Positions Are Genuine; Mondale: A

Liberal Who Sometimes Gives Up," *New York Times*, July 18, 1976, 113; "Give a Little, Take a Little," *Wall Street Journal*, June 25, 1976, 32.

64. Privately circulated copy of memo, Caddell to Carter, December 10, 1976, Papers of President Douglas Fraser, UAW Collection, Walter P Reuther Library, Wayne State University, Michigan, Box 49.

65. "A New Candidate Wins with an Old Coalition," *Congressional Quarterly Almanac*, 1976, 820–821.

66. "Carter Imposes Voluntary Anti-Inflation Plan," *Congressional Quarterly*, October 28, 1978, 3118.

67. Statement by the AFL-CIO executive on the federal budget, February 19, 1979, *Executive Minutes, Meany Library*.

68. AFL-CIO News, March 9, 1980, *Vertical Files, Meany Library*.

69. "Keeping His Options Open," *Argus*, August 12, 1979, C1.

70. "Democrats to Meet in Memphis in '78," *New York Times*, December 10, 1977, 13.

71. Interview with Harold Meyerson.

72. Interview with Jack Clark.

73. Letter, Harrington to Fraser, April 20, 1979, Fraser Papers, Box 53.

74. Interview with Meyerson; leaflet, "Remember November," Fraser Papers, Box 4.

75. Democratic Agenda Budget, undated, Fraser Papers, Box 68, 53; letter, Harrington to Fraser, January 11, 1979, Fraser Papers, Box 53.

76. Interview with Ruth Jordan.

77. Interview with Jack Clark.

78. Interview with Harold Meyerson.

79. Letter, Jordan to Fraser, December 11, 1979, Fraser Papers, Box 53.

80. List, "Mini Plenaries and Workshops," November 5, 1979, Fraser Papers, Box 1.

81. *Democratic Left* VI:10, December 1978, Mandler Papers.

82. Letter, Harrington to initiators of Democratic Agenda, Marjorie Phyfe and Jack Clark, October 24, 1978, Fraser Papers, Box 53.

83. Letter, Harrington to Fraser, November 23, 1977, Fraser Papers, Box 53.

84. Letter, Harrington to Fraser, September 23, 1977, Fraser Papers, Box 53.

85. Letter, Harrington to Fraser, Fraser Papers, Box 4.

86. Interview with Meyerson.

87. Memo, Richard Moe to Rick Hutcheson, undated, Richard Moe Files, Papers of Walter Fitzgerald Mondale, Minnesota Historical Society, St. Paul, Minnesota, Box 2.

88. Interview with Jordan.

89. Interview with Meyerson; letter, Harrington to the initiators of the Democratic Agenda, October 24, 1978, Fraser Papers, Box 53.

90. Memo, Rafshoon to Carter, November 29, 1978, Office of White House Communications, Jimmy Carter Library, Atlanta, Georgia, Box 55.

91. "Democrats Girding for Midterm Parley," *New York Times*, December 7, 1978, A20.

92. "Now's the Time, Party Is Told, to Aid Carter," *LA Times* December 7, 1978, A2.

93. "For Democrats, a Madhouse in Memphis," *LA Times*, December 6, 1978, E7.

94. Agenda, Cook convention center floor, December 8, 1978, Lipshutz Papers, Jimmy Carter Library, Box 13.

95. List of workshop, undated, White House Press Office, Jimmy Carter Library, Box 17.

96. Letter, Harrington to Fraser, October 26, 1978, Fraser Papers, Box 53.

97. "Democratic Agenda Resolutions," undated, Papers of the Special Adviser on Inflation, Jimmy Carter Library, Atlanta, Georgia, Box 13.

98. Resolution supported by petition, December 10, 1978, First Lady's Files, Jimmy Carter Library, Box 5; for the validity of this statement, see "Key Members Question Need for Higher Defense Spending in Fiscal 1980," *Congressional Quarterly*, February 10, 1979.

99. "Liberals Press Floor Fights before Democratic Parley," *New York Times*, December 8, 1978, A21.

100. "Miniconvention," *New Republic*, December 23–30, 1978, 13.

101. "Debate over Domestic Budget Cuts Heats as Democratic Parley Nears," *New York Times*, December 6, 1978, A16.

102. Arkansas Herald, December 10, 1978, reprinted in Clymer Papers, Box 24.

103. "President Links Budget Austerity and Social Goals," *Washington Post*, December 9, 1978, A1.

104. "Carter's Dual Role in Memphis: A Politician as Well as President," *New York Times*, December 10, 1978, 42.

105. "Carter's Inflation Plans Draw Fire as Democrats Convene at Midterm," *New York Times*, December 9, 1978, 1.

106. Memo, Jane Fenderson to Tim Kraft and Richard Hutchenson, December 15, 1978, First Lady's Files, Jimmy Carter Library, Box 5.

107. Timetable for final day, undated, Lipshutz Papers, Jimmy Carter Library, Box 15.

108. "Kennedy Warns of a Party Split by Arms Outlays," *Washington Post*, December 10, 1978, A1.

109. "Memphis Blues," *New Republic*, December 23–30, 1978, 2.

110. Interview with Meyerson.

111. "The Nation; Carter Fights for Hearts and Minds of Democrats," *New York Times*, December 17, 1978, E4.

112. "New Deal Dems Fight Raw Deal Dems," *Democratic Left* VII:1, January 1979, Mandler Papers.

113. Interview with Stillman.

114. Letter, Harrington to Fraser, April 20, 1979, Fraser Papers, Box 53; "Miniconvention," *New Republic*, December 23–30, 1978.

115. Letter, Fraser to regional UAW directors, October 25, 1979, Papers of the UAW Region 1 Local, Walter Reuther Library, Wayne State University, Michigan, Box 232.

116. "Labor Dissidents Confront Carter with a 'High Noon' Challenge," *LA Times*, December 14, 1978, D11.

117. "Labor Joins the Dissidents," *Washington Post*, December 12, 1978, A1.

118. Memo, Schlossberg to Fraser, October 9, 1978, Fraser Papers, Box 62.

119. "From Memphis: A Liberal Message to Carter," *Washington Post*, December 20, 1978, A1.

120. "Socialism Is No Longer a Dirty Word for Labor," *Business Week*, September 24, 1979, 130.

121. Booklet, "Capitalism, Socialism and Democracy" by Sydney Hook, Shanker Papers, Box 62; Leaflet, "Building on the Past for the Future," by Lane Kirkland, Kirkland Papers, Box 52.

122. Except when subsumed within other organizations and campaigns—it was only its own future it could not manage: "DSOC Helps Liz to Victory," *Democratic Socialist New York Newsletter*, October 1980, Mandler Papers.

123. "Whom Should the Left Support in 1980?" *Yankee Radical*, February 1980, Mandler Papers.

124. Letter, Harrington to Fraser, January 16, 1980, Fraser Papers, Box 53.

125. Letter, Harrington to Fraser, December 11, 1979, Fraser Papers, Box 53.

126. *Democratic Socialist New York Newsletter*, November–December 1980, Mandler Papers; special newsletter: "DSOC Members Running for Kennedy Delegate Slots," undated, Mandler Papers.

127. 1981 *DSOC Convention Journal*, Maxine Phillips Papers.

128. "DSOC Convention: New Goals Set, Anti-Carter Mood," *Democratic Left* VII:3, Mandler Papers.

129. *DSOC Michigan Newsletter* No. 8, December 10, 1978, UAW Regional 1 Papers, Box 232.

130. "Citizen's Party," *LA Left*, August 1979, Mandler Papers.

131. A good indicator of the tempo of debate can be taken from *Socialist Forum* 1:2, undated, Mandler Papers. One activist argued "we must cultivate our own leadership," another that the Democratic Agenda is "an unprecedented success," and yet another that "Democratic Agenda deserves a decent burial."

132. "Citizen's Party Born in Unorthodox Way," *New York Times*, April 13, 1980, 15.

133. Interview with Meyerson; letter, McGovern to Darrel G. Wells, October 22, 1979, McGovern Papers, Box 323.

134. Letter, Victor S. Kamber to Fraser, July 18, 1979, Fraser Papers, Box 68.

135. Letter, Winpisinger to members, undated, Fraser Papers, Box 68; the National Call raised $750,000 in 1979, with an average donation of $19 per respondent: letter, Wimpisinger to National Call supporters, late 1979, McGovern Papers, Box 323.

136. "ABC/Harris Poll: President Carter's Chances of Re-election in 1980 Seem Dim," July 5, 1979, Clymer Papers, Box 18; "Kennedy Beats Them Both," *Public Opinion Magazine*, October-November, 23; "Many Republicans Are Fearful of a Kennedy Candidacy," *New York Times*, October 24, 1979, A18.

137. "Poll Shows Carter Gaining Support on Afghan Moves," *New York Times*, January 16, 1980, A1.

138. "Jimmy Strikes Back," *Newsweek*, October 8, 1980, 26–27.

139. "Kennedy Won Popular Vote," *New York Times*, June 5, 1980, B8.

140. Interview with Jack Clark.

141. Letter, Bill Dodds and Bob Carolla to Doug Fraser and Jerry Wurf, June 26, 1980, Fraser Papers, Box 68.

142. "Kennedy's Performance at Convention Met with Widespread Approval," Louis Harris Poll, August 25, 1980, Mondale Papers, Box 4.

143. Jordan, *Crisis*, 329.

144. Isserman, *Other American*, 339–340.

145. Kenneth S. Baer, *Reinventing Democrats: The Politics of Liberalism from Reagan to Clinton* (Lawrence: University Press of Kansas, 2000), 2.

146. "Democrats Seek Election Reform," *New York Times*, July 3, 1981, A10; "Workshops at Democratic Mini-Convention Mix Hoopla and Cynicism," *New York Times*, June 26, 1982, 12.

147. Manning Marable, *Beyond Black and White: Transforming African-American Politics* (New York: Verso, 1996), 61.

148. Interview with Maxine Phillips.

149. Jonathan Bell, *The Liberal State on Trial: The Cold War and American Politics in the Truman Years* (New York: Columbia, 2004), 273–274; Thurber, *The Politics of Equality*, 233; Jonathan Bell, "'To Strive for Economic and Social Justice': Welfare, Sexuality, and Liberal Politics in San Francisco in the 1960s," *Journal of Policy History* (Spring 2010): 193–225.

150. Alan Brinkley, *The End of Reform: New Deal Liberalism in Recession and War* (New York: Knopf, 1995), 3.

151. Interview with Mike Dukakis.

152. Memo, Eizenstat and Bill Johnston to Carter, undated, White House Central Files: LA-7, Jimmy Carter Library.

153. David Butler and Dennis Kavanah, *The British General Election of 1983* (London: Macmillan, 1999), 52.

4

From Friends to Foes

George McGovern, Hubert Humphrey, and the Fracture in American Liberalism

BRUCE MIROFF

A few days after Hubert Humphrey died of cancer in January 1978, George McGovern drafted two tributes to him for publication in newspapers and magazines. In one of these tributes, McGovern took time to reflect on how much his own life was enmeshed in Humphrey's:

> Sometimes I have thought that Hubert Humphrey's life has been a testing ground for mine. Our lives have frequently moved along similar lines. We were both born and reared in depression and drought-scarred South Dakota. We both educated ourselves to become college professors. We both felt the lure of prairie politics and eventually emerged as the presidential nominee of our party—Hubert in 1968 and I in 1972. Although we were divided over the war in Vietnam and became presidential rivals for a brief time, the bonds of personal friendship survived that division. It was not possible to hold a grudge against Hubert. He healed the wounds of political rivalry with humor and love.

The friendship of George McGovern and Hubert Humphrey was more than the normal bond of two midwestern progressives in the U.S. Congress. For a decade, these two men had been nextdoor neighbors in Chevy Chase, Maryland, "where our children grew up together, our wives visited daily, and Hubert and I rode together to Capitol Hill." Humphrey was a political mentor to McGovern—and an exemplar of "the joy of being alive." "Once on a warm summer night," McGovern fondly recalled in this tribute, "I heard him singing happily at two o'clock in the morning while he scrubbed the walls of his kitchen."[1]

As McGovern testified, it was the war in Vietnam that led to a rift between these friends and turned them into rivals in presidential politics both in 1968 and 1972. Yet the sources of the fracture in such a close personal and political friendship ran deeper and began earlier than the conflict in Vietnam. And despite the reconciliation of these old friends after the 1972 campaign, the reverberations of their rift have continued to affect the development of contemporary American liberalism.

My article examines the McGovern-Humphrey relationship on two distinct levels, which have some intriguing interconnections. The first level is personal and psychological, while the second is ideological and political. That a close friendship between two major political leaders is shaken by their opposite reactions to a historical crisis is an interesting story in its own right. The story is given a larger significance in the development of contemporary American liberalism because these men became the leaders of two warring wings in the Democratic Party, were spokesmen for alternative liberal visions and coalitions that emerged in the 1960s, and were still perceptible in the struggle for the 2008 Democratic presidential nomination. In this regard, the fracture in the McGovern-Humphrey friendship may cast new light on the most important fracture in liberal politics since the New Deal.

Fracture Foreshadowed

In the two memorials that McGovern wrote, there was only one critical remark about Humphrey, but it was revealing of what McGovern perceived as a fundamental difference between the two men:

> He had limitations, as we all do. He seldom read a thoughtful book and he was too much in awe of official briefers. But when it came to the great issues of social justice, Hubert's instincts were not only sure, they were enunciated with a passion, earthiness, wit, and force that we are not likely to see exceeded in all the days of our lives.[2]

McGovern praised Humphrey's warm heart but pointed out the limitations of his head (thinking). Humphrey, he was hinting, had absorbed the basic axioms of New Deal and Cold War liberalism as a young academic and politician, but had not exposed himself to the critiques of that liberalism that were published in later years. Perhaps even more important, Humphrey had become part of a governing liberal establishment that was thoroughly uncritical of its own official pronouncements. McGovern never doubted that

Humphrey's heart was in the right place, but he believed that Humphrey's ideological stance was frozen in the past. It is to the past, specifically the 1940s and 1950s, that we must first turn to see the fracture between McGovern and Humphrey foreshadowed.

In searching for sources of this fracture that predated the war in Vietnam, three topics seem particularly suggestive: academic influences, the earlier liberal fracture of 1946–1948, and the respective congressional roles assumed by the two friends. Since both Humphrey and McGovern studied to become academics (although only McGovern completed a doctorate), it is instructive to compare their own reports about intellectual mentors during their time as undergraduates and graduate students. Humphrey's account in his autobiography, *The Education of a Public Man* (first published in 1976), is briefer and less informative, but the figure who stands out in Humphrey's political science training at the University of Minnesota is Evron Kirkpatrick. "While I have never really had an alter ego, politically or intellectually," Humphrey wrote, "the man politically closest to me in that period of my life was Evron Kirkpatrick.... He was an exciting professor, with great interest in practical politics, who was extremely well read and imaginative about the problems of government."[3]

Humphrey remained close to Kirkpatrick (and later to his wife Jeane) throughout his career. Kirkpatrick went on from the University of Minnesota to become a pillar of the political science establishment. After serving in the Office of Strategic Services during World War II, he spent eight years in the state department. From 1954 until 1981, he was the executive director of the American Political Science Association (APSA). In that position, he was a staunch defender of the reigning behavioralist paradigm in the discipline, which claimed the authority of objective scientific method. And as a new generation of political scientists challenged the APSA during the late 1960s to become politically relevant and take an official stand against the war in Vietnam, Kirkpatrick led a successful effort to keep the association out of politics.[4]

Although Arthur Link was McGovern's dissertation adviser in American history at Northwestern, his autobiography, *Grassroots* (published in 1977), emphasized the impact of another professor, Lefton "Lefty" Stavrianos:

> The professor I came to know best at Northwestern ... was Lefton Stavrianos, whose speciality was the Balkans but whose interests ranged broadly across the whole spectrum of human civilization.... He was no apologist for the Soviet Union, but his lectures gave one a more balanced view of the Cold War that was then beginning to develop. Collateral readings stimulated

by his courses [including books by such authors as Edgar Snow and Owen Lattimore] . . . made it impossible for me to accept the conventional view of American Cold War policy.[5]

Robert Sam Anson, who wrote a campaign biography of McGovern, described Stavrianos as "the furthest left" of the Northwestern history faculty.[6] McGovern remained close to Stavrianos (and Link) throughout his own political career.

From this—and later—evidence, it appears that Humphrey and McGovern were steeped in different intellectual cultures, at least with respect to U.S. foreign policy. Humphrey absorbed the Manichean view of the emerging Cold War in the 1940s, in which the United States was the defender of freedom against global communist aggression, whereas McGovern learned an alternative Cold War narrative that highlighted more limited communist aims and a greater measure of American culpability. An unconventional perspective on the Cold War made McGovern a skeptic toward the war in Vietnam from the beginning. It also explained much of his appeal to a younger generation of New Politics liberals in the 1960s, whose own reading—whether revisionist historians such as William Appleman Williams and his students or critics of U.S. foreign policy like Richard Barnet, Ronald Steel, and Noam Chomsky—contained analyses that echoed the largely forgotten dissenters of the 1940s.

Closely related to the respective intellectual perspectives of Humphrey and McGovern were their different stances in the fracture during the immediate postwar years between anticommunist liberals and supporters of Henry Wallace. During the closing years of World War II, Humphrey, just then emerging as the leader of Minnesota liberals, was an admirer of Wallace. As a delegate to the 1944 Democratic convention, he supported Wallace over Harry Truman as Roosevelt's running mate. And when FDR died in April 1945, Humphrey wrote to Wallace: "'I simply can't conceal my emotions. How I wish you were at the helm.'"[7] But Humphrey's position toward Wallace shifted after the left wing of the new fusion movement in Minnesota, the Democratic-Farmer-Labor Party (DFL), pulled off a coup and took over the Party. Battling successfully to take back control of the DFL from Communists and other radicals, Humphrey became vocally anticommunist in his politics. He became one of the founders of the anticommunist Americans for Democratic Action (ADA), and like fellow liberals in ADA, he swallowed hard and campaigned for the unpopular Truman against Wallace in 1948.[8]

Eleven years younger than Humphrey, McGovern was a World War II veteran and graduate student in history during the 1948 campaign. Like many of his graduate student colleagues, he worked enthusiastically for Wallace's election.[9] McGovern and his wife were delegates from Illinois to the 1948 Progressive Party convention, where they were dismayed by the dogmatism of the communists in the Party. Nonetheless, McGovern never accepted the common judgment that Wallace had become a tool of the Reds. In his autobiography, McGovern insisted that the former vice president was "an old-fashioned free-enterprise capitalist and a practical internationalist."[10] Moreover, writing amid the Truman craze after Nixon's downfall, McGovern unapologetically held to his original position in 1948: "I believed in the late forties and I believe now that both the domestic health of the nation and the peace of the world would have been better served by the hopeful and compassionate views of Wallace than by the 'Get Tough' policy of the Truman Administration."[11]

Humphrey was first elected to the U.S. Senate in 1948; McGovern was elected to the House in 1956 and, after a stint as director of Food for Peace under President Kennedy, to the Senate in 1962. One of the most famous liberal leaders in the nation after his passionate speech on behalf of a strong civil-rights plank at the 1948 Democratic convention, Humphrey soon found that he paid a steep price from the conservative southern Democrats who dominated the Senate: the freshman senator was frozen out and marginalized.[12] Miserable in his enforced haplessness, Humphrey was thrown a lifeline by Lyndon Johnson, who shrewdly recognized his usefulness as the Texan's bridge to the liberals in the Senate. With Johnson's support, Humphrey gradually won acceptability from colleagues and became a member of the fifties Senate's famous "club." He was still a strong liberal in most of his policy positions, but his liberalism was sometimes tempered by the need to stay in Johnson's good graces. On occasion, biographer Carl Solberg observes, Humphrey's responses to Johnson, "can only be described as 'abject.'"[13]

Neither in the House nor in the Senate was McGovern ever the insider that Humphrey became after his initial marginalization. In part a matter of temperament, McGovern's more modest congressional role also reflected an electoral base in conservative South Dakota that was far less secure than Humphrey's in Minnesota. McGovern thus concentrated on agricultural and nutrition issues, even though only the latter subject really engrossed him, while Humphrey ranged across a wide array of issues and became one of the most influential legislators in the modern history of the Senate. Yet what McGovern gained from a backbencher's position and the gratification of South Dakotans' material interests was the freedom to pursue what most interested him: a critical posture toward American foreign and defense policy. In his quiet way, McGovern was a national-security "dove" in Congress long before that term came into use to describe opponents of the war in Vietnam.[14]

Several of the positions that Humphrey and McGovern respectively took during their congressional careers clearly previewed their later conflict in presidential politics. Running for reelection in 1954, amid the fearful climate of McCarthyism, Humphrey surprised and dismayed his friends in the ADA by sponsoring the Communist Control Act. Proclaiming that the Communist Party in the United States was the instrument of a global conspiracy against American democracy, the act criminalized membership in the Party.[15] Red-baited when he ran for Congress in 1956, McGovern was not one to raise rhetorical alarms about the communist "menace." One of his first votes in the House in 1957 was in opposition to President Eisenhower's request for broad authority to combat communist influence in the Middle East. Rebuffing the advice of Humphrey to go along with Eisenhower in the name of bipartisan foreign policy, McGovern expressed the same skepticism toward reactionary anticommunist allies that he would later voice toward the South Vietnamese regime.[16] "The lack of any real domestic reform program within the Arab states," he said on the floor of the Senate, "will render our proposed Middle East economic aid program largely ineffective in stopping the internal threat of communism."[17]

The defense budget was another area of disagreement between the two men as presidential rivals that was signaled during their years in Congress. Like most liberal Democrats, Humphrey was troubled by the irrationality of the arms race. One of his creative accomplishments as senator was his introduction of the legislation that established the Arms Control and Disarmament Agency. Yet, as a believer in the Cold War, Humphrey's objections to the defense budget were limited. As biographer Carl Solberg observed, Humphrey "prided himself that he never voted for a cut in a military budget."[18] By contrast, cutting the defense budget was perhaps McGovern's signature issue in the Senate, at least until he became one of its most outspoken opponents of the war in Vietnam. Influenced by the ideas of Columbia University economist Seymour Melman, who argued that excessive military spending, especially on nuclear "overkill," was significantly distorting the American economy, McGovern introduced yearly measures in the Senate to reduce the defense budget and to establish a commission to plan the conversion from a militarized economy to a civilian one. Although he never mustered the Senate support to enact his plan, McGovern kept alive an important debate in the face of the prevailing tendency to treat the defense budget as a sacred cow.[19]

Friends and Neighbors

These differences in the character of their liberalism were not apparent to either man when their friendship began in 1956. That year, McGovern challenged the Republican incumbent, Harold Lovre, in the First Congressional District of South Dakota. Humphrey made campaign appearances for McGovern and solicited funds for his race from the Democratic establishment in Washington. McGovern was grateful, thanking Humphrey for "the substantial help that you provided in my recent campaign."[20] In turn, Humphrey was delighted by McGovern's upset victory: "For me, your victory helped overshadow the national landslide for Ike. The Republican smear attacks in South Dakota were soundly repudiated."[21]

The part that Humphrey played in 1956 led him to claim paternity for McGovern's political career. In a letter to an associate written two weeks after the election, Humphrey spoke of how "'a young friend named George McGovern, teacher at Dakota Wesleyan University, was elected to Congress. He is tops, a liberal, intelligent, articulate, and plenty of personality. I campaigned extensively, and in fact got McGovern to run.'"[22] Five years later, Humphrey jocularly repeated the claim that he had recruited McGovern into politics. Speaking at an American Food for Peace Council meeting, Humphrey nodded to Eleanor McGovern and said: "I think Eleanor feels that I sort of talked George into politics, or at least had something to do with it. I remember one time, when I told George that I thought it would be a great idea for him to run for Congress, Eleanor was reaching for the poison bottle—for me."[23]

Humphrey's claim of paternity is revealing about his attitude toward McGovern, for it is strangely at odds with the facts. Contrary to Humphrey's account, McGovern was not a teacher at Dakota Wesleyan in 1956. He had resigned his academic position in 1953 to take a seemingly thankless job as executive secretary of the South Dakota Democratic Party. By 1956, McGovern had been in politics for three years, rebuilding a moribund party from the grassroots and laying the groundwork for his own run for office.[24]

Humphrey's fabricated version of McGovern's entrance into politics expressed both his own fondness for the younger man and his enduring sense of political superiority. That latter sense would eventually show up in Humphrey's difficulty in taking McGovern seriously as an opponent and resentment that McGovern would presume to challenge him for the presidency. Once McGovern became a champion and leader of the New Politics liberalism that spurned Humphrey, champion of Cold War liberalism, for his fervent advocacy of the war in Vietnam, it was all the harder for Humphrey to recognize him as a political equal.[25]

Several weeks after McGovern was elected to Congress, Humphrey informed him that the house next door to his own in Chevy Chase, Maryland, was for sale. The McGoverns purchased the house, and as neighbors for the next decade, Humphrey and McGovern grew very close. Not surprisingly, given Humphrey's greater age and political stature, the friendship was, at least at first, one of mentor and protégé. As Anson relates, "Hubert, then in his second term as Minnesota's junior senator, schooled George in the vagaries of getting around Capitol Hill . . . They spent hours talking about the issues, over coffee in the Humphreys' kitchen or, once the weather warmed, stretched out in lounge chairs in the backyard. Humphrey naturally did most of the talking, and he had a most receptive listener in the young Congressman."[26]

During the early years of their friendship, McGovern looked up to Humphrey as a liberal hero. Surveying the large field of presidential candidates who sought to restore the Democratic Party to power after Eisenhower's second term, McGovern had no trouble in choosing Humphrey as his man. In January 1959, he wrote to Humphrey: "I intend, with your approval, to give a major part of my spare time in the next two years to what I regard as the most important project open to liberal young Democrats today—your election to the Presidency."[27] McGovern worked to persuade other young liberals in the House to endorse Humphrey's presidential bid. Once John F. Kennedy drove Humphrey out of the race through his victories in the Wisconsin and West Virginia primaries, McGovern, while shifting his support to Kennedy, expressed his disappointment that the most committed liberal would not be the Party's nominee.[28]

Humphrey was always ready to reciprocate when it came to supporting McGovern in these years. After McGovern was narrowly defeated in his attempt to move up to the Senate in 1960, Humphrey lobbied the new Kennedy administration to appoint his neighbor as head of the Food for Peace program. His greatest service to McGovern came in 1962, after McGovern had resigned his position at Food for Peace and was making a second bid for a Senate seat. About a month before the election, McGovern was incapacitated by a bout of hepatitis. Already helping out, Humphrey stepped up his efforts in stumping and raising funds for McGovern. He could not resist assuming something of a paternal tone with the younger man as he urged him not to rush back to the campaign trail: "I am sorry and worried for you. Don't overdo. You know that you can't afford to take any chances with over-exhaustion, no matter what happens in this election."²⁹ Yet Humphrey's assistance was important in what proved to be an extremely narrow McGovern victory (by 597 votes after a recount). In gratitude, McGovern wrote to his friend: "How do I love thee. Let me count the ways. Honestly, Hubert, you are the greatest. You always seem to come through just when we need you most."³⁰

Over the course of the two years (1963–1964) in which they were senate colleagues, Humphrey and McGovern continued to express mutual admiration. Even though he had recently been a member of the Kennedy administration, McGovern as a freshman senator was not shy in criticizing its policies toward Cuba and Vietnam. In September 1963, he told the Senate: "The U.S. position in Vietnam has deteriorated so drastically that it is in our national interest to withdraw from that country our forces and our aid."³¹ Yet in the brief Cold War thaw that followed on the Cuban missile crisis the difference between McGovern's critical stance and that of the Cold War liberals was not as evident as it would shortly become. Hence Humphrey was still full of words of praise for McGovern's senate speeches. In response to one of Humphrey's accolades in 1963, McGovern wrote: "I need not tell you, Hubert, that you have not only been my long-time inspiration, but that all of the new Senators feel you are a truly great and effective leader."³²

Humphrey continued to live next door to McGovern for almost two years after he was elected vice president in 1964 (there was not yet a government-owned residence for vice presidents). But if the two men were still neighbors, their friendship was soon profoundly strained. What came between them not only was a war but a man: President Lyndon Johnson.

War and Estrangement

In December 1964, Dwayne Andreas, the millionaire agribusinessman who was one of Humphrey's close associates, wrote to McGovern: "Martin Sorkin suggested to me that there would be an excellent chance for Hubert to win the Nobel Peace prize next year. . . . I believe the best approach would be for you to nominate Hubert, if you would care to do so."³³ McGovern quickly agreed to put his friend forward for the Nobel prize for his work on disarmament, but he did not hear anything further about the subject for several months. In March 1965, Max Kampelman, Humphrey's chief political adviser, finally notified McGovern that "the consensus [in the Humphrey camp] is that the matter ought to be dropped."³⁴ By this point, Humphrey was the vice president in an administration that was dropping bombs on Vietnam.

After Viet Cong attacks in February 1965 led the Johnson administration to plan a retaliatory bombing campaign against North Vietnam, Humphrey weighed in verbally and with a memo urging delay and recommending a negotiated settlement of the conflict. The president was angered by the dissent from his vice president, from whom he expected unquestioning fealty, and Humphrey was frozen out of subsequent inner circle discussions about the war. His banishment lasted nearly a year. It ended when Johnson calculated that Humphrey could be useful to him in countering mounting liberal criticisms of the war—and when Humphrey got on board with the policy and became an enthusiastic advocate for it.[35] As Solberg writes, "The vice president who had opposed the president's war policy persuaded himself that Johnson was right, and emerged as the leading spokesman for the president's course in Vietnam."[36]

McGovern advocated a strategy of negotiations as well, and he went to the White House to warn President Johnson that the path on which he was embarking was strewn with dangers. The president brusquely dismissed the senator's arguments with standard Cold War refrains. Shortly afterward, the Humphreys went to their neighbors' house for Sunday breakfast. As McGovern describes the scene in his autobiography, he told Humphrey of his disagreement with Johnson's war policy.

> This set off the first real argument Hubert and I had had in a decade as neighbors and friends. He replied heatedly that he believed in the policy—that we had to stop the Communists in Vietnam or they would take over all of Asia. He continued that if I heard others say he wasn't with the President all the way, they weren't doing him any favor—it wasn't true. He had been fighting Communists, he added, ever since he had helped drive them out of the Democratic Farmer-Labor Party in Minnesota in the forties; liberals had to be anti-Communist and Vietnam was the test.[37]

For the remainder of Humphrey's vice presidency, the two men were estranged. In McGovern's recollection: "As time went on, Hubert and I stopped talking about Vietnam. We tried to remain friends, but the war was 'off-limits' in conversations between our families. Gradually we saw less of each other."[38] As the war in Vietnam escalated in carnage and cost between 1965 and 1968, it produced a widening rift between these old friends that was mirrored in the larger liberal community.

Between 1965 and 1968, Humphrey and McGovern were moving in opposite directions. With his trademark exuberance, once Humphrey became committed to Johnson's war in Vietnam he portrayed it as a historic advance for liberal values. Speaking at the U.S. Embassy in Saigon in 1967, Humphrey famously intoned: "I believe that Vietnam will be marked as the place where the family of man has gained the time it needed to finally break through to a new era of hope and human development and justice. This is the chance we have. This is our great adventure—and a wonderful one it is!"[39] Meanwhile, McGovern's experience of meeting with the victims of violence, American and indigenous, in Vietnam hospitals in late 1965 deepened his dissent, giving his intellectual and political case against the war an intense emotional edge. Ending the war became his self-proclaimed "obsession."[40]

Delighting initially mistrustful liberals with his progressive domestic policies in 1964–1965, Lyndon Johnson subsequently fractured the liberal coalition in the Democratic Party by escalating the war in Vietnam. On one side of the new divide were the president's loyalists, dubbed by the press as Vietnam "hawks," with Humphrey now preeminent among them. On the other side were the growing ranks of Vietnam "doves." While Humphrey enjoyed LBJ's favor (in an association that may well have cost him his lifelong dream of the presidency in 1968), McGovern was persona non grata in the eyes of the administration. "After 1965," he notes, "Johnson never invited me back to the White House." [41]

Allard Lowenstein, the driving force behind the "Dump Johnson" movement among antiwar Democrats, approached McGovern in fall 1967 about challenging the president in the upcoming nomination contest. Anticipating a difficult reelection effort in South Dakota in 1968, McGovern demurred and suggested Eugene McCarthy. McGovern subsequently adopted the position of official neutrality between McCarthy, Robert Kennedy, and Humphrey. But it was plain to anyone listening to him that he favored Senator Kennedy. In 1960, McGovern had supported Humphrey over John Kennedy on the grounds that Humphrey was the more liberal candidate. By spring 1968, it was another Kennedy whom he perceived as the liberal standard-bearer, while Humphrey was affiliated with the more conservative elements of the Democratic Party.[42]

After Kennedy was assassinated in Los Angeles in June 1968, a number of his supporters asked McGovern to declare for the nomination as a means of holding together Kennedy delegates for critical convention votes. It was in his role as candidate that McGovern joined with Humphrey and McCarthy in a televised debate at Chicago before the California delegation, a hotbed of antiwar sentiment. In this exchange, Humphrey, not surprisingly, was on the defensive. He attempted to placate the California delegates by voicing abstract liberal sentiments and by reminding them of his pioneering civil rights stance as mayor of Minneapolis and at the 1948 convention. Largely skirting the subject of Vietnam, he insisted: "There is no man that can claim that he is the peace candidate. Every one of us [has] dedicated his life" to peace. It was McGovern who captured the sentiments of the audience with his antiwar message. He reminded the Californians (and the national TV audience) that from the outset of the conflict in Vietnam he had expressed his "concern on the floor of the United States Senate about young men dying 10,000 miles away from our shores, trying in a desperate effort to save a regime out there in Southeast Asia that cannot, or will not, command the respect and confidence of its own people."[43]

For Humphrey, the event was a minor setback, albeit indicative of the major problem he soon faced in generating enthusiasm for his candidacy during the fall from antiwar Democrats. To McGovern, however, it represented a milestone in his relationship with Humphrey. In his eyes, as well as in the eyes of outside observers, he bested both Humphrey and McCarthy in the debate.[44] The former protégé now matched up well against his erstwhile mentor. Considering the vice president's misguided passion for the war and disastrous entanglement with LBJ, McGovern believed he was capable of equal standing with Humphrey. It was not an equality that Humphrey or his advisers would ever come to acknowledge.

Presidential Rivals

After the fury and outrage of the Chicago Democratic convention, antiwar Democrats had a hard time stomaching Humphrey's presidential candidacy. Eugene McCarthy refused to endorse the Democratic presidential nominee until nearly the eve of the fall election, while the nominee was greeted on the campaign trail by demonstrators' signs proclaiming "Dump the Hump." McGovern too was irate at the brutality of the Chicago police, directed by Mayor Richard Daley, Humphrey's ally, and he was urged by many of his backers to withhold his endorsement. Nonetheless, he stood with Humphrey on the rostrum as the vice president accepted the nomination and clasped his old friend's hand in the traditional sign of unity.[45]

McGovern's gesture of residual affection for Humphrey in 1968 was reciprocated on occasion. After watching McGovern's appearance on the *Today* show in April 1970, Humphrey wrote him with high praise. "George," Humphrey wrote, "you are one of the great Senators, and I mean this with all sincerity." Humphrey complimented his old friend for his work on the issue of hunger and his role as chair of the Democrats' reform commission. More surprising, he singled out McGovern's stance on Vietnam: "The whole nation is indebted to you for your sincerity and conviction in the cause of peace."[46] The rift between the two men opened by the war in Vietnam was not so wide as to eradicate their earlier bond. But a greater strain on their relationship soon developed once they became rivals for the 1972 Democratic presidential nomination.

Amid the crowded field of Democratic contenders for the chance to oppose President Nixon at the start of 1972, the frontrunner was Senator Edmund Muskie, whose strategy was to bridge the destructive gap between the regulars and the New Politics reformers that had opened four years earlier. McGovern was positioned on the left, heading a grassroots insurgency that focused on mobilizing antiwar sentiment for the enlarged schedule of primaries and open caucuses that were the product of the Party's reformed rules on delegate selection. Humphrey was positioned to the right of Muskie; the new party rules necessitated that he run in primaries, which he had avoided in 1968, but otherwise his organization and funding practices reflected the thinking of the prereform era. Further to the right was Senator Henry Jackson, and on the far right of the ideological spectrum was George Wallace. McGovern and his staff believed that if the contest eventually came down to their candidacy versus Humphrey's, they would have the advantage. For his part, Humphrey, seemingly still regarding both McGovern and New Politics liberalism with an attitude of superiority, could not really believe that McGovern would be his chief competition. As he wrote in his autobiography: "[W]hile I like George McGovern personally and respect his abilities and humanitarianism, I quite honestly did not take him seriously as a presidential candidate."[47]

Once Muskie, whose bridging strategy left both traditional Democrats and New Politics liberals cold, faded after a string of disappointing primary performances, McGovern and Humphrey emerged as the principal contenders for the nomination. As the contest headed toward the decisive showdown in California, McGovern, the former protégé, was now the frontrunner, while Humphrey, the erstwhile mentor, had become the underdog. McGovern cast himself as the voice of a fresh new liberalism, seeking to topple the Democratic establishment from the bottom up and to redirect the Party's ideological orientation toward a sixties vision of peace and social justice. Humphrey was the last hope of the party establishment and a standard-bearer for the Cold War liberalism that had reigned from Truman through Johnson.[48]

The competitors in the California primary represented two distinct electoral coalitions. Media commentators naturally focused on the youthfulness of McGovern supporters. His coalition included followers of the new social movements of the sixties, among them antiwar activists, civil rights activists, feminists, and gays, along with suburban reform liberals. What was most notable about the coalition that Humphrey assembled was also its age. Humphrey was the candidate of the old—the old labor of AFL-CIO president George Meany, older blacks, older Jews, and senior citizens in general. The much-discussed generation gap of the sixties and early seventies was reflected in the fracture in liberalism.

Humphrey entered the California primary extremely short of funds for paid media, and he had no field organization to match McGovern's grassroots army. Earlier, he had told his staff to avoid personal attacks on his old friend McGovern, but his closest advisers, feeding on a growing sense of desperation, persuaded him to take off the gloves in California and give McGovern a pounding. The new tactic was to portray McGovern as the spokesman for a foolish and dangerous radicalism, and Humphrey, always good at screwing himself up into bursts of rhetorical enthusiasm, went after his rival with ideological accusations that had once been hurled against him.[49]

The centerpiece of the McGovern-Humphrey confrontation in California was the first of three nationally televised debates. Even though Humphrey had already gone on the offensive in his California campaign events, McGovern "wasn't prepared for him to open up right out of the box with a series of attacks on everything I had stood for."[50] After attempting to deflate McGovern's signature boast that he had been "right from the start" about the war in Vietnam, Humphrey pivoted to an assault on McGovern's proposal for a large-scale reduction in the defense budget. McGovern's approach to military spending, Humphrey alleged, would cut "into the very security of this country" and "make America into a second class power." Humphrey hammered on the welfare issue as well, exaggerating the size and scope of McGovern's "demogrant" proposal and claiming that it amounted to "putting everybody on welfare" and "having the government in everything." On the issue of McGovern's proposal to raise taxes on the wealthy, Humphrey insisted that "it would drive away any possible incentive for the American enterprise system."[51]

Humphrey probed some genuine weaknesses in McGovern's campaign proposals. However, as Solberg observed, "to raise [these issues] was to put Humphrey on the side of the status quo, of big business, of the military-industrial complex."[52] The one-time prairie populist had already moved toward a more probusiness perspective as Johnson's vice president. As a presidential candidate, he held to the economic growth philosophy of the Kennedy-

Johnson years and wanted nothing to do with the income-redistribution approach that New Politics liberals like McGovern were touting. Even in the issue area of civil rights, in which he was most proud of his past accomplishments, Humphrey positioned himself in 1972 to the right of McGovern. As Timothy Thurber writes, Humphrey disappointed his allies in the black community "by flip-flopping on Nixon's call for a one-year moratorium on court orders to enforce busing and permanent legislative restrictions on busing."[53]

McGovern captured the winner-take-all California primary despite Humphrey's attacks, but the Minnesotan and his allies, invoking the reform spirit of the McGovern-Fraser rules, challenged the results and demanded a proportional distribution of California delegates. As a stop-McGovern coalition formed among his Democratic rivals, Humphrey's allies were the spark plugs of the effort, and Humphrey was the likely beneficiary if the California challenge was upheld by the Party. As Humphrey kept up his barrage against McGovern's supposed radicalism and the California challenge threatened to deny the nomination to the insurgent from South Dakota, McGovern at last hit back with the harshest words he ever used about his old friend and neighbor:

> It is sad to see a nationally-known figure like Hubert Humphrey undermining his reputation and jeopardizing his party by the kind of misleading statements he has been making about my positions. He knows that I am a reasonable man, yet he persists in twisting my positions to serve his own desperate purposes. ... I am afraid that my old friend has forgotten that there is such a thing as wanting too much to be elected.[54]

When the opening session of the Democratic convention in Miami Beach finally upheld California's winner-take-all process, McGovern's nomination was assured. But the stop-McGovern forces were not, for the most part, reconciled to his candidacy. Humphrey's most important political allies, George Meany and Richard Daley, were particularly bitter toward the McGovern forces. Humphrey himself withdrew from the race the next day. But Scoop Jackson remained in the contest, and most of the delegates that Humphrey had collected in the spring voted for Jackson when the convention roll was called.[55]

Like McGovern in 1968, Humphrey campaigned for the Democratic nominee in 1972. In light of his inflammatory remarks about McGovern in the spring, some McGovern supporters doubted the sincerity of his support. Writing to a Southern California Democratic official in September 1972, Humphrey sought to dispel such doubts:

I know that things got a little rough out in California in the primary; but quite frankly, some of the positions announced by McGovern in that primary just won't hold up on a national scale. That is why George has modified his positions.... Enough of this. I'll be doing all I can to heal wounds to see that McGovern is elected. I want him elected. I surely don't want Nixon, and I'll be in there pitching.[56]

How hard was Humphrey "pitching"? On the basis of a new Nixon tape released in the summer of 2007, Rick Perlstein argues that Humphrey did not actually want McGovern to win in 1972. According to Perlstein, Humphrey's congratulatory phone call to the president on Election Night suggested that Nixon was more likely to bring peace in Vietnam than was McGovern. Discussing his campaign efforts on McGovern's behalf, Humphrey told Nixon: "'I did what I had to do. If not, Mr. President, this whole defeat would have been blamed on me and some of my associates.'" Then, Perlstein relates, the two men "share[d] a hearty laugh."[57]

After 1972

On the heels of McGovern's landslide defeat in November 1972, the forces that had combined in the stop-McGovern coalition swiftly moved to take control of the Democratic Party away from the new liberal coalition and return it to the hands of the Cold War liberals. Along with electing a centrist Texas Democrat, Robert Strauss, as the chair of the Democratic National Committee, Humphrey and Jackson allies were at the forefront in the creation of the Coalition for a Democratic Majority (CDM). Humphrey and Jackson became honorary cochairs of the new organization, while their top aides, Max Kampelman for Humphrey and Ben Wattenberg for Jackson, actively ran it. Through CDM—and the Committee on the Present Danger that it helped to spawn a few years later—a number of prominent Cold War liberals began their transition to neoconservatism.[58]

But Humphrey was not among their ranks. In his final years in the Senate, his principal achievement was cosponsorship of the Humphrey-Hawkins full employment bill. Although the bill proved to be ineffectual, Humphrey's work for it represented something of a return to his roots. The plan harkened back to New Deal liberalism with its provision for public sector jobs in the absence of sufficient employment opportunities in the private sector. It also restored Humphrey's close ties to African American politics; its cosponsor was a black congressman from Los Angeles and it was backed by the Congressional Black Caucus.[59]

Neither McGovern nor Humphrey was the type to hold a grudge, and the two achieved a reconciliation of sorts after the 1972 campaign. As he had done so many times in the past, Humphrey campaigned for McGovern during the 1974 Senate race in South Dakota, helping him win what would prove to be his final term in office. Still infected with the presidential bug despite his painful defeat in 1972, McGovern approached Humphrey with an unusual proposition in the summer of 1975. He suggested a Humphrey-McGovern ticket for 1976 that would bring the warring wings of liberalism back together. Humphrey appeared to be moved by McGovern's offer, but he did not seriously consider it.[60]

Humphrey was just as infected as McGovern. He was prepared to run his fourth campaign for the presidency in 1976. But this time, with Jimmy Carter rather than George McGovern as the insurgent candidate, Humphrey could position himself to the left of the frontrunner. Indications were that he was to announce his entrance into the New Jersey primary, scheduled for June 7, on the final open day, April 30. His staff booked the Senate Caucus Room for the announcement. But when Humphrey took the podium, it was to opt out of the race. He told his supporters that he did not have the organization or the funding to challenge Carter. Left unspoken was perhaps the ultimate reason for the decision: Humphrey's ill health. Only a few months later, he received the diagnosis of the cancer that would kill him.[61]

Conclusion

The fracture in liberalism that became embodied in the rivalry of George McGovern and Hubert Humphrey never fully healed. It took new and complicated forms in the years that followed. Ironically, some of those who came to oppose the more leftward version of liberalism that McGovern championed were his former campaign staffers, most prominently Gary Hart as neoliberal and Bill Clinton as New Democrat. If the aging acolytes of Hubert Humphrey and Scoop Jackson gravitated to the right (with some even becoming Republicans), Hart and Clinton shaped a new Democratic center. They were not heirs of Cold War liberalism, but they shared with the Humphrey of later years a skeptical view toward the economic and cultural postures of the Democratic left. As for fading memories of the McGovern insurgency of 1972, they were primarily kept alive by the centrists, who invoked them as admonitions of what would happen to the Democratic Party if it ever allowed the liberal-left again to capture its presidential nomination.

The fractures of 1972 were still detectable in the most recent round of Democratic primaries and caucuses. With Barack Obama and Hillary Clinton as the chief competitors, race and gender politics inevitably played out differently in 2008 than in 1972. The issue differences between Obama and Clinton also were less pronounced than in the McGovern-Humphrey contest. Obama had been an original opponent of President Bush's war in Iraq while Clinton initially supported it, but by the time of their competition they were largely agreed in their critiques of the president's policy. On the hottest domestic issue during the Democratic primaries and caucuses, health care, Clinton was, if anything, positioned to Obama's left.

Nonetheless, there were striking parallels between the Democratic nomination contests of 1972 and 2008. In many respects, the rival electoral coalitions of 2008 resembled their predecessors of thirty-six years earlier. Like George McGovern, Barack Obama had greater support from the young, from antiwar activists, and from Democrats with more education and higher incomes. Like Hubert Humphrey, Hillary Clinton had greater backing from the old, from foreign-policy traditionalists, and from Democrats with less in the way of education and income. Fortunately for Obama, the split among Democrats was easier to bridge for the general election of 2008. Obama benefited from a unity in Democratic ranks that had totally escaped McGovern.

In one of the tributes McGovern composed after Humphrey's death, he wrote: "We were not only warm friends, but we shared the legacy of American liberalism."[62] This legacy was ambiguous and capacious enough that McGovern, Humphrey, and their backers fought a fierce battle over its meaning. Since that battle was waged, with destructive consequences for the viability of the Democratic Party, it has taken decades of increasingly conservative Republican rule to remind liberals of what they still have in common. The story of the relationship between McGovern and Humphrey is revealing of some of the underlying differences that still divide Democrats. But it also points to the moral convictions, shared struggles, and personal good will that can bring together liberalism's often-warring wings and give the Democratic Party a fighting chance against the more cohesive conservative ranks of its Republican adversary.

Notes

1. George McGovern, tribute to Hubert Humphrey sent to various newspapers, January 15, 1978, George S. McGovern Papers (hereafter GMP), Seeley G. Mudd Manuscript Library, Princeton University, Princeton, New Jersey, Box 483.

2. George McGovern, "Final Tribute" (written for *New Times*, dated January 16, 1978), GMP, Box 483.

3. Hubert Humphrey, *The Education of a Public Man: My Life and Politics* (Minneapolis: University of Minnesota Press, 1991), 36.

4. David M. Ricci, *The Tragedy of Political Science: Politics, Scholarship, and Democracy* (New Haven: Yale University Press, 1984), 135, 283–284; David Binder, "Evron Kirkpatrick, 83, Director of Political Science Association," *New York Times*, May 9, 1995.

5. George McGovern, *Grassroots: The Autobiography of George McGovern* (New York: Random House, 1977), 40.

6. Robert Sam Anson, *McGovern: A Biography* (New York: Holt, Rinehart and Winston, 1972), 62.

7. Humphrey quoted in Carl Solberg, *Hubert Humphrey: A Biography* (New York: W. W. Norton, 1984), 112.

8. Solberg, *Hubert Humphrey*, 93–123; Steven M. Gillon, *Politics and Vision: The ADA and American Liberalism, 1947–1985* (New York: Oxford University Press, 1987), 3–56.

9. Anson, *McGovern*, 59–60.

10. McGovern, *Grassroots*, 43.

11. Ibid., 45.

12. Solberg, *Hubert Humphrey*, 133–149.

13. Ibid., 171. On the Johnson-Humphrey relationship, see Solberg, 160–164, 169–171; Robert A. Caro, *The Years of Lyndon Johnson: Master of the Senate* (New York: Alfred A. Knopf, 2002), 439–462.

14. Anson, *McGovern*, 86–91, 128–136.

15. Gillon, *Politics and Vision*, 107–109.

16. McGovern, *Grassroots*, 79.

17. Speech delivered in the U.S. Senate, January 31, 1957, GMP, Box 1035.

18. Solberg, *Hubert Humphrey*, 182.

19. Anson, *McGovern*, 129–134.

20. George McGovern to Hubert Humphrey, November 27, 1956, GMP, Box 501.

21. Hubert Humphrey to George McGovern, November 8, 1956, GMP, Box 501.

22. Humphrey quoted in Solberg, *Hubert Humphrey*, 177.

23. Hubert Humphrey, Remarks at First National Conference, American Food for Peace Council, June 28, 1961, GMP, Box 1048.

24. For accounts of McGovern's early political career, see Anson, *McGovern*, 66–85, and McGovern, *Grassroots*, 51–71. Humphrey is not mentioned in either account.

25. Max Kampelman, Humphrey's chief political adviser, told me in 2005 that "McGovern would have had no career had it not been for Hubert Humphrey." Author's telephone interview with Max Kampelman, September 19, 2005.

26. Anson, *McGovern*, 85.

27. George McGovern to Hubert Humphrey, January 30, 1959, GMP, Box 1048.

28. George McGovern, Press Release, May 13, 1960, GMP, Box 1048.

29. Hubert Humphrey to George McGovern, October 8, 1962, GMP, Box 464.

30. George McGovern to Hubert Humphrey, October 20, 1962, GMP, Box 464.

31. George McGovern, speech in Senate, *Congressional Record—Senate*, September 26, 1963.

32. George McGovern to Hubert Humphrey, August 3, 1963, GMP, Box 1049.
33. Dwayne Andreas to George McGovern, December 18, 1964, GMP, Box 496.
34. Max Kampelman to George McGovern, March 4, 1965, GMP, Box 496.
35. Solberg, *Hubert Humphrey*, 267–300; Robert Mann, *A Grand Delusion: America's Descent into Vietnam* (New York: Basic Books, 2001), 499–503.
36. Solberg, *Hubert Humphrey*, 285.
37. McGovern, *Grassrooots*, 105. Humphrey does not mention the conversation—or his rift with McGovern over Vietnam—in his own autobiography.
38. Ibid., 106.
39. Humphrey quoted in Solberg, *Hubert Humphrey*, 312.
40. McGovern, *Grassroots*, 106–107.
41. Ibid., 105.
42. Ibid., 108–116.
43. Transcript of exchange before the California delegation at the 1968 Democratic convention, GMP, Box 922.
44. McGovern, *Grassroots*, 123.
45. Anson, *McGovern*, 208–212.
46. Hubert Humphrey to George McGovern, April 29, 1970, GMP, Box 492.
47. Humphrey, *The Education of a Public Man*, 327.
48. On the 1972 Democratic nomination contest, see Bruce Miroff, *The Liberals' Moment: The McGovern Insurgency and the Identity Crisis of the Democratic Party* (Lawrence: University Press of Kansas, 2007), 41–71.
49. Solberg, *Hubert Humphrey*, 432–433.
50. Author's telephone interview with George McGovern, November 1, 2002.
51. Transcript of first California debate on *Face the Nation*, May 28, 1972, GMP, Box 830.
52. Solberg, *Hubert Humphrey*, 432.
53. Timothy N. Thurber, *The Politics of Equality: Hubert H. Humphrey and the African American Freedom Struggle* (New York: Columbia University Press, 1999), 229.
54. McGovern Campaign Press Release, June 20, 1972, GMP, Box 830. On the California challenge, see Miroff, *The Liberals' Moment*, 72–76.
55. Gordon Weil, *The Long Shot: George McGovern Runs for President* (New York: W. W. Norton, 1973), 145.
56. Hubert Humphrey to M. Larry Lawrence, September 20, 1972, Papers of Frank Mankiewicz, McGovern Campaign, John F. Kennedy Library, Boston, Box 19.
57. Rick Perlstein, "The Myths of McGovern," *Democracy: A Journal of Ideas* 7 (Winter 2008).
58. Miroff, *The Liberals' Moment*, 262–265.
59. Thurber, *The Politics of Equality*, 233–247.
60. McGovern, *Grassroots*, 260–262.
61. Solberg, *Hubert Humphrey*, 451–453.
62. McGovern, "Final Tribute," GMP, Box 483.

PART II

Liberals and Urban Policy

5

New York Liberalism and the Fight against Homelessness

ELLA HOWARD

The modern American welfare system reflects its architects' desires to assist the poor as well as their fear of fostering dependency on relief. Its programs, forged and expanded during periods of liberal political dominance, have shifted over time, as resource allocations and attitudes toward poverty have changed. The urban homeless have long slipped through the cracks of this system, struggling to navigate the complex terrain of overlapping and sometimes conflicting policies.[1]

Although charitable impulses are not confined to liberal politics, the expansion of the scope of the government in order to provide such charitable programs, whether at the municipal, state, or federal level, has been a core tenet of modern liberalism. As the meaning of the term *liberalism* in America shifted from its early-nineteenth-century orientation toward protecting the rights of the middle and upper classes to its twentieth-century focus on the expansion of the regulatory state, it represented a growing political consensus that individuals should be protected from the previously unchecked power of the business sector. At each juncture in the development of urban liberalism, the contemporaneous policies toward homelessness reflected political commitments to the equality of opportunity, belief in human potential for reform and rehabilitation, attitudes toward the poor, and definitions of the role of government itself.

This essay explores the development of homeless policy in New York during two periods of liberal expansion of the welfare state. During the 1930s, in response to the crisis of the Great Depression, liberal politicians expanded the power and responsibility of the federal government, regulating the business sector and providing assistance to the nation's needy. Most of the specialized New Deal programs faded as the U.S. entry into World War II restored the nation's economic prosperity. But increased faith in the expanded role of the federal government continued, facilitating the unprecedented tactics adopted under President Lyndon Johnson in the 1960s to end American poverty. Johnson's philosophies and strategies were far from those adopted by Roosevelt; the Johnson administration was much more willing to make fairly radical, long-term interventions into the economic landscape.

Although the poverty programs of the Roosevelt and Johnson administrations have been widely and cogently analyzed, relatively little attention has been paid to the treatment of the poorest of the poor during these periods. Studying the homeless offers a new perspective on the development of the nation's welfare system. Utterly destitute, the urban homeless of the midcentury era were often male, unemployed, and sometimes heavy drinkers. As profoundly unsympathetic subjects to many Americans, they tested the limits of liberalism. Although neither vulnerable women, nor deserving children, most skid-row homeless were American citizens. As such, to what aid were they entitled and how must they behave in order to receive assistance?

Focusing on New York City, one of the nation's most politically liberal cities, this essay analyzes the changing experience of homelessness during these two pivotal eras in the development of urban liberalism. It examines the programs that were developed to aid the homeless while also exploring the effects on the indigent of other period interventions into the urban landscape, in order to clarify the attitudes of urban liberals toward the homeless and, ultimately, toward poverty. It argues that most lasting programs designed to combat urban poverty offered little aid to the poorest of the poor. This pattern of neglect reflected the political motivations and limitations that defined liberal programs, whose proponents routinely abandoned the urban homeless when supporting them might prove unpopular. While American liberalism achieved many laudable goals, including providing assistance to many impoverished individuals and families, it operated within the confines created by a voting public committed to specific visions of a work ethic and economic self-sufficiency.

Early Welfare Systems and Homelessness

The tumult of the nineteenth century had sparked new understandings of the role of government. As industrialization transformed the nation and cities rose alongside factories, the population faced a changing and unfamiliar world, in which industrial labor proved physically difficult, dangerous and repetitive, and often paid abysmally low wages. The existing system of poorhouses struggled to contain the indigent population. The facilities had been developed in the United States in the late eighteenth and nineteenth centuries to aid as well as contain the poor. Yet as industrialization relied upon new labor supplies, temporary workers between jobs joined the ranks of the nation's homeless population. Many such individuals resisted the prospect of institutionalization. Taking to the roads, these migrant homeless traveled the country in search of work. Furthering the mobility of this new generation of "tramps," the nation's railroad network expanded dramatically in the decades following the Civil War.[2]

By the turn of the century, single homeless men began to congregate in urban centers, forming a relatively stable population. Skid rows formed in the nation's major cities. In New York, the Bowery housed flophouses, religious missions, cheap restaurants and bars, and other institutions targeting the homeless. The homeless were encouraged (sometimes forcibly) to remain within the confines of these poverty districts. Their enclosure shielded the city's middle and upper classes from interacting with the homeless.

Nineteenth-century charity reformers such as Charles Loring Brace had judged the character of the poor with a moral compass. They believed that work obligations and means tests for all charity recipients would limit dependency on relief, a fate they feared more even than the immediate suffering of the poor. Many Progressive reformers, however, considered these priorities to be skewed. For reformers like Jane Addams, overt moralizing toward the poor mattered less than providing comfort and lobbying for expanded governmental protections of their interests.[3]

As a result of such efforts, by the 1920s, New York City was home to an elaborate charity network. The local Charity Organization Society's 1920 *New York Charities Directory* required over four hundred pages to explain the roles of the thousands of area organizations. Aid to the homeless was local in nature and primarily privately funded. Dozens of the directory's entries promised help to the homeless, but most did so according to strictly delineated mission statements. Women, children, and ethnic minorities in need turned to agencies scattered across the city's five boroughs, while much assistance for white men clustered on or near the Bowery. Alongside the commercial establishments, these charitable organizations coded the Bowery as increasingly white and male.

Three types of charitable enterprises offered assistance to the Bowery's homeless. Ethnic associations sprang from the tradition of immigrant aid societies, designed to ease new arrivals' transition to American life. Religious charities most often approached the homeless with the dual goals of alleviating their suffering while saving their souls. Public facilities, such as the municipal shelter, were few in number. Their operation reflected nineteenth-century efforts to aid the homeless while also ensuring social control and social order. For decades, such organizations had worked in tandem, both on and off the Bowery, to address the problem of homelessness.

Regardless of their location and purpose, however, charitable and commercial establishments designed for use by the homeless and destitute were unprepared for the ravages of the depression. By 1929, the existing network of assistance and commercial lodging that had been sufficient for decades strained under the rising tide of poverty and homelessness. City officials and charity administrators looked on in horror as poor people spread across the city landscape, squatting in shacks, lining up for bread, begging for cash, and even marching in protest. The events of the late 1920s and early 1930s shocked city and state officials into action, prompting them to begin developing a new philosophy of relief.

Across the country, those dislocated by the economic crisis faced struggles similar to those of the Joad family featured in John Steinbeck's novel, *The Grapes of Wrath*. Destitute families arriving in communities nationwide were often greeted with suspicion and even outright hostility. Lacking the one year of local residency required of relief recipients by many states, homeless individuals were deemed ineligible for assistance.[4]

Coming into office, President Franklin Roosevelt and his administration charged headlong at many of the problems gripping the nation. Amid the whirlwind reforms of their legendary first hundred days in office, the Roosevelt administration launched the Federal Transient Program in August 1933. The program pledged fifteen million dollars to the support of the mobile indigent masses in an effort to end transiency. Fearful that the roaming groups of destitute unemployed would prove demoralizing to the national character, the administration reasoned that the homeless would be easier to monitor as well as care for if they became more stationary. Even as support services for the homeless expanded to their most elaborate level to date, program directors were careful to explain to the public that the program would be aiding the worthy, temporarily homeless, rather than the persistent homeless whose poverty had begun before the onset of the economic crisis.[5]

The FTP expanded quickly, soon boasting nearly three hundred facilities. With few exceptions, the program's centers offered clients little more than food and lodging. The grand scale of the operation facilitated the housing and feeding of many homeless people but afforded the time needed for intensive one-on-one work with none. Little casework was provided to clients, most of whom were considered only temporarily homeless and thus less in need of such services.[6]

Some localities launched labor programs, which ranged from a mineral mining program in Colorado to more traditional work camps in locations across the country. New York State's Temporary Emergency Relief Administration had launched Camp Bluefield, a work program, in 1933. Homeless male clients of the municipal shelter and area flophouses were sent to Palisades Interstate Park, where they were lodged, fed, and set to work. Eventually, over two hundred single, homeless men were earning fifty cents per hour felling trees, maintaining roads, and performing other construction tasks.[7]

A similar program for the homeless operated out of Camp Greycourt, located north of the city, in Chester. Launched in 1934, the program soon employed six hundred men chosen from the clientele of the municipal shelter. Depending on the season, the men farmed or performed road construction and maintenance, earning less than fifty cents per day. Similar FTP camps soon opened across the state of New York and across the country. By 1934, nearly two hundred camps had been established nationwide.[8]

These programs complemented the logic of the broader New Deal, as the popular Civilian Conservation Corps and other programs used federal funds to put unemployed Americans back to work. Such programs promised the poor not only financial support, but also restored dignity in labor. Although criticized for inefficiency, the programs resonated with traditional national ideals of self-sufficiency and allowed clients to avoid the discomfort of receiving a "handout."[9]

Some of the era's homelessness programs proved remarkably innovative, including the TERA's operation of Hartford House, a midtown Manhattan program that had been launched by the YMCA in 1931. The program offered employment placement and enrichment activities to white-collar New York men.[10]

In large part, however, New Deal money funded "warehousing" of the homeless. State and local officials used federal funds to establish or continue large-scale sleeping shelters, such as the Gold Dust Shelter, a Salvation Army facility lodging over two thousand men in a building on loan from the Gold Dust flour company. Young, healthy men participated in the new work programs and camps outside the city, leaving the elderly and the weak to return to skid row. Those individuals received meal and lodging vouchers for the city shelter, hotels, and area restaurants. In New York and Chicago, as well as other cities, those vouchers offered a way to house the homeless temporarily without having to build new, costly facilities. Although limited in these aspects, the FTP was the only federal intervention into the problem of homelessness. Such involvement resulted from the new understanding of homelessness as a national problem worthy of large-scale reduction efforts.[11]

In 1935, Roosevelt famously announced the transition of the New Deal from relief programs to the construction of a social welfare system grounded in wage labor. The focus now would be on a social insurance system funded by employer and employee contributions that would protect those unable to work, due to age or injury. For those able to work, the Works Progress Administration provided jobs, with the goal of generating full employment. This new system of social insurance, although limited in comparison to programs in Western Europe, emerged as the central achievement of the New Deal, benefiting millions of Americans.[12]

The resulting postwar American welfare system has drawn distinctions between Social Security and public assistance, leaving many voters supportive of the "earned" benefits of the former, but critical of the "unearned" benefits of the latter. For many homeless, this new system of public welfare offered little hope. Men who had been homeless for some time often found themselves too weakened to perform WPA jobs and were often refused entry to the program altogether. Social Security, too, excluded most working homeless, who found employment only as day laborers and transient workers, in jobs cut off from the program. During the postwar years, some homeless drew Social Security benefits, and some had earned benefits through the Veterans Administration. But most experienced the expansion of the federal government's welfare provisions primarily through vouchers distributed by city officials that were redeemable for a night at the municipal shelter or a meal at a local cafeteria. In that regard, the landscape of skid row remained largely unchanged from its appearance in the 1920s.[13]

But the true impact of the expanding welfare system was found in the untold numbers who avoided homelessness altogether due to the public assistance, subsidized housing, and Social Security programs of the postwar era. New Deal liberalism constructed an impressive and effective security net that prevented many Americans from facing the depths of destitution, even if those who slipped through that net found few publicly funded programs to meet their needs.

During the postwar era, urban liberals would reconsider the legal rights of the impoverished. They would also reprise the construction of large-scale, federally funded poverty programs. This time, however, the homeless would find little relief through their plans. Even as postwar liberals embraced the notion of boundless economic growth, they shied away from truly redistributive welfare policies and avoided dealing directly with the problem of homelessness.

Midcentury Liberal Urban Policies

Midcentury liberalism encompassed a range of overlapping and sometimes conflicting approaches to urban problems. At the judicial level, liberal justices focused on expanding the rights of members of groups that had been previously excluded from political equality. Simultaneously, other groups of urban liberals worked to remake city centers. These varied objectives affected the lives of the homeless, whose concerns were seen as peripheral to the central goals of liberal politicians and urban planners.

During the 1950s and 1960s, the Supreme Court led the government in progressive change. After the Warren Court's verdict in *Brown v. Board of Education* mandated the racial integration of the schools and other public facilities, it went on to expand the rights of the indigent to an attorney if charged with any felony in *Gideon v. Wainwright*. In the well-known case of *Miranda v. Arizona*, the Court established the rights of the accused to be informed of their rights and obligations during arrest. The courts during this era at the state/federal level also expanded other rights specific to the homeless, including those governing vagrancy and public intoxication.[14]

Modern vagrancy laws had originated in the 1837 *City of New York v. Miln* verdict, in which the Supreme Court had supported the exclusion of the homeless from the city. Justice Barbour had likened such vagrants to "an infectious disease" that might jeopardize the safety of other city residents. Well into the postwar era, vagrancy remained a crime, reflecting the persistent belief that the homeless posed a credible threat to the community in which they lived. The court ruled in *District of Columbia v. Hunt* (1947) that "A vagrant is a probable criminal."[15]

But by the 1960s, courts yielded in the face of pressure from legal scholars and advocates for the rights of the homeless. New York's Court of Appeals ruled against such vagrancy ordinances in *Fenster v. Leary*, arguing that such ordinances led to the unjust persecution of those vagrants who left the designated skid-row area, and that their true crime was that of inconveniencing the more monied classes of the city through their presence. The social-control aspects of homeless policy were anachronistic during an era of expanded personal liberties. By the 1970s, the nation's remaining vagrancy laws were overturned by the Supreme Court as violating the due process clause of the Fourteenth Amendment.[16]

The homeless had attained a legal right to exist, but their behavior remained under constant scrutiny. President Lyndon Johnson's Commission on Law Enforcement and Administration of Justice analyzed "Drunkenness Offenses." By the mid-1960s, approximately one-third of the nation's arrests were for public intoxication. Police departments in cities such as Atlanta and Washington, D.C. strictly enforced such ordinances, resulting in over three-fourths of all arrests relating to drunkenness, disorderly conduct, and vagrancy. In the face of such data, which documented a massive waste of public resources, the commission called for the prosecution of disorderly conduct, but not public intoxication.[17]

The courts took a similar stand on public drunkenness during these years. A series of rulings, including *Robinson v. California*, *Driver v. Hinnant*, and *Easter v. District of Columbia* considered drug addiction and habitual drunkenness to be symptoms of a disease rather than criminal actions. These rulings gave legal backing to the rising cultural tide of the alcoholism movement, which had begun in the 1940s at the Yale University Section of Alcohol Studies. There, Elvin Jellinek and other researchers had promoted the theory that alcoholism was a progressive disease, whose victims could not regulate their consumption of alcohol. As such, they were worthy of assistance and efforts at rehabilitation, rather than criminal prosecution.[18]

The well-known *Powell v. Texas* ruling tested the limits of these new approaches toward public drunkenness. Larry Powell, an Austin resident, had been arrested seventy-three times for public intoxication since 1949. The Supreme Court supported these arrests, rejecting Powell's counsel's argument that they constituted cruel and unusual punishment. Justice Thurgood Marshall noted that defining such arrests as cruel and unusual punishment could complicate future prosecutions of those committing crimes while intoxicated.[19]

These rulings called into question national attitudes toward homelessness, prompting many to reconsider their core assumptions about the indigent. The nineteenth-century policies that anticipated crime as a logical result of the presence of homeless people in a community were out of place in an era in which the courts and politicians alike were working to increase equality of opportunity. Decriminalizing vagrancy also established the right of an individual to remain in his area of residence, even without an official home.

The era's new interpretations of the drunkenness statutes also reflected changing understandings of the nature of substance abuse. As the disease theory of alcoholism became popular not only within the medical community but also within the legal profession, intoxicated vagrants were seen less as criminals and more as sick individuals in need of compassion and understanding.

The homeless were, at last, receiving legal acknowledgement of their right to occupy the streets of the nation's cities, due to the steps toward equality taken by the liberal courts of the era. At the same time, however, the homeless faced new challenges from those who were committed to using dramatic renewal strategies to change the urban landscape. Midcentury liberals supporting urban renewal hoped to improve city living conditions, but did so with little concern for the homeless.

The urban renewal initiatives embodied the core principles of postwar urban liberalism. Such programs set out to remake America's cities through the development of public-private development partnerships. The federally sponsored program originated in the 1930s, with the initial goal of expanding the quality housing options available within cities. By the time the federal legislation was enacted and implemented, however, the program was focused less on housing development than on slum clearance. The program reshaped urban life nationwide.[20]

In New York City, urban renewal brought dramatic change to several neighborhoods. The program was headed by Robert Moses, whose ambitious urban renewal agenda proceeded largely unchecked for years, due to the wide berth he was granted by city officials. As the head of multiple city agencies, Moses held the power to fell entire city blocks. As dilapidated buildings were destroyed, they were often replaced with middle-income housing developments, displacing poor and minority residents. Moses prioritized the needs of the city as a whole over those of any individual resident. He envisioned an urban core populated primarily by the middle and working classes. Moses set out to clear the Bowery of the homeless and the establishments that catered to them. His proposal for the Cooper Square District called for leveling all of the buildings on the east side of twelve Bowery blocks, from Ninth Street to Delancey Street. Instead of the flophouses, bars, restaurants, and gospel missions that characterized skid row, Moses wanted to build apartment buildings designed to house the middle class. Moses was aware of the effect this development would have on the area's homeless population and actively embraced their departure. He hoped the homeless would abandon not only the Bowery, but also the city of New York, migrating away once the environment proved inhospitable.[21]

Community activists rose up in protest against the Bowery plan, much as had other protestors in other cities. Concerned residents argued that the Cooper Square Plan would unjustly displace many longtime area residents.

Area activist Thelma Burdick's flyer expressed the demands of many New Yorkers alienated by urban renewal: "We need low cost housing and low middle income housing, with no down payment in our neighborhood for ourselves."[22] The activists' Cooper Square Committee went so far as to hire city planner Walter Thabit to draft a new proposal for the area, the "Alternate Plan for Cooper Square." The new plan would raze a smaller area and would implement gradual, deliberate phases of urban renewal. The CSC emphasized the negative effects Moses's plan would have on the neighborhood's Puerto Rican population. They also worried about the future of the area's homeless residents. Rather than displace all of the homeless area residents, the CSC argued, the city should keep key institutions, like the Salvation Army's recently opened Alcoholic Rehabilitation Center, in place. If city officials implemented work programs and other opportunities for Bowery men, the CSC argued, fewer would remain homeless, leading to improvements in the Bowery area.[23]

The odds looked long for the activists as they began their struggle. For one, Moses wielded a daunting amount of power within the city's bureaucratic machinery. Fortunately for the activists, however, Moses's power had finally begun to erode when the Cooper Square Plan was scheduled for implementation. By the late 1950s, the urban renewal program was slowing, and by 1959, the criticism of the program had rendered the Title I program, in Moses's words, "a dead duck." As Moses exited urban renewal work, city planners abandoned the original Cooper Square project. A series of modified and compromise plans for the area followed, but were ultimately crushed by the fiscal crisis of the 1970s.[24]

In other cities, urban renewal advocates prevailed, demolishing numerous skid rows. The Philadelphia Redevelopment Authority razed skid row in its Independence Mall Urban Renewal Project; Minneapolis's Housing and Redevelopment Authority cleared a modest area of skid row through its Lower Loop Redevelopment Plan. Chicago, Detroit, St. Louis, and Boston also used urban renewal programs to revitalize skid row areas.[25]

Even as urban renewal projects uprooted many of the poorest residents of the nation's cities, President Lyndon Johnson declared war on poverty itself. Although postwar economic growth ushered in an era of affluence, estimates placed just under 20 percent of the country's population in poverty in 1963. Liberal poverty analysts saw the widespread economic prosperity as a reason to tackle the persistent problem of poverty. A nation as powerful and wealthy as the United States, they reasoned, possessed the resources needed to end poverty altogether. As analyst Mollie Orshansky observed, "The legacy of poverty awaiting many of our children is the same as that handed down to their parents, but in a time when the boon of prosperity is more general, the taste of poverty is more bitter." Inspired by such sentiments, analysts identified possible causes of "poverty amid affluence." Perhaps capitalism itself was not functioning properly. Maybe capitalism required the development of vital institutions and services that would compensate for the inequities inherent to the system. Others worried that the causes of poverty originated within the impoverished individuals themselves. Between the late 1950s and the mid-1960s, these debates continued between "structuralists" and anthropologists, fostering not only lively dialogue, but also a wide array of attempts to solve the problem of poverty.[26]

Turning their attention to the homeless, sociologists launched an eight-year study through Columbia University's Bureau of Applied Social Research. The research team opened their initial proposal noting that the modern welfare state left some individuals surprisingly "lost." Sociologists Theodore Caplow and Howard Bahr sought to determine the extent to which "disaffiliation," or the lack of social ties, rendered individuals homeless.[27] Their research stemmed from a fundamental conviction that the homeless differed inherently from the rest of society. Not merely the poorest people in any given area, the homeless were suspected of bearing some deeper flaw, trait, habit, perspective, or way of life that set them apart. Anthropologists, sociologists, and psychiatrists developed distinct hypotheses and theoretical frameworks, reflecting the approaches and methods of their academic disciplines, but shared the goal of tracing the causes of homelessness beyond simple economic deprivation.

On one level, researchers sought an answer to the alleged problem of dependency, long a focal point for those involved with social welfare programs. Nineteenth-century charity discourse had framed "paupers," the dependent poor, as individuals possessing flawed characters. In the postwar era, as "dependency" came to refer to those assisted by public aid, recipient males were frequently viewed as especially degraded, stripped of their traditionally masculine role as providers. Bahr, reviewing hostile public attitudes toward the homeless man, speculated that it was, in part, his very powerlessness that rendered him repugnant to most Americans. In designing the project's research methods, Bahr set out to understand how and why a man became willing to depend upon public assistance for survival.[28]

The Columbia faculty and their graduate students employed various research strategies, ranging from participant observation in a Bowery bar to "passing" as a homeless man seeking employment, but they focused on collecting detailed life history interviews from the homeless in an effort to develop a profile of the average skid-row resident. The remarkable analytical attention focused on Bowery men in this era led writer Elmer Bendiner to quip, "Sociologists have counted their noses, tabulated their previous occupations, the first names of their grandparents, and the color of their skins."[29]

Through the Columbia project and others, social scientists combed the streets of the nation's skid rows, finding some "disaffiliated" homeless men, whose lives had contained few lasting relationships. On the whole, though, they discerned no broad pattern of disaffiliation or dependency. Instead, they met hopeless, impoverished men with few other places to go. Nonetheless, they marshaled their slim findings in support of conclusions that the homeless were largely disaffiliated, and they offered vague recommendations for social programs designed to intervene in their lives before their arrival on skid row.

The Columbia Homelessness Project emphasized the importance of social affiliations in understanding the experience of homelessness. The research paradigm dictated an emphasis on the affiliative aspects of various relationships in the lives of the homeless under study, rather than the economic ramifications of such relationships. The loss of a job, severed family ties, the dissolution of a marriage, strained relationships with adult children, and limited personal friendships also signaled closed avenues of potential economic assistance. This catalog of "failed" relationships explained quite clearly how some individuals slipped through the informal assistance networks generally provided by family and friends to those in need. No single factor explained the plight of the homeless, yet these constellations of factors highlighted the limited options and resources available to many poor individuals. The intellectual orientation of the project steered the results away from such structural causes of homelessness, focusing instead on the "social problem" aspect of the topic. In the end, the copious research conducted for eight years on the Bowery and elsewhere produced no overarching sociological explanation of homelessness.

As social science research into homelessness and poverty proved largely inconclusive, the war on poverty at the federal and municipal levels was also losing support. Johnson's declaration of war on poverty had been fueled by the optimism and confidence of a successful nation. The federal urban programs sponsored by the Office of Economic Opportunity brought money into the nation's cities, creating new programs aiding many residents. But even as it began, the battle against poverty and the liberal philosophies and programs that undergirded it had drawn criticism. In New York, when Mayor Robert Wagner declined to run for a fourth term in 1965, liberal Republican

John Lindsay campaigned successfully on a platform of "fiscal responsibility," criticizing Wagner's budget deficits and pattern of borrowing funds. Once in office, Lindsay's own liberal welfare policies would facilitate the expansion of the number of New York City residents receiving public assistance from 531,000 in 1965 to 1.25 million by 1972. The amount of benefits paid to welfare recipients grew alongside the welfare rolls, heightening tensions surrounding the city's public assistance system. This situation was not limited to New York, as cities across the country struggled with "welfare crises" of their own during these years. But even this expansion of the welfare system brought little change to the lives of the urban homeless, who continued to live on the margins of society.[30]

As public vagrancy and intoxication cases were increasingly dismissed in the mid-1960s, the police complained of a lack of facilities to which they could direct the homeless. After a nighttime tour of the Bowery, Commissioner of Corrections George F. McGrath echoed Mayor Lindsay's call for the establishment of a "drying-out" center for homeless alcoholics. Drawing on the resources provided by social investigators, officials strove to develop meaningful services for the homeless. The struggles they faced highlight the marked difference between scholarly investigations and the pragmatic concerns of service providers.[31]

New York's Vera Institute of Justice had been founded in 1961 as an independent nonprofit organization, developing programs to improve the relationships between individuals and the justice system. In May 1966, Mayor Lindsay approached the Vera Institute about planning a program for the homeless. A Ford Foundation planning grant enabled the organization to begin their project. Initial discussions of a rehabilitation program soon gave way to plans for a temporary detoxification center allowing anyone who had been on a drinking binge (or "bender") the time and space to repair his or her health. Social scientists assisting in planning the project sought to modify the behavior of homeless individuals by altering their sense of "norms." They hoped that homeless individuals approached by a street patrol and transported to a detoxification center would stop sleeping in public upon recognizing "a new norm . . . that one doesn't sleep on the sidewalk." This crude plan exemplified the social control the era's program staff wished to exert over the homeless.[32]

After initial efforts to house the detoxification center in an area hospital failed, space was secured at the Muni, where homeless men had previously been lodged, but now received only day services. The State Department of Mental Hygiene balked at the Bowery location, fearing that skid-row alcoholics would succumb to temptation, but granted approval after St. Vincent's Hospital agreed to provide support services including laboratory and x-ray work and admission for men in crisis.[33]

Before officially launching the program, concerned the homeless might prove unwilling and difficult participants, organizers staged a daylong demonstration of the proposed procedures. On a Thursday in October, George and Patricia Nash of the Columbia project, accompanied by a New York Police Department lieutenant, two hotel clerks, and representatives from the Vera Institute proceeded down to the Bowery, where the fourth floor of the Muni had been furnished as a temporary detoxification facility, complete with an infirmary, recreation room, showers, toilets, and interview offices.[34]

Driving a rented station wagon with a New Jersey license plate (in an effort to remain inconspicuous), and an unmarked police car filled with observers, the team set out to pick up homeless recruits. They first approached a homeless man sprawled on the street outside the Muni covered in urine and blood, his ear filled with pus and lice. When shaken awake, Robert K., a fifty-three-year-old laborer who had spent seventeen years on the Bowery, refused their offer of assistance, saying, "I don't want to eat. I don't want to see a doctor. I don't need anything. Just leave me alone! . . . I know the Men's Shelter and I don't want any part of it." Demonstrating their experience working with homeless alcoholics, the hotel clerks offered him a cigarette and engaged him in conversation. Ultimately he agreed to accept their offer, accompanying them to the temporary center where staff treated wounds over his eye and in his ear, and deloused him. Robert K.'s case proved fairly representative; after some convincing, over three-fourths of the men approached agreed to visit the detoxification facility. The sweep tactics of the staff so alarmed passersby that one onlooker, fearful he had witnessed a kidnapping, telephoned a report to the Ninth Precinct. Marked cars and staff uniforms were planned to avoid confusion on future outings.[35]

Some critics worried about the dangers of detoxification for Bowery men, fearing the "DTs," delirium tremens, would kill over 15 percent of the men treated. But the project's medical director correctly predicted the program would maintain a fatality rate lower than 1 percent. Other opponents cited cost and the high rates of recidivism among homeless alcoholics. But ultimately, the Commissioner of Social Services, the Police Department, the Department of Hospitals, and the Department of Corrections agreed to donate staff and equipment, and the fifty-bed Manhattan Bowery Project center opened within a year.[36]

Upon arrival at the facility, a client was screened by a physician, showered and deloused, assigned a bed near the nurse's station, given a physical examination, and sedated. If necessary, he was fed intravenously during this period. After three days, most patients were moved to the "recuperative ward," where they had access to the recreation room. The third day included a caseworker interview, which was used in conjunction with feedback from other staff members to develop an individualized referral plan.[37]

Many clients suffered from serious medical conditions. Almost one-fourth were diagnosed with neurological diseases, almost two-thirds with pulmonary diseases, 9 percent with cardiovascular disease, and over one-fifth with dermatological disease; 23 percent had liver disease and 4 percent late latent syphilis. They suffered mental and emotional problems as well; of the first two hundred men treated, one-third were diagnosed schizophrenics, nearly 40 percent had personality disorders, almost 9 percent had anxiety neurosis, and over 17 percent suffered from depression. Overall, the men proved relatively easy to treat and only 3 percent left the program against medical advice; their compliant state stemmed largely from the fact that they were placed on "drug therapy" and given phenobarbitol.[38]

By 1968, 73 percent of the men approached by the project's rescue teams accepted assistance. But African Americans proved far less receptive to the staff's advances, and fully half refused services. Previous negative experiences with police and hospitals, or fear of such experiences, left many homeless African Americans suspicious of outreach efforts. Once MBP staff began a concerted initiative to recruit African American men into the project, they increased the number of African American clients from less than 10 percent to approximately one-quarter.[39]

A follow-up survey conducted among one hundred men who completed the five-day program revealed that three months later, thirteen remained sober, seventeen were in other rehabilitation programs, twenty-two had stayed sober for at least five weeks before relapsing, thirty-five were drinking heavily, and thirteen had lost contact with officials. Most clients were referred to the state hospital rehabilitation units, the psychiatric wards of Central Islip State Hospital, Camp LaGuardia, an AA sponsor, Bellevue Hospital, the Bowery Mission, Bridge House, the Brooklyn State Hospital Alcoholism Unit, Camp LaGuardia, Graymoor, the McAuley Water Street Mission, Operation Bowery, the Quaker Assistance Program, the Rikers Island TB Unit, the Salvation Army, the Veterans Hospital TB Unit, or the MBP's own aftercare clinic. The MBP clinic offered psychiatric sessions and caseworker visits, as well as Antabuse (a drug rendering one ill upon consumption of alcohol), vitamins, and tranquilizers to ninety men per day.[40]

The program's long-term success remained difficult to gauge. Almost 40 percent of the men completing the program returned later. The MBP staff insisted that even limited behavior change, such as a longer "average time between benders" reflected a victory for both the program and the individual participant. They intentionally employed recovered alcoholics on the rescue teams as well as in other staff positions, where possible, to keep the program grounded in the realities of life on skid row.[41]

Excited by the successful results achieved on the Bowery, the MBP looked around the city for ways to expand its programs and services. In the early 1970s, the organization launched a pilot program of "supported work," through which six homeless, alcoholic men cleared vacant lots for six salaried weeks. The men performed their duties consistently and did not immediately resume drinking. Buoyed by their participation, the MBP ambitiously established a toy truck factory to employ Bowery men. But the toys failed to sell, the men found the work oppressive, and the program folded.[42]

Through an agreement with the city, the MBP next launched Project Renewal to employ homeless men clearing lots that the city was converting to playgrounds. Initially, ten participants lived in the Salvation Army Hotel; later they moved to a group home in Brooklyn. In addition to performing part-time salaried work in the lots, the men participated in group therapy, individual and vocational counseling, and educational and recreational activities. In 1974, the Project's fifteen trainees and four graduates maintained ninety-one playgrounds, collecting eighteen thousand fifty-gallon sacks of garbage. In its four years of operation, over one-fifth of participants completed the program, and three-fourths of those men stayed sober.[43]

In 1973, the MBP launched STEP (Supportive Therapeutic Environment Program). Coordinated by a psychologist, the program made counseling services, group meetings, vocational rehabilitation and recreational activities available to participants. During the six-month residency, public benefits programs paid for the men's lodging in fourteen designated rooms of a single-room occupancy hotel.[44]

Moving groups of homeless men into residential communities often required difficult negotiations. Project Renewal's move from one Brooklyn home to another, for instance, sparked initial community protest. Learning from that experience, when the MBP staff brought the STEP program to Greenwich Village, they reached out to the block association, which became a strong ally later, during the city's financial crisis. Once settled in the Village, program staff strove to integrate the participants in local activities, having the men maintain a community garden and staff a table at the neighborhood block party.[45]

During the 1960s, city officials attempted to merge the findings of social investigators with the goals of social service providers in developing services for the homeless. Comprehensive programs included mental health services, medical care, job training and employment assistance, and traditional shelter facilities. Several of the new programs proved successful and enduring, fostering positive change in the lives of many homeless individuals.

Despite such success stories at the local level, by the early 1970s, the midcentury federal struggle against poverty had lost political and popular support. In part, it had been flawed from its inception, its scope and efficacy limited by what historian Alice O'Connor has described as "poverty knowledge," the body of social scientific expertise that shaped understanding of poverty and welfare systems. Acting on their preconceived notions, poverty analysts placed blame on the perceived flaws of the poor themselves rather than the structural inequalities propagated by the American economic and political system. With few exceptions, such logic had blunted the potential usefulness of many urban programs.[46]

Fundamentally, the definitions of the "problem" of homelessness at midcentury had varied too widely, leaving no consensus on the appropriate response. Homelessness was identified as undesirable within New York and other cities, but for reasons ranging from the suffering of the poor to the urban deterioration of the neighborhoods they inhabited. To some observers, the contact between the indigent and middle-class and working-class city residents seemed the greatest problem associated with homelessness. With no common definition of the problem, few practical solutions had emerged.

Public welfare systems, in general, and the problem of homelessness, in particular, tested the popular understanding of the parameters of the common good at midcentury. Those who were deemed "abnormal" because the structure of their lives violated social norms especially pressed the boundaries of public sentiment. The extensive homelessness relief program of the 1930s Federal Transient Program was not continued after the Depression's end. Postwar American rhetoric posited that prosperity was attainable for those who were motivated enough to seek it out. As a result, no similar system for housing the homeless was established. To many observers, the postwar skid-row homeless were undeserving of public assistance. Their concerns were largely ignored by the Social Security system and by the advocates of urban renewal. The homeless benefited from the legal expansion of their rights under the Warren Court, gaining more from the era's judicial liberalism than its expanding welfare system.

The homeless remained outside most protections provided by the welfare state into the 1970s. Liberals had attempted to revitalize urban centers through the massive urban renewal program, and had expanded the safety net of public assistance to encompass more impoverished families. But despite this unprecedented expansion of the welfare state, the poorest of the poor remained dependent on private charities and city shelters, as they had been for decades.

Notes

1. Portions of this essay are drawn from Ella Howard, "Skid Row: Homelessness on the Bowery in the Twentieth Century" (PhD diss., Boston University, 2007).

2. Michael B. Katz, *In the Shadow of the Poorhouse: A Social History of Welfare in America* (New York: Basic Books, Inc., 1986), 3–35.

3. Joel Schwartz, *Fighting Poverty with Virtue: Moral Reform and America's Urban Poor, 1825–2000* (Bloomington: Indiana University Press, 2000), 109–120.

4. Morris Dickstein, "Steinbeck and the Great Depression," *South Atlantic Quarterly* 103:1 (Winter 2004): 111–131.

5. Joan M. Crouse, *The Homeless Transient in the Great Depression: New York State, 1929–1941* (Albany: State University of New York Press, 1986).

6. Boyden Sparkes, "The New Deal for Transients," *Saturday Evening Post*, October 9, 1935, 94.

7. "Park Experiment Is a Big Success," *NYT*, March 12, 1933. Research Bureau, The Welfare Council of New York City, "Temporary Shelter of Homeless Persons in New York City, Confidential Report," March 1933, Box 131, Folder: Homeless 1927–33, Community Service Society Papers, Columbia University Archives, New York.

8. The Welfare Council of New York City, "Summary of Minutes, Meeting of the Executive Committee of the Coordinating Committee on Unemployment," May 16, 1934, Box 185, Folder: Welfare Council—Coordinating Committee on Unemployment, 1934–35, CSS Papers. "Summary of Minutes, Meeting of the Executive Committee of the Coordinating Committee on Unemployment," October 10, 1934, Box 185, Folder: Welfare Council—Coordinating Committee on Unemployment, 1934–35, CSS Papers. Joan Crouse, "The Remembered Men: Transient Camps in New York State, 1933–1935," *New York History* LXXI:1 (January 1990): 68–94.

9. Edward Robb Ellis, *A Nation in Torment: The Great American Depression, 1929–1939* (New York: Kodansha America, 1995), 288–307.

10. "School for Young Transients," *The Survey*, August 1935, 241.

11. Esther H. Elias, "Gold Dust Lodge," *The War Cry*, December 31, 1932, 3, 15. Jean Johnson, "Pure Gold at Gold Dust Lodge," *The War Cry*, November 4, 1933. Errol

Lincoln Uys, *Riding the Rails: Teenagers on the Move during the Great Depression* (New York: TV Books, 1999), 79.

12. Franklin D. Roosevelt, "Annual Message to the Congress," January 4, 1935, vol. 4 of *The Public Papers and Addresses of Franklin D. Roosevelt* (New York: Random House, 1938), 19–20. Albert U. Romasco, "Relief As Recovery," ch. 4 in *The Politics of Recovery: Roosevelt's New Deal* (New York: Oxford University Press, 1983), 52–66.

13. Katz, *In the Shadow*, ix–xiv.

14. Robert G. McCloskey, *The American Supreme Court*, 4th ed. (Chicago: University of Chicago Press, 2005), 148–194.

15. 36 U.S. (11 Pet.) 102, 142–143 (1837) quoted in William O. Douglas, "Vagrancy and Arrest on Suspicion," *Yale Law Journal* 70:1 (November 1960): 1–14; 2. See Gary V. Dubin and Richard H. Robinson, "The Vagrancy Concept Reconsidered: Problems and Abuses of Status Criminality," *New York University Law Review* 37:1 (1962): 102–136. In 1941, Miln had been reversed by the Court in *Edwards v. California*. 314 U.S. 160, 177 (1941). S. Rep. No. 821, 77th Cong, 1st Sess. 2 (1941) quoted in Douglas, 8. *Columbia v. Hunt*, 163 F.2d 833,835 (D.C. Cir. 1947). Harry Simon, "Towns without Pity: A Constitutional and Historical Analysis of Official Efforts to Drive Homeless Persons from American Cities," *Tulane Law Review* 66:4 (March 1992): 632–676.

16. Gary V. Dubin and Richard H. Robinson, "The Vagrancy Concept Reconsidered: Problems and Abuses of Status Criminality," *New York University Law Review* 102 (1962): 102–136. Caleb Foote, "Vagrancy-type Law and Its Administration," *University of Pennsylvania Law Review* 603 (1956): 104. Madeline R. Stoner, *The Civil Rights of Homeless People: Law, Social Policy, and Social Work Practice* (New York: Aldine de Gruyter, Inc., 1995), 23. Simon "Towns without Pity," 634, 642. *Fenster v. Leary*, 229 N.E. 2d 426, 430 (N.Y. 1967). The Supreme Court struck them down in *Papchristou v. City of Jacksonville* (405 U.S. 156 [1972]) and *Kolender v. Lawson* (461 U.S. 352 [1983]).

17. "Skid Row Cleanup: Some Big Cities Switch from Arresting Drunks to Try Rehabilitation," *Wall Street Journal*, February 14, 1967. "Drunkenness Offenses," ch. 9 in *The Challenge of Crime in a Free Society: A Report by the President's Commission on Law Enforcement and the Administration of Justice* (U.S. Government Printing Office, Washington, D.C., February. 1967), 233–238. LBJ established the Commission through Executive Order 11236, July 23, 1965.

18. *Easter v. District of Columbia*, 361 F.21 50 (D.C. Cir 1966). *Driver v. Hinnant*, 356 F.2d 761 (4th Cir. 1966). *Robinson v. California*, 370 U.S. 660 (1962). E. M. Jellinek, "The Alcohol Problem: Formulations and Attitudes," *Quarterly Journal of Studies on Alcohol* 4:3 (1943–1944): 446–461.

19. *Powell v. Texas*, 392 U.S. 514 (1968). Simon, "Towns without Pity,"660–663. "Chronic Alcoholics' Jailing for Intoxication Is Upheld," *NYT*, June 18, 1968. Gerald R. Garrett, "Alcohol Problems and Homelessness: History and Research," *Contemporary Drug Problems* (Fall 1989): 301–323.

20. Jon C. Teaford, *The Rough Road to Renaissance: Urban Revitalization in America, 1940–1985* (Baltimore: The Johns Hopkins University Press, 1990), 122–167.

21. "Plan of Sections Containing Areas Suitable for Development and Redevelopment," Item CP-11256, City Planning Commission Minutes 1957, 72. "Bowery's 'Skid Row' Going for Housing and Factories," *New York Herald Tribune*, March 15, 1959. "Bowery Area Changes: A Review as of August 18, 1959, Based upon Minutes of Community Meetings and Newspaper Articles of 1959," RG 4.5, Box 208, Folder 2, Salvation Army Archives, Alexandria, Va.

22. Cooper Square Development Committee and Businessmen's Association, *An Alternate Plan for Cooper Square*, 1959, 1. Thelma J. Burdick and Staughton C. Lynd, Co-Chairmen, Committee on Community Development, flyer, RG 4.5. Box 208, Folder 2, Salvation Army Archives.

23. Interview with Walter Thabit, New York City, December 17, 2003. *Alternate Plan*, 69.

24. Charles Grutzner, "Moses Says Title I Is a 'Dead Duck'; Decries Charges," *NYT*, July 4, 1959. Thomas W. Ennis, "Cooper Square Plan Set for Decision," *NYT*, August 31, 1969. Iver Peterson, "Project in Bowery Is Approved Following 10-Year Controversy," *NYT*, February 14, 1970.

25. Stephen Metraux, "Waiting for the Wrecking Ball: Skid Row in Postindustrial Philadelphia," *Journal of Urban History* 25:5 (July 1999): 691–716. Joseph Hart, *Down and Out: The Life and Death of Minneapolis' Skid Row* (Minneapolis: University of Minnesota Press, 2002), 39, 40–42. *The Homeless Man on Skid Row* (Chicago: Tenants Relocation Bureau, 1961), 57–61. Charles Hoch and Robert A. Slayton, *New Homeless and Old: Community and the Skid Row Hotel* (Philadelphia: Temple University Press, 1989), 117–119, 121.

26. Robert J. Lampman, "Population Change and Poverty Reduction, 1947–75," in *Poverty amid Affluence*, ed. Leo Fishman (New Haven: Yale University Press, 1966), 18–31. Lampman, "Ends and Means in the War on Poverty," in *Poverty amid Affluence*, 212–229. Mollie Orshansky, "Consumption, Work, and Poverty," in *Poverty As a Public Issue*, ed. Ben B. Seligman (New York: Free Press, 1966), 52. James T. Patterson, *America's Struggle against Poverty 1900–1985* (Cambridge: Harvard University Press, 1986), 99–125.

27. Howard M. Bahr and Gerald R. Garrett, *Women Alone: The Disaffiliation of Urban Females* (Lexington, Mass: Lexington Books, 1976), 1. Theodore Caplow and Howard M. Bahr, *Old Men Drunk and Sober* (New York: New York University Press, 1974).

28. Howard M. Bahr, *Skid Row: An Introduction to Disaffiliation* (New York: Oxford University Press, 1973), 29, 44.

29. Elmer Bendiner, *The Bowery Man* (New York: Thomas Nelson and Sons, 1961), 93.

30. Charles Brecher, Raymond D. Horton, with Robert A. Cropf and Dean Michael Mead, *Power Failure: New York City Politics and Policy since 1960* (New York:

Oxford University Press, 1993), 83-84. Vincent J. Cannato, *The Ungovernable City: John Lindsay and His Struggle to Save New York* (New York: Basic Books, 2001), 539, 542.

31. "Police Here Halt Derelict Arrests," *NYT*, July 29, 1966. "Derelicts in City's Parks to Get a Boon of Sorts," *NYT*, August 18, 1966. "A Tour in Bowery Stirs Night Mayor," *NYT*, October 6, 1966.

32. Manhattan Bowery Project (MBP), *First Annual Report*, April 1969, 13. George and Patricia Nash, "The Planning and Operation of the Experimental Detoxification Center, October 1966," 114, Box 79, BASR Records.

33. MBP, *First Annual Report*, 16.

34. George and Patricia Nash, "The Planning and Operation," 1-2.

35. Ibid., 3, 6-9.

36. Ibid. Steven S. Manos, "The Manhattan Bowery Project," *Alcohol Health and Research World* (Winter 1975/76, experimental issue): 11-15. MBP, *First Annual Report*,1, 13, 19-21. The MBP opened November 27, 1967, and was overseen by Lindsay's Criminal Justice Coordinating Council.

37. MBP, *First Annual Report*, 25.

38. MBP, *First Annual Report*, 30-31. Dr. Robert Morgan and Dr. Charles Goldfarb, "Medical Complications," in *First Annual Report*, March 2, 1969, 56-57.

39. After three years, the MBP split from the Vera Institute, becoming a separate entity, the Manhattan Bowery Corporation. "City Helping Bowery Derelicts to Discover a New Way of Life," *NYT*, June 22, 1968.

40. Elaine Palusci, "After-care Plans of Patients Admitted to the Manhattan Bowery Project between November 27, 1967 and November 30, 1968," in MBP, *First Annual Report*, 63-65.

41. MBP, *First Annual Report*, 37, 40, 36, 26-27. In 1968-1969, the program's budget totaled $635,800, $175,800 of which came from the city in the form of staff and services. The estimated cost per patient was $38.50. Keeping a physician on duty made the program expensive, accounting for approximately 20 percent of the project costs. The Bureau of Alcoholism, the city's Community Mental Health Board, agreed to fund the MBP. For the first year, they were assisted by the Office of Law Enforcement Assistance of the U.S. Department of Justice. For 1972, MBP was to run Project Renewal, a residential work program funded through the Manpower and Career Development Agency (previously run by Vera). Manhattan Bowery Corporation (MBC), *Annual Report*, July 1, 1970-June 30, 1971.

42. By the late 1960s, homeless alcoholics increasingly congregated in midtown Manhattan. The first expansion plan proposed a limited midtown facility offering preliminary medical examinations and phenobarbitol for withdrawal symptoms. MBC, *Annual Report*, July 1, 1970-June 30, 1971.

43. Manos, "The Manhattan Bowery Project," 13-15. In 1994, the MBC's Bowery program was renamed "Project Renewal." Now in operation almost thirty years, Project Renewal assists more than 20,000 individuals annually.

44. STEP placed less emphasis on counseling and analysis than did Project Renewal, but participants in both programs took Antabuse and were encouraged to participate in Alcoholics Anonymous. Manos, "The Manhattan Bowery Project," 14.

45. Manos, "The Manhattan Bowery Project," 15.

46. Alice O'Connor, *Poverty Knowledge: Social Science, Social Policy, and the Poor in the Twentieth-Century U.S. History* (Princeton: Princeton University Press, 2001), 3–22.

6

Liberalism in the Postwar City

Public and Private Power in Urban Renewal

LIZABETH COHEN

When President Barack Obama announced the appointment of Adolfo Carrión Jr. as director for his newly created White House Office of Urban Affairs soon after his inauguration in 2009, the *New York Times* ran a story entitled, "From Bronx to Washington, after Mixed Results."[1] The article contended that Carrión, a former teacher, city planner, community activist, New York City councilman, and two-term Bronx Borough president would be bringing a mixed reputation to his new job coordinating national urban policy, particularly federal investment in jobs, housing, and urban infrastructure. According to the article, his defenders praised his ability to channel private development funds toward projects that have helped the Bronx revitalize, such as a new Yankee Stadium and shopping center and an expansion of jobs and housing for low- and moderate-income borough residents. His critics charged that his prodevelopment approach "often sacrificed community concerns to please business interests and failed to follow through on many of his ideas." Undoubtedly, the new president's creation of an office for Urban Affairs highlighted the importance of cities to his administration's liberal agenda. But the controversy surrounding Carrión's record revealed a critical tension within postwar liberalism, particularly visible in the urban setting: how to balance public and private authority and resources in achieving liberal notions of the common good.

Since the dawning of the New Deal Era, liberalism, I would argue, has not only advocated for individual liberties, social tolerance, and ideological openness (as Alan Wolfe has emphasized in his recent book *The Future of Liberalism*), but it has also promoted greater economic and social equality, within the constraints of a capitalist market economy.[2] I would define the liberal vision of the post–World War II era as aiming to improve the social, economic, and political quality of life for as many Americans as possible by leveling the playing field to facilitate individuals' access to social goods such as housing, education, medical care, and jobs, and to the rights of citizens in a democracy. Subsidizing housing rentals and ownership, providing college loans, supplementing private medical insurance, registering more people to vote: postwar liberalism has focused on strategies like these to improve the means to broader social and economic participation rather than a more progressive focus on securing the ends of equality or a more conservative commitment to leaving things to market forces. What remains unresolved in this liberal aspiration for broader participation in the American good life, however, is exactly how those means should be defined, specifically the relative importance of action by the government and the private sector. Over the more than six decades since the New Deal marked a new baseline for twentieth-century liberalism, liberals have disagreed among themselves over the appropriate balance of government dirigisme and capitalist investment, and prevailing attitudes have shifted with the times. Throughout the postwar era, the city—buffeted by rampant suburbanization, crippling deindustrialization, and exploding globalization—has proved a fertile setting for conflicts over how best to calibrate public and private interests. While some liberals have been willing to accept urban decline as part of the natural evolution of things, most have not. They have argued instead that cities matter too much as engines of capitalism, beneficial to entrepreneurs and workers alike, and as incubators of liberal, democratic values, being centers of pluralistic populations and intellectual and cultural creativity. The dynamism and diversity of cities has been hard to duplicate in the more segmented suburbanized world I wrote about in my book, *A Consumers' Republic: The Politics of Mass Consumption in Postwar America*.[3] Hence, the liberal Obama administration's concern to save American cities, and the debate over Adolfo Carrión's approach to balancing public and private power in achieving that goal, is only the latest example of a decades-long struggle.

Liberals have not been the only historical actors in the postwar period to view cities and the city building process as ideal laboratories for carrying out experiments in calibrating desirable levels of government intervention and private sector management. In the aftermath of the destruction of New Orleans in the wake of ferocious hurricane Katrina, that city's reconstruction became a test case of the conservative, so-called "neoliberal" ideas (not to be confused with postwar *liberalism*) that have gained strength over the last three decades, which preach that the public interest is best served through empowering private markets and their agents and retreating from the kind of top-down, government-funded—and orchestrated—social, economic, and physical planning that had characterized the more social democratic regimes that preceded this era, what we often call the "New Deal Order" lasting from the 1930s into the 1970s. As part of this neoliberal approach to rebuilding New Orleans, the whim and profit calculations of private interests and the initiatives of individual homeowners determined much of what happened. Tourist hotels in the French Quarter reopened while public housing—whether ruined or not—was closed down to low-income renters as part of a deliberate strategy to eliminate it or remake it, supposedly as "mixed-income." The meager state government relief program, "The Road Home," favored homeowners over renters, and particularly those homeowners with the most private insurance to cash in, making it quite clear which route back—and which returnees—were preferred. Private developers faced little public sector pressure to coordinate their rebuilding schemes and instead were assisted with no-bid contracts, the suspension of prevailing wage and affirmative action requirements for labor, the lifting of environmental restrictions, and the creation of tax-advantaged enterprise zones. When the worst physical disaster in American history hit, the U.S. government was hard to find, outsourcing the job of reconstruction to private companies.[4] As one local resident involved in the effort to save New Orleans' historic architecture put it in August 2007, "There is nothing the government is doing to encourage the recovery.... They're not managing it, they're not directing it, they're not assisting it. In fact, they're in the way. And as a result, everything you see right now is citizen-driven. And that's pathetic."[5] In fact, neoliberals' denunciation of what they saw as excessive governmental interference in cities during the long New Deal Order served as crucial justification for advocating a more private-sector–driven type of urban redevelopment after Katrina. The mantra went: Let's not allow government to overreach and repeat the mistakes of federal urban renewal. Federal urban renewal, which prevailed from the early 1950s into the 1970s, served as a negative example not only of urban policy, but also of liberal government more broadly.

To a large extent, city building has always resulted from combined public and private activity. Indeed, most urban development historically in Western capitalist democracies, and particularly in the United States, has blended public and private initiative and financial investment. Whether Boston, New York, Chicago, or Los Angeles, the growth of American cities from the eighteenth into the twentieth centuries was through joint public-private ventures. Nor do I mean to imply that private market forces bear most of the blame for the urban crisis of the postwar era that government then stepped in to solve with urban renewal. Indeed, government intervention contributed significantly to the metropolitan decentralization that threatened the survival of American cities in the 1950s, when in the twenty largest metropolitan areas, cities grew by only 0.1 percent and their suburbs by a whopping 45 percent, as residents, employers, and retailers fled. Federal mortgage insurance programs that favored newly built suburban homes, tax policies that gave real estate developers and retailers more incentive to build anew than renovate downtown, and the construction of the federal highway system were among the initiatives that literally paved the way to suburban growth and urban crisis.[6] Nonetheless, even private enterprise with strong ties to downtown pressured government to play a new kind of savior role in cities during the postwar era. Richard C. Bond, president of John Wanamaker of Philadelphia, called his department store colleagues to arms in 1960: if America's great cities are not to become ghost towns, he urged, merchants, "should be heading the list of dedicated, aroused, and enlightened business leaders, for we have more at stake than perhaps any other group to see that our cities thrive rather than shrink and die." Only a multimillion dollar program of federal spending, Bond went on, can "check this urban erosion before it reaches catastrophic proportions."[7]

Liberals throughout the postwar era have struggled with achieving the right balance between public and private activity in revitalizing cities. Since the heyday of urban renewal from the late 1940s through the 1960s, and still today, planners and government officials have weighed *one*, direct state intervention in improving urban infrastructure against *two*, incentivizing private interests to invest against *three*, heeding the warnings of prominent urban renewal critic Jane Jacobs and her heirs that cities are best left to evolve naturally without much government planning.

The career of a major figure in the urban renewal of American cities, redevelopment "czar" Edward J. Logue, provides useful insights into how liberals in the postwar period strategized to revitalize the urban built environment and the lessons their actions might hold for liberals in the present and future. Logue moved from New Haven in the 1950s to Boston in the 1960s to New York State and City from the late 1960s through the mid-1980s, with his last major job there an effort to resuscitate a crumbling South Bronx. Crowned "one of the top three urban renewal men in the U.S." by *Time* magazine in 1964, dubbed "Mr. Urban Renewal" by the *New York Times* in 1970, described as "one of the most impressive movers and shakers of subsidized construction since the time of King Tut" by *Newsweek* magazine in 1972, Logue embodied federal urban renewal in its most progovernment, liberal form.[8] True to role, he told an interviewer late in his career, "I've always felt [you] can't trust the private sector to protect the public interest."[9] Despite ongoing commitment on Logue's part to the federal government playing a critical role in urban policy, over the almost half century he worked as urban redeveloper, his approach changed as a result of political necessity and experience on the ground. Thus the trajectory of Logue's career from his entry into the field in 1954 until his death in 2000 reveals the evolution of the liberal city-building project over the postwar period, with particular attention to the shifting balance of power between the public and private realms.

Ed Logue's first of four major projects in urban redevelopment was New Haven, Connecticut, where he arrived in 1954 at age thirty-three to work closely with newly elected reform Mayor Richard Lee. He brought a range of experiences to the job of heading the New Haven Redevelopment Agency that would shape how urban renewal unfolded in New Haven, and by example, elsewhere in the nation as this city became a laboratory for federally funded urban renewal. As a former Yale undergraduate and law student he had pushed the university, the city's major business, in progressive directions—on civil rights, in recognizing organized labor on its own campus, and in protecting academic freedom in the Cold War forties. Urban redevelopment became in his mind one more progressive undertaking, not the probusiness, antidemocratic effort that later critics frequently charged. As a bombardier in the American military during World War II, he had reveled in aerial views of European cities and appreciated the virtues of large-scale planning and maneuvers. And just before his arrival in New Haven in 1954, he had served as special assistant to Ambassador Chester Bowles in India, well positioned to observe State Department- and Ford Foundation–funded infrastructural improvements and social programs that aimed to modernize villages and make India a democratic, anticommunist ally of the United States. Modernizing the built environment struck him as an inseparable part of perfecting democracy and fulfilling promises of greater equality. Under Logue and Mayor Lee's watch, New Haven, a relatively small city with a long-declining industrial base, became the nation's "model city" of urban renewal in the 1950s—receiving more federal dollars per capita than any other American city, by 1965 two and a half times greater than the next highest, Newark—a surprise to many familiar with the city's problems in recent years.[10]

Logue's work in New Haven raised all the hard questions and epitomized all the flawed solutions of the early, heavy-handed era of urban renewal. Implemented during the heyday of the Eisenhower-era stress on commercial redevelopment rather than the more housing-oriented, slum clearance of the previous Democratic administrations of Roosevelt and Truman, revitalizing the city's economic centrality to the region became a major priority. With a paucity of deep private pockets to dig into, the federal government's investment became crucial; Logue's genius became figuring out how to maximize federal investment and minimize expenditures by a financially struggling local government. His New Haven Redevelopment Agency became so well heeled with federal funding, so powerful, and so independent that it was known locally as "the Kremlin."[11] The plan involved putting a major highway, the "Oak Street Connector," through a physically deteriorating but still socially intact low-income neighborhood to facilitate bringing retreating suburbanites back downtown; constructing high-rise luxury apartments to keep the middle class living in New Haven; replacing much of New Haven's ninety-three–acre downtown core of small stores and modest service establishments with a mix of suburban-style department stores, an enclosed mall, hotel, office tower, and massive attached parking garage to compete better with the new suburban shopping centers; and replacing rundown housing with new modernist complexes or rehabbing existing structures that often—intentionally or not—encouraged gentrification. In most of the residential projects, land was cleared and new townhouses or low-rise apartment buildings were constructed, requiring significant relocation of current residents—in some cases temporarily, in other cases permanently. The major exception was the Italian neighborhood of Wooster Square, one of the first examples in the nation of housing rehabilitation rather than demolition and new construction, permissible under a change in federal law in 1954. Logue always took great pride in his agency's pioneering work in the Wooster Square neighborhood, even though critics charged that rehab favored better-off homeowners over renters and removed poor black residents from an adjacent area.

Although Logue optimistically believed that "we're on our way...to...a slum-free city" when he left New Haven in 1961, it is clear today that urban renewal did not save New Haven, although it is unlikely that the city would have fared much better without it, given its deep economic problems and the State of Connecticut's favoring of suburban over urban development through its tax structure and other policies.[12] Few would claim that urban renewal in New Haven was a success. Downtown continues to struggle; much of the replacement housing has not worn well; and the city remains a poor, minority-dominated core surrounded by affluent white suburbs. As true believers in the power of federal urban renewal, Logue and Lee thought that federal urban renewal dollars could buy a future for New Haven. They learned two important lessons: first, that displacing residents with massive clearance only breeds resentment and despair; racial tensions, some rooted in the disruptions of urban renewal, flared dangerously in the riots of August 1967 and continued to fester long thereafter. And second, like it or not, within a capitalist economy, private investment, ranging from the individual homeowner to the deeper-pocketed industrialist, must complement public spending for urban revitalization to work. New Haven's urban renewal failed on many levels, including in calibrating an effective mix of public and private resources. It is not clear, however, where—outside of Yale University, which in the mid-1990s began investing deeply in a troubled New Haven out of necessity—this private investment would have come from.[13]

Logue was recruited to Boston, his second urban renewal site, by newly elected Mayor John Collins in 1960 to help him turn around a near bankrupt Boston that in the previous decade had lost 13 percent of its population and 8 percent of its jobs to booming suburbs and had built only two new office buildings in the previous thirty years. Boston's tax base was declining precipitously and its tax rate was the highest in the nation. Recognition of the failure of New Haven's urban renewal lay in the future, and Ed Logue was considered a leading young star of what seemed like a landmark effort to revive America's cities. Collins gave Logue unprecedented centralized authority over the city's planning *and* redevelopment as head of the Boston Redevelopment Authority (BRA). By 1968, the BRA would be staffed by seven hundred employees, where there had only been sixteen when Logue arrived, and Collins gave his blessing to a renewal plan that involved half of the city's acreage. Needless to say, Logue's arrival made a big splash in the conservative old seaport city of Boston. Over seven years, Logue became widely credited with launching the "New Boston," which has since flourished as an urban mecca.

In Boston, Logue sought to improve upon his New Haven strategies and Boston's own sorry episode a few years earlier of the wholesale demolition of the city's West End immigrant neighborhood, which resembled on a larger scale the destruction of New Haven's Oak Street area. Having learned from the excessive leveling and unapologetically top-down approach to urban renewal in New Haven, Logue experimented in Boston with strategies that would achieve more buy-in from capitalist interests on one side and neighborhood residents on the other. In Boston, Logue worried less about bringing middle-class people back into the city to live and focused instead on creating jobs downtown, specifically in a sixty-acre Government Center complex of federal, state, and municipal headquarters built on the side of Scollay Square, Boston's former red-light district. He then used that leverage to pressure Boston's business leaders to erect new office towers nearby. With the promise of more workers downtown, he next goaded existing merchants to help renovate the city's retail core and launched plans to rehab and reuse Faneuil Hall and Quincy Market, the decaying old wholesale markets whose eventual renovation provided the prototype for the urban festival marketplace phenomenon nationwide. In Boston, Logue also became more committed to achieving high design standards in his projects, which inevitably led to modernist structures on superblocks such as the new Boston City Hall. Simultaneously, in the face of growing popular criticism of urban renewal nationwide, he became more vigilant about implementing what he called a "planning with people" policy, consulting neighborhood residents about project planning (with differing degrees of conviction and success), including in Roxbury, the center of Boston's growing African American population; Charlestown, a bastion of working-class Irish; and the South End, a mixed ethnic, poor neighborhood close to downtown. Some of this community consultation was pure window dressing, but in a neighborhood such as the Washington Park district of Roxbury, residents were actively engaged in contemplating their community's future. Moreover, rehabilitation supplanted demolition as the BRA's first line of attack.

As Boston's urban renewal took off, the federal dollars poured in, moving Boston from seventeenth to fourth in per capita renewal grants nationally. In a matter of years, a "New Boston" emerged for which Logue received credit, though his failure to win election as the city's mayor in 1967 provided disappointing evidence to him that not everyone in the city viewed his tenure favorably. Whereas there is no question that Boston's potential as the economic heart of the New England region made Logue's job easier there than it had been in New Haven, still, urban renewal in Boston succeeded in combining federal dollars and private investment to support a more dynamic Boston economy and built environment. And although there were legitimate criticisms, such as that Logue's BRA planned with some people and not others (homeowners over renters, for example) and favored large-scale commercial redevelopment over sustaining small merchants and existing neighborhoods, in Boston government officials like Logue kept control over the planning process while still encouraging private investment and cushioning to a noteworthy degree the dislocating effects of economic revival, in many cases by working closely with nonprofit community organizations. Boston's balance sheet still registered discontented and dislocated residents as it negotiated the fragile tension between growing an economy and shielding longstanding communities, but the city did turn around economically while retaining much of its historic fabric and diversity of population.

Having resigned his post at the BRA to run for Mayor, Logue found himself jobless in the fall of 1967 and saddled with a substantial campaign debt. By winter he had perched as the visiting Maxwell Professor of Government at Boston University while he contemplated his next career move, entertaining overtures from Los Angeles, San Francisco, Cleveland, and Baltimore, among other opportunities. Soon he would get a job offer that propelled him into the third phase of his urban redevelopment career and allowed him to address two frustrations he was increasingly encountering in his urban renewal work: the difficulty creating mixed income urban communities and, relatedly, the limitations of single city-based redevelopment for making more socially and economically integrated metropolitan areas. America's urban problems, he argued, could be solved only by developing projects that crossed social class and city boundaries. So when New York's liberal Republican Governor Nelson Rockefeller called in the winter of 1968, first to seek Ed Logue's advice on drafting legislation to create a new kind of powerful statewide urban renewal agency and soon after to offer him the job as its president, Logue jumped at the opportunity.

Rockefeller, for his part, was also frustrated with the usual way of doing business, as he watched his bond issues to build badly needed subsidized housing and other industrial, commercial, and civic infrastructure keep getting defeated at the polls. For the first time in the nation, the semiautonomous redevelopment agency, a common structure for overseeing urban renewal in cities, would be tried on the state level. Rockefeller and Logue designed what they called the New York State Urban Development Corporation (UDC), a public benefit corporation, funded with an initial appropriation of $17 million and the authority to self-finance through issuing its own bonds up to $1 billion (later increased to $2 billion), to be backed by the "moral obligation" of the state. (As an aside, it is interesting to note that the concept of the "moral obligation bond" was developed by John Mitchell, later Richard Nixon's notorious attorney general, while he was a municipal bond lawyer in New York City and serving as bond counsel to Governor Rockefeller in the 1960s. In an effort to circumvent the voter approval process for increasing state and municipal bond limits, Mitchell invented this type of revenue bond that indicated the state's intent to meet bond payments even though it was not legally obligated to do so.[14]) Most controversially, at Logue's insistence, the UDC had the power to employ eminent domain, to override local zoning laws and building codes, and to make its projects tax-exempt. New York State legislators adamantly resisted the creation of such an independent agency over which they would have little control, but Rockefeller shrewdly took advantage of the political opening created by Martin Luther King's assassination and the riots that it precipitated to ram the UDC through the New York State Legislature.

From 1968 until 1975, Logue presided over massive building in New York State, providing exciting opportunities for architects to innovate, putting up thirty-three thousand units of housing—most of it subsidized for low- and moderate-income residents and the elderly, constructing three "new towns" (two upstate and Roosevelt Island in the East River), and creating ten industrial parks and more than a dozen downtown renewal projects. I will focus here on the two projects that addressed most directly Logue's larger political agenda for the UDC of social reengineering and metropolitan planning.

The first project, Logue's pride and joy, was the car-free, mixed-income "new town in town" of Roosevelt Island, planned for the nearly abandoned Welfare Island by Philip Johnson and John Burgee to house eighteen thousand residents in five thousand apartments, though the demise of the UDC in 1975 stunted its full development. Logue wanted the Welfare Island location so badly that he agreed to Mayor John Lindsay's demand that he develop several other difficult New York City sites in addition. "I got the goat sites, and I got the island," is how he bluntly recalled the deal.[15] What I call Logue's "Great Society Utopia on the East River" provided him with the opportunity to create from scratch the kind of socially integrated community that he had long idealized by mixing subsidized housing for low-income and elderly tenants with market-rate rental and co-op apartments, by scattering small-scale public schools and day care facilities throughout the buildings, and by providing for large families and physically disabled residents fifteen years before the latter was mandated by the Americans with Disabilities Act of 1990.[16] New construction like Roosevelt Island and the upstate new towns appealed to planners like Logue as ways of avoiding the complex politics stemming from clearance and dislocation of already inhabited sites. These projects also offered unique opportunities to create socially integrated communities, so difficult to achieve within an existing, socioeconomically segmented, urban setting.

The second UDC project that expressed Logue's social priorities was an effort in 1972 to introduce a metropolitan solution to the state's housing crisis by establishing a bold "Fair Share" housing program. The plan involved putting one hundred units of affordable housing in nine wealthy Westchester towns, threatening if necessary to use the UDC's power to override local zoning. The response of these communities was quick, thunderous, and unyielding. Not only were the UDC's proposals rejected outright (and Logue himself subjected to death threats), but the state legislature curtailed the UDC's override powers in New York's villages and towns as punishment.

Over the next two years, the convergence of a number of factors threatened the UDC's survival as an aggressive statewide agency that coordinated public and private investment around progressive social priorities: growing antagonism in Albany toward the UDC's independent power; President Richard Nixon's impounding of congressionally approved housing subsidies (upon which the UDC depended) as he redirected Washington away from LBJ's "Great Society" to his own "New Federalism"; and a severe fiscal crisis in New York City and State that made New York bankers less willing to lend to the UDC. Even without a financial crisis, however, the bankers were increasingly uncomfortable with the UDC's way of operating. They charged that Logue was spending beyond the UDC's means by not making its projects self-supporting; Logue retorted that he had a social mission and was not running a for-profit business. In early 1975, Logue was forced to resign by New York's new Governor Hugh Carey, who also called for a Moreland Act Commission investigation into possible corruption at the UDC. Ed Logue and Nelson Rockefeller's great experiment was ending in public inquisition and disgrace, marking not only the fall of Logue's UDC empire but also the end of an era of large-scale public investment in the urban built environment. The Commission's final report exonerated the UDC of corruption but concluded that the state's oversight of UDC's finances had been too lax and Logue's UDC so single-minded in pursuit of a social agenda that it had taken unwise financial risks. (Logue reflected later, "It was too good to last, and that's why I so cordially despise bankers.... They felt threatened.... I was engaged in—bankers said this—social engineering. As if that's a mortal sin. I was very proud of the fact that Roosevelt Island was a total piece of social engineering."[17]) In a searing analysis of what went wrong with the UDC, housing analyst Joseph Fried concluded that depending too much on the private sector to fund renewal on this scale, with the requirement that projects prove themselves good financial investments, was a deeply flawed concept. "Rebuilding the slums is a long-term and financially risky endeavor at best," not well suited to the "private investment market, skittish and volatile.... Rather the job must be done by American society generally, and that means sufficient public funds for subsidized housing and redevelopment programs to begin with, as well as a willingness by government to take the ultimate risk when it does seek to draw private capital into the effort."[18]

The defeat of the UDC marked the end of government control over the physical development of the nation's cities, and it sent shock waves through redevelopment circles nationwide.[19] From here forward, rebuilding cities to make them more receptive to the postindustrial economy and to cushion their citizens from the deepening inequities that would accompany that new economy would increasingly be left to the private sector. What housing was not in the hands of private enterprise was left to poorly funded, small-scale but scrappy, nonprofit Community Development Corporations (CDCs). Logue's fourth major phase of urban redevelopment work would take place in this new era of city building and his work there is instructive for how he adjusted his liberal agenda to the new political and economic realities of the late 1970s and onward. After three years as a consultant, trying to keep his hand in what he considered his life's work, Logue finally got back in the urban redevelopment saddle when, in 1978, New York City Mayor Ed Koch appointed him executive director of the South Bronx Development Organization (SBDO). This was a job that Logue desperately wanted. As he put it, "I'm not going to let that son of a bitch Hugh Carey write the last chapter of my public life."[20]

In truth, there were not many competitors eager to tackle the near impossible job of rebuilding the ravished blocks of the South Bronx, decimated by arson, impoverishment, and population loss. Here, Logue faced the worst urban devastation of anywhere he had ever worked and with fewer financial resources than he had ever had at his disposal. But where many of his former colleagues in Boston and New York's UDC saw a humiliating career comedown, Logue sensed a unique opportunity to make a difference and threw himself into the job. In its smaller scale and make-do strategies, the SBDO reflected a major shift in the nation's approach to its urban crisis. Logue marshaled whatever federal, state, city, and private foundation resources he could muster and collaborated more than he ever had before with truly grassroots community organizations, such as Father Louis Gigante's South East Bronx Community Development Corporation, the Banana Kelly Community Improvement Association, and the Mid-Bronx Desperadoes Community Housing Corporation, to name the most influential. Ironically, forced to operate within the limited and market-oriented emphasis of President Ronald Reagan's urban agenda, Logue came closest here to fulfilling his longtime motto of "planning with people." But the scale was small and the effort to turn around the South Bronx for him frustratingly incremental—an industrial park promising jobs here, a block of new houses there, the need to advocate for greater social services for impoverished residents everywhere.

Ed Logue is best remembered in the South Bronx for his unorthodox plan to repopulate the abandoned, rubble-strewn Charlotte Street neighborhood with owner-occupied, single-family, prefabricated, conventional suburban ranch-style houses with picket fences. Logue had been impressed that amid the decay of the Bronx, some homeowners persisted in caring lovingly for their homes, and many new immigrants from the Caribbean and other developing countries wanted to own their own land. Making use of the federal mortgage subsidies now becoming available in the new era of market solutions to urban problems, Logue's "Charlotte Gardens" offered houses at $52,000 ($30,000 less than they cost), with only 10 percent down. The project's opening won front-page attention in the *New York Times* and many other publications, an enthusiastic reception from the lower middle-class New Yorkers it was aimed at, and rejection from the national community of planners and architects whose approval Logue had carefully cultivated throughout his career. They dismissed this suburban housing tract within an urban setting as a harebrained scheme, too low in density and lowbrow in aesthetics. Logue acknowledged that "this stuff will not win the architectural awards that I have so enjoyed receiving," but he felt this prefabricated housing was the best hope for reviving the South Bronx. Prefabrication brought down the price and quickened the pace of rebuilding. The single family structure was what was readily available in prefabricated buildings, but it also was cheaper to put up than multiple dwellings, which had stiffer building code requirements and more expensive hookups to main utility lines. Logue's long-term plans included establishing a factory to manufacture houses to create new jobs as well as new dwellings, which could then have been designed to fit better with an urban setting.[21]

In October 2007, the thirtieth anniversary of President Jimmy Carter's famous visit to devastated Charlotte Street in 1977, which led to what became the SBDO, current Charlotte Street homeowners proudly showed off their homes to reporters. These journalists were impressed with the well-kept houses, the health of the neighborhood, and the South Bronx's recovery more generally, which the SBDO is often credited with having helped make possible.[22] In the South Bronx, Ed Logue, limited financially and isolated professionally, had used whatever subsidies he could tap into to push privatization and other market approaches to urban development in more democratic social directions. The product of collaboration between the SBDO and the local, nonprofit Mid-Bronx Desperadoes Community Housing Corporation, Charlotte Gardens—small in scale, bootstrapped in implementation, modest in impact—became a prototype for whatever city building was not in the hands of a profit-oriented private sector as the twentieth century ended and the twenty-first century began. A further departure from the ambition, some would say hubris, of New Haven's massive urban renewal of some thirty years earlier, is hardly imaginable. But while we might applaud the success of small-scale, public-private interventions like Charlotte Gardens, in contrast to the arrogant master planning of the urban renewal heyday, we should note two things. First, the aesthetic consequence of the government's retreat from its role as modern-day Medici was a decline in modernist architecture and its replacement with rather anodyne American domestic tastes, which many Americans, of course, may have welcomed but which undercut the most fruitful experiments in architectural innovation. And second, despite the soundness of banks' mortgage lending in these early regulated years, the story culminated with President George W. Bush's "ownership society" where consumers were pushed to purchase homes they could not afford while their subprime mortgages became a source of irresponsible profit-making by private financial institutions.

What can we learn from city builder Ed Logue's experience in urban redevelopment over more than three decades and particularly his liberal effort to balance public and private power to keep American cities viable, even flourishing? Whereas his first foray into urban renewal in New Haven suffered from a lack of both private investment and engagement with the communities affected by redevelopment, in Boston he achieved more buy-in from the private sector and neighborhood residents, albeit with louder complaints from the latter. But he also recognized the intractability of inequality produced within cities undergoing urban renewal, and he aimed through the UDC in New York to tackle this problem by designing new, socially mixed urban communities like Roosevelt Island and by redressing urban woes with metropolitan solutions like the "Fair Share" affordable housing program. After the era of federally funded urban renewal ended and Logue struggled to improve the South Bronx with the minimal tools provided by the Reagan administration, he saw his job as using what limited power he had to steer private resources in the direction that Bronx residents wanted.

I hope it is clear from Logue's career that first, it is an enormous distortion to paint the federal engagement in "urban renewal" with one condemning brush, as the neoliberal reconstructors of New Orleans and, it must be said, the Jane Jacobs–inspired antiplanners tend to do. Rather, urban renewal varied tremendously over time and setting and had more positive attributes than its critics might acknowledge and more detriments than its defenders at the time would have admitted.

Second, it should be evident that whatever the scale or ambition of the urban development project, whether rebuilding the downtown of New Haven or Boston or a few streets of the South Bronx, there was no escaping the necessity of balancing public resources and planning and private investment, the liberal dilemma with which this essay began. This dilemma left planners like Logue, who considered themselves experts deserving of the power and resources to fix problems, frustrated and vulnerable to criticism and constraints from three sides: first, from private capitalists like the New York bankers who balked at investing without the most profitable of returns; second, from ordinary city residents understandably fearful of threats to their communities; and third, from critics of urban renewal, often propelled by Jane Jacobs's influential critique in *Death and Life of Great American Cities* of 1961, who rejected planning in favor of her call to preserve the "spontaneous and untidy" "ballet of the sidewalk" on what she called the "organic" city street, at its best blessed with its mixed uses, short blocks, varied building types, and population density.[23]

Not surprisingly, Jane Jacobs and Ed Logue did not like each other. They had several angry exchanges, included a celebrated face-off at a forum on city planning at the Museum of Modern Art in March 1962, soon after the publication of her *Death and Life*. Jacobs considered Logue the epitome of the bulldozing urban renewer ("a very destructive man—he thought it should all be wiped out and built new. Boy, in my books he went down as a maniac"), while Logue argued that Jacobs's call not to interfere with the natural evolution of blocks and neighborhoods perpetuated the status quo, thereby—intentionally or not—abandoning the cities and relieving uncaring, and increasingly suburbanizing, elites of all responsibility for urban recovery. He accused Jacobs of speaking as a resident of the safe, relatively well-off neighborhood of Greenwich Village, a privilege that slum dwellers did not enjoy. "Not surprisingly," he went on cynically, "this approach has won her many new friends, particularly among comfortable suburbanites. They like to be told that neither their tax dollars nor their own time need be spent on the cities they leave behind them at the close of each work day."[24] To make the politics of the Jacobs critique even more complicated, Jacobs is not only a heroine of a populist Left; the conservative Right has also made her its patron saint in matters urban. For example, the libertarian magazine *Reason*, devoted to "free minds and free markets," named Jacobs to its gallery of thirty-five heroes of freedom for her embrace of the marketplace and "detest[ation of] the intrusiveness of government, big or small." On the more traditional Right, William F. Buckley Jr. included Jacobs's writing in his anthology, *American Conservative Thought in the Twentieth Century*. Jacobs's defense of the natural evolution of the organic street, with all its political ambiguity, has become a foundation stone of neoliberal urban policies.[25]

The Logue and Jacobs standoff brings us back to where we began, to the tensions surrounding the proper balance between public and private initiative in liberal social thought and urban policy. These spokespeople represent two very different and well-meaning conceptions of how best to achieve a more egalitarian, democratic society where cities are economically viable and where their residents enjoy decent places to live and interact with each other, regardless of class or race. One—the Ed Logue approach, if you will—might be considered social democratic in its embrace of the power of the public sector and government to bring about positive change. This position need not ignore popular input; in fact, as time went on Logue and his peers became committed, often through popular pressure, to inviting more and more of it. Still, their approach did run the risk of imposing too much top-down authoritative decision making on city dwellers, as Jacobs and her supporters claimed. The other approach, articulated powerfully by the Jacobsonians, could be characterized as antistatist, antimodernist, and potentially (though not necessarily) market-oriented in its rejection of state intrusion, preference for "natural" evolution, and call for more decentralized, localized decision making. It has the virtue of getting closer to community sentiments, but it cannot necessarily be counted on to improve people's urban environments. In a relatively healthy neighborhood like Jane Jacobs's own Greenwich Village that may not be bad, but in a less privileged and less prosperous city community, a lack of public investment might perpetuate an unacceptable status quo or a private-development–driven solution.

The case of city-building in the post–World War II era thus illuminates well a fundamental tension in postwar American liberalism—between state-centered intervention and populist decentralization. The former, as seen in the strategies of Ed Logue, aims to use the power and resources of government to deliver a more socially and economically egalitarian urban America. The latter, wary of what anthropological theorist James Scott has recently labeled "high modernist urban ideology," rejects efforts by state officials and planners to impose rationalist "legibility" in place of the local knowledge of indigenous populations. States, he warns, "driven by utopian plans and an authoritarian disregard for the values, desires, and objections of their subjects, are indeed a moral threat to human well-being," forcing judicious weighing "of the benefits of certain state interventions against their costs." It should be noted, however, that in a postscript to his argument, Scott acknowledged that post-1989, the kind of states he criticizes "have for the most part vanished or have drastically curbed their ambitions," while "large-scale capitalism," particularly global capitalism, has become the most damaging standardizer and homogenizer.[26] In the end, then, the social democrats and the antistatists converge in their common distrust of capitalist interests. They seek to check them, however, with very different interventions—through strengthening the federal government for the New Deal liberals, through empowering the local community for their opponents.

Only months into Obama's presidency, The New York Times had already begun to warn of the dire consequences in articles like "All Boarded Up: How Cleveland Is Dealing with Mass Foreclosures" and "The Effort to Save Flint, Michigan, by Shrinking It."[27] Whatever Carrión's critics might have preferred for the Bronx, it was clear that in this urban crisis, as in earlier ones, private investment was essential. The question became, as it has been throughout the postwar era of liberal city rebuilding, what role government—big and small—should play in the process. Ed Logue would have argued that while all his projects combined public and private investment, he succeeded best when the public side called most of the shots. What public funding gave him, he often claimed, was the leverage to push private investment in a more socially responsible direction, in contrast to the neoliberal era, when what got built was what private developers thought would turn a profit. That dependence on the private market meant that while Manhattan, San Francisco, Boston, and Dallas have thrived, Detroit, Hartford, Cleveland, and Newark did not. And what John Kenneth Galbraith called "social goods" in The Affluent Society of 1958—the public infrastructure of roads, bridges, schools, and trains that yield no profit—continued to deteriorate.

Logue would not have considered his liberal collaboration with the private sector the same thing as recent calls for "public-private partnerships." This lingo has crept into the discourse surrounding improving the urban built environment, but it represents something quite different. It comes out of the privatization drive of the 1980s and is really aimed at enhancing the private sector's role by encouraging it to assume more of the responsibilities traditionally performed by government. The National Council for Public-Private Partnerships was founded in 1985 to advocate actively for these arrangements. Most recently, the George W. Bush administration's Department of Transportation responded by actively encouraging private investors to lease roads and bridges from states and run them at a profit.[28] Were Ed Logue still alive as liberals returned to Washington in 2009, he would have been ecstatic at Barack Obama's election as president, he would have encouraged his commitment to cities, and he would have told him to make sure that he and his Director Carrión rejected the neoliberal approach and stayed safely buckled in the driver's seat for what was sure to be a long, rocky but worthwhile ride. And then we would hope that some of the lessons that Logue should have learned during his long career in rebuilding cities—to heed some of Jacobs's and Scott's cautions and truly plan with people on a local level—would also become part of the new rules of the road. The melding of social democratic government leverage and community-based democratic participation into a truly "public" sector—as fraught as that marriage might prove—will likely be required to counterbalance the enormous influence that private development interests have gained since 1980 if American cities are to have a liberal future.

Notes

1. "From Bronx to Washington, after Mixed Results," *New York Times*, March 2, 2009; see also "Two New Yorkers Picked by Obama," City Room: Blogging from the Five Boroughs, *New York Times*, February 19, 2009, 10:45 AM.

2. Alan Wolfe, *The Future of Liberalism* (New York: Alfred A. Knopf, 2009).

3. Lizabeth Cohen, *A Consumers' Republic: The Politics of Mass Consumption in Postwar America* (New York: Alfred A. Knopf, 2003).

4. My understanding of New Orleans is based on: Special Issue of *The Nation*: "New Orleans Struggles Back," September 10, 2007, and an insert, "After Katrina: Redemption and Rebuilding," in *The American Prospect*, March 2009, A1–A23; AFL-CIO blog (http:blog.aflcio.org, accessed September 12, 2011): James Parks, "A 'Disposable Workforce' in New Orleans after Katrina," October 19, 2007; Brookings Institution, "The New Orleans Index: Tracking Recovery in the Region," August 2007, http://www.brookings.edu/reports/2007/08neworleansindex.aspx, accessed September 12, 2011; "Road to New Life after Katrina Is Closed to Many," *New York Times*, July 12, 2007; from the *Times-Picayune*: "City to Unveil Targets for Redevelopment," and "Developers Picked for Revamping Public Housing," March 28, 2007; "N.O. Post-K Blueprint Unveiled," March 29, 2007; "City's Redevelopment Planned Unveiled," March 29, 2007; and tremendous help from Andrew Horowitz, director of the Imagining New Orleans Project of Yale University, which did extensive interviews and collected memorabilia in New Orleans in the Spring of 2006. Also see his paper, "Imagining New Orleans: Oral History after Katrina," Princeton University, Spring 2007. On the decision not to reopen public housing, see also the comment in September 2005 by Rep. Richard H. Baker, a ten-term Republican from Baton Rouge, "We finally cleaned up public housing in New Orleans. We couldn't do it, but God did." http://www.washingtonpost.com/wp-dyn/content/article/2005/09/09/AR2005090901930.html, accessed September 12, 2011.

5. Meg Lousteau, interviewed in Transcript to American Radio Works, "Routes to

Recovery," by Kate Ellis and Stephen Smith, August 2007, 7; http://americanradioworks.publicradio.org/features/nola/, accessed September 12, 2011.

6. On highways, Jon C. Teaford, *The Rough Road to Renaissance: Urban Revitalization in America, 1940–1985* (Baltimore: The Johns Hopkins University Press, 1990), 93–94. On mortgages favoring suburban properties, see Kenneth Jackson, *Crabgrass Frontier* (New York: Oxford University Press, 1985) and Cohen, *A Consumers' Republic*, 204–205; on accelerated depreciation in the tax code, see Thomas W. Hanchett, "U.S. Tax Policy and the Shopping-Center Boom of the 1950s and 1960s," *American Historical Review* 101:4 (October 1996): 1082–1110.

7. "Pressure by Business Urged for U.S. Aid to Urban Areas," *Women's Wear Daily (WWD)*, February 8, 1960. For similar encouragement of department stores to engage in downtown renewal, see summary of a speech by the president of Abraham & Straus to the Harvard Graduate School of Business Administration in "Rebuilt Cities Held Retailers' Downtown Key," *WWD*, March 22, 1957; "Ralph Lazarus Stresses Faith in Downtown," *WWD*, May 27, 1957; "Suburban Figures at Federated Nearing 25%," *WWD*, May 16, 1959; Federated Department Stores, Inc., *1964 Annual Report*; Federated Departments Stores, Inc., *1965 Annual Report*. For valuable discussion of the importance of retail to downtown urban renewal, see Alison Isenberg, *Downtown America: A History of the Place and the People Who Made It* (Chicago: University of Chicago Press, 2004), 166–202.

8. "The City: Under the Knife, or All for Their Own Good," *Time*, November 6, 1964, 71; "Ed Logue—The Master Rebuilder," *Washington Post*, April 15, 1967; "New York's Mr. Urban Renewal," *New York Times*, March 1, 1970, and "'Mr. Urban Renewal' Acts to Rebuild His Image," *New York Times*, May 10, 1980; "Housing: How Ed Logue Does It," *Newsweek*, November 6, 1972; Richard Heath, "An Act of Faith: The Building of the Washington Park Urban Renewal Area, 1960–1967," Appendix: A Conversation with Edward J. Logue, December 7, 1990, Edward J. Logue Papers, Yale University (EJL) 2002 Addition, Box 22, Folder: A Conversation with EJL by Richard Heath, 1; "Czar" is used to describe Logue throughout his career; "Bold Boston Gladiator—Ed Logue," *Life Magazine*, December 24, 1965.

9. Linda Corman, "Former BRA Head Takes Another Look at the City He Helped Plan," *Banker and Tradesman*, October 21, 1987, 6.

10. New Haven's leadership in per capita federal funding of urban renewal is well known and can be most easily documented in Douglas Rae, *City: Urbanism and Its End* (New Haven: Yale University Press, 2003), 324.

11. For the "Kremlin," see Rae, *City*, 318–320. For more on New Haven's urban renewal, see Robert A. Dahl, *Who Governs? Democracy and Power in an American City* (New Haven: Yale University Press, 1961); Allan R. Talbot, *The Mayor's Game: Richard Lee of New Haven and the Politics of Change* (New York: Harper and Row, 1967); Jeanne R. Lowe, *Cities in a Race with Time: Progress and Poverty in America's Renewing Cities* (New York: Random House, 1967), 405–551.

12. Logue quote from Interview with Edward J. Logue in Series "Pioneers in Housing," May 24, 1995, by Morton Schussheim, Library of Congress, 20.

13. Jennifer Kaylin, "The Emerging Urban University," *Yale Alumni Magazine*, April 1995, http://www.yalealumnimagazine.com/issues/93_04/urbanu.html, accessed June 4, 2010.

14. "John N. Mitchell," *Wikipedia*, accessed March 8, 2009.

15. Ivan D. Steen, Interview with Edward J. Logue, Lincoln, Massachusetts, March 3, 1986, EJL, 2002 Addition, Box 21, Folder: EJL, Rockefeller Oral Histories, 43–44.

16. Lizabeth Cohen, "Urban Renewal Czar Edward J. Logue and Utopian Visions of the Postwar American City," Paper presented to the Davis Center, Princeton University, March 29, 2007.

17. Frank Jones, Interview with Edward J. Logue, Martha's Vineyard, April 16, 1999, Tape 3, 38, transcript in my possession.

18. Joseph P. Fried, "The Roof Falls In," *The Nation*, August 15, 1975, 102–106.

19. For an excellent discussion of shifts underway in public funding of cities during the 1970s, see Jane Berger, "'There Is Tragedy on Both Sides of the Layoff': Privatization and the Urban Crisis in Baltimore," *International Labor and Working-Class History*, Special Issue, "The Class Politics of Privatization: Global Perspectives on the Privatization of Public Workers, Land, and Services," 71 (Spring 2007): 29–49. For New York State's investigation of the UDC's default, see "Restoring Credit and Confidence: A Reform Program for New York State and Its Public Authorities," A Report to the Governor by the New York State Moreland Act Commission on the Urban Development Corporation and Other State Financing Agencies," March 31, 1976.

20. Frank Jones, Interview with Edward J. Logue, Martha's Vineyard, April 16, 1999, Tape 4, 58, transcript in my possession.

21. Letter from Edward Logue to John Goldman, May 27, 1982, Edward J. Logue Papers, Yale University Manuscripts and Archives, 1985 addition, Box 107, Folder: Manufactured Housing Correspondence.

22. "In the Bronx, Blight Gave Way to Renewal," *New York Times*, October 5, 2007.

23. Jane Jacobs, *Death and Life of Great American Cities* (New York: Vintage, 1961); for thoughtful recent considerations of her career after her recent death, see three essays in *Journal of the Society of Architectural Historians* 66:1 (March 2007): 5–23.

24. See Walter McQuade, "Architecture," *The Nation*, March 17, 1962, 241–242; James Howard Kunstler, "Godmother of the American City: An Interview with Jane Jacobs," *Metropolis*, March 2001, 133; "American Cities: Dead or Alive?—Two Views," *Architectural Forum: The Magazine of Building*, March 1962, 89–91, Logue quote on 89.

25. See *Reason* website (http://www.reason.com, accessed September 12, 2011), particularly obituary April 25, 2006; G. Tracy Mehan III, "Keeping Cities Free: Jane Jacobs Was a Prescient Defender of Stifling, Centralized Government Urban Planning," *National Review*, April 27, 2006 (obituary); Herbert Gans, "Jane Jacobs: Toward

an Understanding of Death and Life of Great American Cities," and David Halle, "Who Wears Jane Jacobs's Mantle in Today's New York City?" *City and Community* 5:3 (September 2006): 213–215, 237–241.

26. James C. Scott, *Seeing Like a State: How Certain Schemes to Improve the Human Condition Have Failed* (New Haven: Yale University Press, 1998), 1–8.

27. "All Boarded Up: How Cleveland Is Dealing with Mass Foreclosures," *New York Times Magazine*, March 8, 2009; "The Effort to Save Flint, Michigan, by Shrinking It," *New York Times*, April 2, 2009.

28. "Social goods" from John Kenneth Galbraith, *The Affluent Society* (Boston: Houghton Mifflin, 1958). On private investors—with the encouragement of the Bush administration's Department of Transportation—leasing roads from states to operate them at a profit, see "They Really Do Own the Road," *Time*, October 29, 2007; website for the U.S. Department of Transportation—Federal Highway Administration, "Public-Private Partnerships—FHWA," http://www.fhwa.dot.giv/PPP/, accessed March 3, 2009. On the National Council for Public-Private Partnerships, see http://www.ncppp.org/aboutus/index.shtml, accessed March 3, 2009.

PART III

Coalitions

7

Albert Gore Sr., Liberalism and the South in the 1960s

TONY BADGER

In 1970, Tennessee Senator Albert Gore Sr. became a prominent victim of President Nixon's Southern Strategy. Democrat Gore was running for reelection after three terms in the Senate and looked like a good target for the White House. He was a New Dealer in economics, had backed the Voting Rights Act and had spoken out against the Vietnam War. The White House sensed that he was out of touch with his Tennessee constituents. In September, Vice President Spiro Agnew visited Memphis and called Gore "the Southern regional chairman of the Eastern Liberal Establishment."[1] The Republican candidate, William E. Brock III, ran a populist conservative campaign that brilliantly exploited the racial and cultural fears of a state in transition. Gore was defeated by 51–47 percent.

Gore's loss represented the end of Southern New Deal liberalism, perhaps even of New Deal liberalism in general. As this essay shows, he was undone by the policy agenda of the 1960s. Gore pushed a New Deal economic liberalism, a combination of populism and social democracy. But he couldn't navigate his way out the racial conflicts stirred up by the civil rights movement. Conservative Republicanism came of age in the 1970s, and the negative campaign against Gore foreshadowed the tactics of the New Right that would pave the way for the Reagan Revolution of the 1980s—a revolution built in part upon the reddening of the South.

The story of Gore's slow detachment from mainstream southern opinion took place in a remarkably short period of time. In 1956, he was popular enough to be considered a potential running mate for Adlai Stevenson. In 1960, journalist Robert Novak recalled the Senator asking him, "Why would the Democratic Party pick Jack Kennedy when they could have had me?"[2] Just ten years later, Gore was fighting for his political life.

The liberal establishment understood the importance of his reelection. Ted Kennedy organized a fundraiser for Gore at his house in McLean, Virginia. Clark Clifford and Averell Harriman attended. Labor was represented with officials from the Machinists, the Auto Workers, the Electrical Workers, and the Teamsters. Senator Daniel Inouye from Hawaii said Gore was the only senator to receive such a reception because "this election is of historical importance." Inouye also said, "We are responding to the President [Nixon]. We are picking up his gauntlet." Kennedy praised Gore as courageous for casting votes that were unpopular in Tennessee, adding, "his constituency is all of this great nation." Kennedy also said, "This election is one of the greatest urgency and importance to all of our country and to all of us."[3]

Kennedy later recalled that he organized the fundraiser because of a "kind of a sense that it [the Gore Campaign] was adrift and it was really kind of a question that he didn't want to be turned out but it was a question how much he really wanted to remain in." Kennedy put Gore in contact with the Kennedys' favorite filmmaker, Charles Guggenheim, who produced a series of beautifully crafted cinema verité ads for the incumbent, evocatively staged in the hills of middle Tennessee. Kennedy reflected that Gore "had been a giant in the Senate." Kennedy was particularly impressed by "two very hard decisions" that Gore had made on southern judges nominated by Nixon to the Supreme Court, Clement Haynsworth and Harold Carswell. Kennedy, a key figure on the Judiciary Committee in the battle, knew that Gore was under tremendous pressure in the Carswell nomination. There is no doubt that Gore would have greatly preferred to be able to back the President's second nomination of a southern judge. Even his staff was not certain how he would vote even at the last minute. But, as Kennedy recalled, "Gore was just terrific on both of these. You had a sense having been very much involved in that fight and seeing what was happening in terms of the war issue and how he is being targeted. I wanted to be able to help that cause indeed. And during that period we developed some relationship. Although it was very much generational separated. I was still relatively young, and he was a senior member."

But Kennedy also recalled his family's friendship with Gore. He remembered that Gore had helped him in his efforts to eliminate the poll tax in the 1965 Voting Rights Act, rather than by constitutional amendment. Support for a junior member was "incredibly significant" because Gore was "both enormously knowledgeable about and passionate about these issues." For Kennedy, Gore and Paul Douglas were "really two giants on tax justice" and

Gore "was as influential in getting the Medicare thing passed as anybody around here." The chamber always filled, Kennedy claimed, when Gore spoke on finance: his expertise was recognized.[4] In return, Gore seconded Kennedy's nomination for whip in 1968 and refused to criticize him at the time of Chappaquiddick.

Gore had not lost his liberal evangelical zeal in 1970. Republican gubernatorial candidate, Winfield Dunn had never heard Gore make a campaign speech before. But at a hustings of all the candidates for statewide office, Gore's eloquence reminded Dunn of the Mississippi orators of his boyhood:

> His voice was strident from the beginning, his Tennessee twang was crisp and generous, his conviction was clear that his reelection to the Senate was pivotal in terms of the economic and military security of the nation, his guardianship of the rights and benefits of the working man was irreplaceable, and his statement was emphatic that the mothers, babies, and veterans of the state of Tennessee would be in some kind of jeopardy were he not sent back to Washington. His delivery overall exposed an evangelical zeal that was unmatched by any other speaker that evening. And at the conclusion, his shirt was soaking wet from perspiration.[5]

But, for all the enthusiasm of his liberal colleagues, Gore still lost. Gore was a longtime senator who had not kept his political fences mended at home and was at odds with his local party. He ran a highly personal, disorganized, old-fashioned campaign against a media-savvy, well-financed opponent who hammered away at four main issues that would become conservative standards throughout the 1970s—busing, gun control, the Supreme Court judges, and prayer in schools. This appeal to social and cultural values, often indistinguishable from issues of the war and civil rights, offset Gore's appeal on economic issues to his traditional coalition of lower-income white and black voters. Jonathan Daniels, the veteran North Carolina liberal newspaperman understood the significant of the election. His old iconoclastic soul mate, Thad Stem Jr., wrote to Daniels that "As old and as feeble as I am, I'd walk from here [Oxford, N.C.] to Tennessee, backwards, if Albert Gore could whip Brock, the chocolate candy scion." Daniels, who had been FDR's and Truman's press secretary, replied that Gore's defeat left him "sick."[6]

Gore and Great Society Liberalism

Gore had made his reputation in the 1940s and 1950s as an advocate of federal investment in the South (and the nation's) infrastructure. Like so many of Roosevelt's "New Generation" of southerners, Gore had a profound faith in the capacity of the federal government to transform and modernize the South as it had the Tennessee Valley. His passionate involvement in the TVA and his close friendships with first David Lilienthal and, later, Frank Smith came not from the patronage opportunities that attracted old-style Tennessee politicians like Kenneth D. McKellar but from the policy model that the TVA provided for the development of the South. Rural electrification, cheap power, and water resource development would modernize southern agriculture and bring industrial development. He had been equally enthusiastic about atomic energy. Gore wanted to make Tennessee the atomic capital of the nation. After visiting the U.K. and Japan, he wanted the U.S. government, rather than private industry, to build nuclear power stations. (He also became an authority on nuclear disarmament.) Finally, he wanted the new limited access roads that would stop the nation from being clogged by the postwar expansion of automobile ownership and would open up cities like Nashville as a transport and marketing hub for the whole nation. The Gore family has always been proudest of Albert Gore's role as Senate sponsor of the 1956 Interstate Highway Act. In 1992 Albert Gore, about to celebrate his eighty-fifth birthday, noted that Nashville was one of the few cities in the nation where three interstates intersected. In 2005 Al Gore proudly illustrated the dramatic impact of those interstates and his father's achievement:

> Last year, this past year, Nashville was the number one city in the nation for the recruitment of new industries and the relocation of industries and businesses from other places to Nashville. Number one in the entire nation. Nissan located here, Saturn located here, Dell Computer located here, not all of those three in the last year, but why? And why has Nashville been so prosperous even during the downturn? Because there's interstate 40, interstate 65, interstate 24. And if you look at the market of the United States there's the eastern two-thirds and then the scarcely populated Rockies and then the west coast, Nashville is at the center, the center of gravity, particularly as the population has shifted towards the Sunbelt. . . . And the confluence of those three major interstates right here has made it one of the most attractive places to locate businesses in the nation.[7]

But infrastructure issues were not at center stage in the 1960s. They were not contentious issues. There were battles, to be sure, to ensure maximum appropriations but the structural innovations were largely uncontroversial. Free trade, an issue that Gore inherited from an earlier holder of his congressional seat, Cordell Hull, was also not a major issue. Gore had had to fight off a protectionist challenger in 1958, but he was relatively untroubled on that issue in the 1960s. Again, whereas Gore had been a leading Senate spokesman for the Democratic senators in their attacks on Eisenhower's economic policies and their recessionary impact, the preferred Democratic option for economic growth in the 1960s was the tax cut—and on that issue Gore was not at one with his Democratic colleagues. Atomic energy, highways, and the TVA would all, in their time, arouse the concerns of environmentalists. Most of these concerns (although the TVA was the first to begin to feel the environmentalist heat) became pressing after Gore left office. Gore was, in any case, was too committed to the infrastructure investment that would rescue the South from poverty to be much concerned about the environmental cost.[8]

But Gore was not simply committed to economic growth. Both in the House and the Senate, Gore pursued a consistently New Deal–style stand on domestic policy, supporting redistributive, social justice policies. He was part of what Katznelson, Kryder, and Geiger have described, especially in the House, as a "party based liberal coalition of nonsouthern and southern Democrats on welfare state, fiscal and regulatory issues." Gore like other southern liberals supported "much of the Party's social democratic agenda with a level of enthusiasm appropriate to a poor region with a heritage of opposition to big business and a history of support for regulation and redistribution." Gore's Senate record in the 1950s also suggests a qualification to the picture of post–New Deal liberalism so brilliantly described by Alan Brinkley. The record of Gore and other southerners, like Hill, Sparkman, and Monroney in the Senate, point to the persistence of a social democratic, redistributionist liberalism that paralleled the liberal efforts of northern senators like Paul Douglas, Herbert Lehman, and Hubert Humphrey. Such liberalism was more akin to older New Deal versions of social Keynesianism than the more limited "commercial Keynesianism" that Brinkley rightly identifies as so powerful in postwar America.[9]

In the 1960s Gore fought consistently for a more progressive taxation. Frustrated in the House, he was more successful when he got on the Senate Finance Committee. Eugene McCarthy remembered sitting alongside Gore on that Committee trying to prevent the barons, Robert Kerr and Russell Long, from securing favored treatment for special interests. Gore had always sought to protect a graduated and progressive income tax and to close the tax loopholes "which make a mockery of the concept of an income tax levied fairly and in accordance with the ability to pay." He strenuously opposed the Kennedy-Johnson tax cut. His faith in federal government programs meant that he did not want to see government revenue cut in any way. On the contrary, to do the things that needed to be done, he argued in 1961, "indeed to do the things we are already doing—a substantial increase in revenues of the Federal government is essential." A sometimes lonely crusade to make the income tax more fairly graduated was capped in 1969 when he secured the first increase in the personal tax exemption for ordinary citizens since 1948. In his views on the need for tax reform and his skepticism about the efficacy of the tax cut as an economic stimulus, Gore echoed the views of his old friend John K. Galbraith. Galbraith and Gore had been allies in the battle over price controls in World War II. They remained skeptical through the 1960s about the disinterested attitudes of American business leaders.[10]

In the 1960s Gore enthusiastically backed federal social programs. He was a consistent advocate of federal aid to education and rejoiced in its passage in 1965. He led the battle for Medicare in 1964 and had hoped to see its passage that year. Thwarted by Wilbur Mills then, Gore was a prominent supporter of successful Medicare legislation the following year and an effective advocate on the Senate Finance Committee. He was a completely reliable supporter of Great Society legislation.[11]

What also identified Gore in the 1960s was his consistent opposition to Douglas Dillon and Henry Fowler as secretaries of the treasury who represented, he believed, the interests of Wall Street. The influence of the bankers, he argued, led to the high interest rate policies of the U.S. government in the 1960s, which he relentlessly attacked. Gore's hostility to bankers was unsurprising. His father had put what money he had in a number of different banks in Smith County during the Depression as a precautionary measure. Such prudence was to no avail. All the banks failed. Gore's hostility to high interest rates reflected the historic suspicions of a region whose businessmen and farmers felt starved of credit. One of the achievements of the New Deal had been to make low-cost credit available to regional entrepreneurs in the South through the Reconstruction Finance Corporation. In the 1960s Gore saw the high interest rate policy of successive administrations put that achievement at risk. Once again, Gore and Galbraith had similar ideas. Indeed, Galbraith had favored someone like Gore as Kennedy's secretary of the treasury. There is no evidence that such an appointment was seriously considered. But the very idea gave *Washington Post* publisher, Phil Graham, apoplexy.[12]

Gore's persistent faith in New Deal–style liberalism in the 1960s marked him out from other southern senators, even those who had been "TVA liberals" like John Sparkman and Lister Hill. Few southerners had been more committed to federal programs to transform the South than the Alabama senators. But when segregationist pressure built up in the 1950s, not only did they abandon any pretense of racial moderation in order to accommodate the demands of Massive Resistance, they abandoned their economic liberalism as well. Gore remained, by contrast, committed to infrastructure investment, social programs, and progressive taxation throughout the 1960s.[13]

Gore and Race

Gore, in his own words, was "No Shining Knight" on civil rights. Like other southern liberals of his generation he believed that the economic modernization of the South would produce gradual racial change as increased employment and education eliminated racial tension between poor whites and blacks. Gradualism, rather than a head-on assault on segregation, was both prudential—it avoided an issue that would split the lower-income white-black coalition that backed liberals like Gore—but it also reflected their personal reluctance to give up the privileges of segregation and their genuine faith in the transformation that would occur if poverty were eliminated in the South.

The race issue scarcely surfaced in Gore's successful race against segregationist Kenneth McKellar in 1952. Gore was largely silent after the *Brown* decision: it was the law of the land but he did not intend that statement to indicate that he approved of the decision. Like other senators, he noted that school desegregation was a matter for state and local officials. Many of his constituents were surprised that he refused to sign the Southern Manifesto in 1956. In 1957 he went further and voted for the 1957 Civil Rights Act. The changes Lyndon Johnson secured in the Act, notably the removal of Title III and the provision of a jury trial in voting rights suits, enabled Gore to argue that he had worked "to modify the bill into one the South could support." The electoral retribution that segregationists threatened did not materialize. Gore was opposed in 1958 by former governor, Prentice Cooper. Cooper waved a copy of the Manifesto every time he spoke and announced that *he* would have signed it. Don Oberdorfer was covering that election as a cub reporter for the *Charlotte Observer*. Traveling on the Cooper campaign bus, he recalled that Cooper, a Harvard graduate, latched on to Oberdorfer and another young Ivy League graduate journalist and would sit with them at the back of the bus as he expounded his progressive ideas for reorganizing the state. But

> then the bus had stopped in the old Court House Square and he got out of the bus and I followed him. He'd go into the centre of Court House Square where there was a crowd, not a big crowd. And his line was "I'm Prentice Cooper, and I'm gonna keep the niggers out of the schools!"[14]

Gore faced hostile crowds in many Black Belt communities in western Tennessee. But he was unapologetic in his defense of his position supporting a voting rights bill. As he said, "I believe in the right to vote for everyman—white or colored, rich or poor, Jew or Gentile—and I hope you do too." He won convincingly. On the 1960 civil rights bill, he was able to repeat the tactic, indicating that he was biding his time hoping to make the bill more acceptable, but finally voting for it.[15]

Balancing racial moderation with white constituency pressure was harder in the 1960s because African American protesters started dictating the timetable of racial change. Gore made no comment on the direct action protests by young African Americans, not even the sit-ins in Nashville. When Kennedy introduced civil rights legislation in 1963 in the aftermath of the Birmingham demonstrations, Gore indicated that he opposed parts of the proposals, but that he would wait in the hope that they would be amended sufficiently, as in 1957 and 1960, to enable him to support a Civil Rights Act. By 1964, it was clear that Lyndon Johnson did not intend to make concessions to defuse southern opposition. Gore, who refused to join Richard Russell's filibuster team, could expect little help from the administration and he was up for reelection against GOP Memphis congressman, Dan Kuykendall, in a year when Barry Goldwater was deliberately seeking the support of disaffected white segregationists.

Gore's mail ran overwhelmingly against the legislation. Correspondents spent most time asserting that the public accommodations sections grossly assaulted rights of private property and would impose great burdens on business. Others, of course, raised issues of communism, black violence, and intermarriage. Unlike 1956 when many correspondents praised his stand against the Southern Manifesto, few encouraged Gore to vote for the 1964 Act. Gore himself focused on what he saw as the arbitrary power of the attorney general in the Act and, particularly on Title VI, which provided for the cutting off of federal funds to agencies that discriminated. Gore complained that there were no guidelines, no standards, by which local school boards, for example, could be judged. Instead, power appeared to reside solely with unelected and unaccountable bureaucrats. He feared, for example, that a school district desegregating under court order would still find itself punished by the loss of federal funds if administrators, not the court, deemed its compliance insufficient. He feared that the token school desegregation that white Tennesseans appeared to accept would fall foul of zealous bureaucrats and that he would find it even harder to contain white anger. No concessions came from the administration. Gore voted against the final measure.

Once passed, he urged compliance with the law, but he also moved quickly to clarify with HEW officials how they intended to interpret their guidelines, so that he could protect Tennessee school boards as best he could.

Gore's stance angered Hubert Humphrey's staff. The *Tennessean* and the local NAACP condemned his vote. Stickers appeared in black communities, "Ignore Gore in 1964." Crusading black lawyer (and Republican) Z. Alexander Looby never forgave Gore and refused to vote for him in 1970. There is little doubt that he was aware of the challenge he faced in his own Senate race and the disaffection of white supporters in Tennessee. John Seigenthaler believed that Pauline Gore, alerted by brother Whit LaFon in Jackson, was fearful of the political fallout in western Tennessee in the election. His administrative assistant Bill Allen would have been cautious. The presence of Estes Kefauver alongside Gore in the Senate had given him a measure of protection in the past: Kefauver was a lightning rod for segregationist criticism. Kefauver was no longer there.[16]

It is certainly true that Gore took his own counsel. It may not have been just political calculation that dictated his vote. His pattern of behavior was not uncommon among southern moderate congressmen. Jim Wright, Jack Brooks, and Dante Fascell all followed the same path—refusing to sign the Southern Manifesto, voting for the 1957 Act, but against the 1964 Act. The right to vote was one thing, dictating to local school districts was another, imposing restrictions on how businessmen ran their daily affairs was yet another.[17]

But reelection and the violence at Selma resolved dilemmas more easily. While many of his constituents blamed King and the protesters for the violence and feared that Johnson's voting rights bill in 1965 would create a "watered down replica of the Russian monstrosity," Gore found Johnson's address to Congress "inspiring" and from the start indicated that he would support the Voting Rights Act. "Freedom of the ballot box is the very essence of democracy," he proclaimed. Indeed, as someone who had supported antipoll tax legislation in 1942, he supported the efforts to add the abolition of the poll tax by legislation rather than constitutional amendments. He received a modicum of support from newspapers and constituents appalled by the vivid televised footage of Bloody Sunday. Southern historian Bruce Clayton wrote him from Bristol, Tennessee, that the "moral and constitutional issue is clear: we Americans must act if we believe in democracy."[18]

White disillusionment in western Tennessee grew over the next five years. The specter of Communism loomed large. "The Communists are our most deadly enemies, our boys died by the 1000s in Korea and now over 400 in South Vietnam so far, why let these boys down by letting these Communist agitators create chaotic conditions as exist in Selma today." A repeated refrain was the double standard applied to whites and to civil rights protesters. King was a lawbreaker "who violates any law he wishes, according to his conscience, while no one else is allowed to." Welfare mothers loomed large. Is it right "for us to be taxed to support the negs to raise bastards. Negro preacher's daughter down here has six bastards. And the US News shows that Washington is full of bastards"[19]

Gore was unmoved. Real estate interests deluged him with mail opposing a housing bill from 1968 onward. There was little chance of passage until King's assassination in Memphis. Then Gore moved to endorse the Open Housing Act. While some Tennesseans lamented King's assassination and were ashamed that it had taken place in their own state, other angry whites believed that King deserved what he got and thought it somehow dreadfully unfair that King had got himself killed in Memphis, which did not deserve national opprobrium. Gore went on to oppose the Supreme Court nominations of conservative white southerners Clement Haynsworth and Harold Carswell. These votes won him much praise from the black political organization, the Tennessee Voters Council. Gore received overwhelming black support in 1970. But there was always a certain distance between black voters and Gore. David Halberstam noted Gore's "failure to make special gestures, his belief that his record speaks for itself." Gore himself acknowledged that "while black leaders almost unanimously supported me, some of them were not all that enthusiastic. For they never felt I was quite their man. While I had supported civil rights legislation generally, I was not the kind of person to 'clear' things in advance with black leaders—or any other kind of leader." Gore's relations with African Americans reflected the general pattern of southern moderates of his generation. They campaigned for black support at one remove, dealing through intermediaries with black leaders who were expected to deliver the black vote. That style of campaigning for black support made it hard for Gore to pick up some of the immediacy and impatience of black demands and to enthuse the black electorate.[20]

Defeat in 1970

At the Democratic National Convention in 1968 Gore cut a lonely figure in the Tennessee delegation. His speech in favor of the Vietnam peace plank for the platform won enthusiastic applause from northern delegations. His fellow Tennesseans sat on their hands or ostentatiously read their newspapers. Gore cast his vote for George McGovern; the rest of the delegation, tightly controlled by Governor Buford Ellington, lined up to support Hubert Humphrey. The governor, a close friend of LBJ's, represented the conservative wing of the Party. He had fought a bitter and divisive battle against the wealthy young "Kennedy man," John Jay Hooker in 1966. Ellington's faction was gearing up for another battle against Hooker in 1970. Ellington considered Gore arrogant and egotistical. Gore despised Ellington. He regarded him as a dolt, according to John Seigenthaler. George Barrett spoke for many in the Gore camp when he said Ellington was "a Mississippi boy that never got over it, never rose above it." In fact, Ellington had come to terms with the civil rights legislation of 1964 and 1965. Working at the Office for Emergency Planning for Lyndon Johnson, Ellington had been the link man to southern governors at civil rights flashpoints across the region. Like fellow "law and order" conservative governors—Dan Moore and Bob Scott in North Carolina and John McKeithen in Louisiana—Ellington guided his state into generally peaceful acceptance of racial change, despite some race riots in Memphis and campus disturbances. But the factional split in the Democratic and Gore's distance from the state administration meant that Gore knew he could not rely on the state Party organization to make up for his own lack of a personal political organization. In the past he had been able to rely on Kefauver's painstakingly constructed county-by-county organization.[21]

Gore also knew that he faced serious Republican opposition in the state. In 1952 and 1958 Gore had received 74 percent and 78 percent, respectively, of the vote in the general election. Tennessean Republicanism remained a largely mountain Eastern Tennessee phenomenon. But new forces were remaking the Republican Party. Whites in western Tennessee in Memphis and the Black Belt responded to Barry Goldwater's appeal to southern segregationists. In 1964 Memphis congressman Dan Kuykendall reduced Gore's share of the general election vote to 54 percent. In the cities businessmen and professionals aimed to eliminate the old-guard one-party control of politics. In 1962 they sent William E. Brock to Congress from Chattanooga.

In 1966 Howard H. Baker Jr. joined John Tower of Texas as the only southern Republican in the Senate. Baker had polled 47 percent against Ross Bass in 1964. Two years later he triumphed over Governor Frank Clement by over one hundred thousand votes. He appealed to his traditional Eastern Tennessee base but also reached out with a fiscally conservative message to business and professional urban voters. He won a majority of white votes but also 15–20 percent of the black vote because of his moderate record on civil rights. Baker then set about building up an organization with Lamar Alexander at his side that would enable him to buck the trend of one-term

Republican senators in the modern South. In 1968 Nixon won Tennessee with 37 percent of the presidential vote. George Wallace polled 24 percent. Gore knew that his opposition to the Vietnam War and his racial moderation would make it difficult to win those disaffected white Wallace Democrats in 1970. He had seen how his political soul mate Mike Monroney had been defeated in Oklahoma in 1968.[22]

At a family council of war at Christmas 1968, the Gores discussed whether the Senator should even run again. But they soon dismissed that argument: the issues were too important to give up on. They briefly considered moving the family home to Memphis but doubted that would make much difference. They did resolve that the Senator would get back to the state more often to try and hit the major TV networks each weekend. For the next two years his weekly schedule was usually to be in Nashville Friday afternoon to catch the chance to be on the local newscast that night, Knoxville and Chattanooga on Saturday to get TV exposure there, Memphis on Sunday for similar television coverage, and his Memphis office Monday morning for constituency work. But it was difficult for someone so committed to playing a role in the national polity to convey an enjoyment of, and enthusiasm for, this week-in/week-out politicking. Future Senator James Sasser and his wife ran Gore's campaign in Davidson County in 1970. Conscious of his own political downfall in 1994, Sasser noted:

> I mean when you spend eighteen years in the Senate as Gore did and I did, you get out of touch without knowing it and as you progress in the Senate, as your responsibilities get heavier you just can't attend to as much of the fence mending and massaging of egos as you could when you had more time. But, having said that, Senator Gore was not any good at that anyway.[23]

By 1970 Gore's political position had worsened in Tennessee. The Democratic Party was even more divided after a bitter gubernatorial primary battle in which John Jay Hooker had earned his revenge for 1966. While the Ellington state administration would do little for either Hooker or Gore, neither would Hooker help Gore, even though Hooker's brother-in-law and campaign finance manager, Gil Merritt, was a Gore protégé. In vain, AFL-CIO director Al Barkan offered to put labor finances into the campaign on condition that the two campaigns worked together. As it turned out, Hooker brought no strength to the Democratic ticket in 1970. His links to the collapsed Minnie Pearl chicken franchise and the unexpected success of an attractive West Tennessee GOP candidate, dentist Winfield Dunn, doomed Hooker's race.[24]

Gore had had firsthand experience of those divisions when he faced unexpectedly strong opposition in the 1970 primary from a political neophyte, Hudley Crockett, Buford Ellington's press secretary. Crockett was not in the race at Ellington's behest—otherwise he would not have announced at the last minute and he would have had significant financial backing. He did not have the money to produce TV ads, but he did produce an effective alternative: a live Crockett Report, where the former TV newscaster, well-known to Middle Tennessee viewers, delivered half an hour of unscripted and unrehearsed talk straight to camera. He harried Gore as out of touch with the views of Tennessee voters and particularly assailed his stance on Vietnam. Crockett attracted young businessmen and politicos about his age. He was supported by businessmen who had been involved in the industrial development drives by governors Clement and Ellington. He tapped into the latent hostility to Gore among moderate and conservative state legislators and local politicians who felt patronized by the Senator and were only too aware of their constituents' unease with what they saw as the unrepresentative liberal views of an arrogant and unresponsive Senator. His campaign manager was Eddie Evins, nephew of the powerful veteran chair of the House Appropriations Committee Joe Evins, who represented Gore's old congressional district. (Ellington had been Evins's first campaign manager). He was supported by future congressmen Bart Gordon and John Tanner.[25]

Gore's campaign manager hoped for a majority of one hundred thousand, which would give Gore momentum for the general election. Instead, Gore won by fewer than thirty-two thousand votes and Crockett won over 45 percent of the vote. It did not bode well for the November election. As *The Tennessean* noted, Crockett's votes "picked up steadily as he moved Westward across the state into the counties that supported George Wallace in 1968." The *Chattanooga News* made the same calculation: Crockett "ran ahead of Gore in those areas carried by George Wallace in the 1968 presidential election." Gore won Alabama border counties, but as R. W. Apple noted from the *New York Times*, "over rural west Tennessee—in backwater counties like Lauderdale, Dyer and Tipton, where the race issue is central—Mr. Crockett matched or bettered Mr. Wallace's vote." Crockett carried Shelby County and the four western congressional districts. If the Wallace vote was to be the key in November then it appeared that Gore had a mountain to climb.[26]

The Republican threat to Gore was formidable. The Republicans had their largest ever primary vote. Tennessee was a testing ground for Nixon's Southern Strategy. In the first place, Wallace's 34 percent of the vote in 1968 had enabled Nixon to win the state with 37 percent. To capture those votes would lock up the state for 1972. The slowdown on school desegregation, the Supreme Court nominations of strict constructionist southerners, and the vocal opposition to "forced busing" were all part of Nixon's strategy to win over the Wallace voters. In the 1970 elections, Nixon above all wanted to be rid of Gore. Gore, along with Ralph Yarborough and Fulbright, was one of the Senators who could be identified by the administration as a "radical liberal"—a liberal whose relentless and superior criticism of the administration's Vietnam policy infuriated Nixon as much as it had Johnson. Gore's remorseless and increasingly scornful attacks on Nixon's Vietnam policy, so Nixon, believed, hurt the chances of Nixon securing an honorable settlement in Vietnam by encouraging the North Vietnamese to stand firm in negotiations.

Harry Dent, Strom Thurmond's former aide, was the point man for the administration in the South. He kept a close eye on Tennessee and worried whether the best candidate would emerge. He mused that Buford Ellington might be persuaded to run against Gore. After all, as Dent commented, Ellington sounded like a Republican and ought to become one. He was pleased that by October 1969 Congressman William E. Brock had emerged as the leading Republican candidate for Gore's seat.[27]

William E. Brock, wealthy son of the Chattanooga candy manufacturer, had been a key figure in expanding the Tennessee Republican Party out of its historic, rural, mountain base in the East. Young businessmen like Brock, fresh from the Navy and inspired by Eisenhower, had challenged local corrupt, complacent establishments in cities like Chattanooga. Brock and his fellow ideologues also chafed at what they took to be the top-down approach of the traditional eastern leadership of the Party, first under B. Carroll Reece, then under Howard Baker. East Tennessee Republicans, they argued, had been too ready to accede to Democratic dominance in the rest of the state in return for local control of patronage. Brock and his allies wanted to make the Republican Party an identifiably conservative and statewide party. They intended to build up from the grassroots and in 1962 they aimed to win a majority of the state offices by 1970, although Brock concedes that probably a few too many beers might have fueled that ambition.[28]

Brock became the first Republican congressman to break out of the Eastern Tennessee mountain redoubt by winning the 3rd district seat in Chattanooga and Hamilton County; his organization became the model for Republican organization across the state. His grassroots get-the-vote-out organization was based on volunteers and paid attention to how the AFL/

CIO organized locally and how Kefauver, who had been friendly to his fellow townsman, functioned.[29]

Brock's conservatism was unequivocal. Unlike Howard Baker, he gloried in Goldwater's candidacy in 1964, even his proposals to sell off the TVA. He sought to prevent the Party swinging to the left in the aftermath of Goldwater's defeat. But, like other southern Republicans, he latched on to Richard Nixon's candidacy in 1968 and was one of ten "surrogate" speakers for Nixon in the campaign.[30]

The White House may not have anointed Brock but his former administrative assistant, Bill Timmons, was working there and Brock had already acquired Ken Reitz of Treleavan Associates who had run Nixon's media campaign in 1968. As early as October 1969, the White House and Ken Rietz agreed that grant announcements, patronage appointments, and presidential visits would be carefully coordinated to aid the Brock campaign. Brock's path to the Republican nomination appeared to have been smoothed and he was running with every sign of White House backing.[31]

From the start, Brock's pollsters and advisers identified three main issues of public concern: support for law and order, particularly in regard to student unrest; opposition to increased welfare support for those who did not look after themselves, especially African Americans; and opposition to the interference of the federal government and the Supreme Court into local affairs. Brock's team translated these into thirty-second or sixty-second spot messages. Harry Treleavan believed in these ads, and spending on them nationally doubled between 1964 and 1968. Even a 60-second spot was thought to be too long by some political consultants: they could become refrigerator visiting time. Under the mantra "Bill Brock Believes" that later turned into "Bill Brock Believes in What We Believe In," they translated those general public concerns into specifics on opposing busing, supporting the President on the war, controlling government spending to curb inflation, combating crime by appointing judges who would put criminals in jail and a Supreme Court that would not tie the hands of the police, opposition to gun control, stronger drug laws and enforcement, and the expulsion of violent student protesters. Brock talked to ordinary Tennesseans: a parent, a veteran, a pensioner, a farmer, hunters, constituents who had been helped, disaffected Democrats, the wife of a POW, a textile worker, a young man. The message was that Brock listened and took local issues seriously, unlike Gore. The implication of course was that Gore did not believe what Tennesseans believed in. Indeed, some in the Gore camp were convinced that the subliminal message of the first billboards was that Gore was not a religious believer whereas Brock was.[32]

Brock also ran what journalist Larry Daughtrey described as "tautly-managed and efficient organization." The itinerary was charted out to the minute. There was even a timetable for "applause by the mini-skirted girls at each rally." Priority was given to the press and broadcast media—helpful handouts and a telephone number in Nashville where journalists could hear a tape-recorded message from the candidate daily.[33]

The contrast with the chaotic Gore campaign was stark. The one concession to modern campaigning was the memorable cinema verité ads produced by Charles Guggenheim. They stressed that Gore grew up in Smith County and still held to the principles he had learned in the hill country of Tennessee. One showed Gore playing checkers with an old-timer in a county courthouse square. He joked that the man beat him because he had been practicing while Gore was in Washington protecting his Medicare. Another old man approaches and reminds Gore that he had voted for him six years previously and promised to do it again if he lived. "Here I am, Albert," he comes to tell the Senator. Another featured Albert and Al riding horses on the farm. Yet another featured Gore telling his uniformed son, Al, to love his country. Tennessee was just one state where Guggenheim and Harry Treleavan were going head to head as political consultants.[34]

Otherwise Gore's campaign was massively disorganized. There were no advance men. The powerful friends and close local allies Gore had relied on in the past were no longer around. Too often supposed local campaign managers were elderly and inactive. Gore's county organization was no match for the county-by-county teams that Brock had spent years assembling for the Republican Party. He only secured a press secretary late in the day when Gene Graham came down from teaching journalism at the University of Illinois and stayed on to serve as the press secretary the campaign did not have. At times even Gore himself seemed resigned. On a Saturday afternoon, Norman Ferris went to a bookstore at Mercury Plaza, one of the two biggest shopping centers in Murfreesboro, which was full of people. Gore was in a bookstore, "sitting in the back at a table and a few people would wander in and maybe somebody would buy his book *The Eye of the Storm* and he would sign it; and I said, 'Senator, all those people out there. Why don't you go out and shake some hands and be visible?' This was not long before the election. He said, something like, 'Well if they don't know what I stand for by now, it seems a little late.'"[35]

Once Gore did get involved, however, he campaigned furiously from dawn to dusk at factory gates, stockyards, and courthouse squares. He campaigned with a flesh and blood fervor that made Brock seem like an invisible candidate manipulated by image makers. David Broder came down from Washington to observe the campaign and concluded that it was really a test of two different styles and theories of campaigning. Broder argued that "Gore... was campaigning in the way that he had always campaigned, which was personal appearances, very folksy, talking to people directly. Brock ran what was one of the really the first modern media campaigns. And as I watched it, the impression that I had was that Gore could not understand really what was happening to him and he couldn't figure out, sort of, what the dynamic was and even though his own people made beautiful commercials, as you've seen in that campaign—the white horse which became sort of a classic thing. So I think it was something done for him, but not really representing anything that which he was personally invested. And he'd go around and, you know, still very much in the old-fashioned, have these kind of conversations with, with voters believing that, you know, that was still how you communicated with the State that he had come to know very well over a long period of time."[36]

The voters Gore was targeting in these conversations were, just like Brock, the Wallace voters. He believed that he could appeal on pocketbook issues to their populist instincts. He hoped to appeal to them by stressing economic issues, not racial or social ones. He called the roll on all Brock's votes against programs that benefited Tennessee and stressed, in contrast, what he had done throughout his career for lower-income voters. Surprisingly and dramatically, he started to claw back so that by mid-October polls for both Brock and Hooker suggested that this bid by Gore to reclaim the Wallace voters was succeeding.

But Reitz and the Brock team had anticipated this surge and were ready for it. They went after the undecided voter "with the four big issues we've saved for the last ten days." Three of those issues—gun control, busing and the judges—were already there. But they had a new one for which they had not prepared TV ads: school prayer. Highlighting a series of technical votes on a rider defending school prayer added to the Equal Rights Amendment by Everett Dirksen and his son-in-law, Howard Baker, newspaper ads proclaimed: "ALBERT GORE HAS TAKEN POSITION AGAINST SCHOOL PRAYER THREE TIMES."[37]

Gore found this an issue from left field. Religion for the family was a private, understated matter. Both Pauline and Albert Gore remembered the religious hatred stirred up against Al Smith in 1928. In 1960 they had experienced the ferocity of the anti-Catholic campaign in Tennessee against John Kennedy. Even Gore's mother found it difficult to vote for a Catholic that year. Public religiosity was something to be avoided. Their Baptist background mandated the separation of church and state. It was difficult to adapt to a new politics where opponents sought out hot-button issues that were largely symbolic, i.e., issues on which the legislative branch could in fact do little, simply to cast the opponent on the "wrong side."[38]

When Gore was defeated, his followers were in little doubt that race had beaten him. All the key Brock issues—busing, guns, and the courts—had a coded, or not so coded, racial element. Gene Graham then added bitterly, "John T. Scopes" for the school prayer issue. David Halberstam, in an eloquent recapitulation of the campaign, described Brock's "candy-coated racism." C. Vann Woodward, the foremost academic authority on southern racial practices, thought Halberstam had it exactly right. Halberstam himself looking back was in no doubt about his analysis. Brock himself saw the campaign in a different light—after all he had helped initiate school desegregation in Chattanooga and he certainly did not run a crude race-baiting campaign like Republican Albert Watson in South Carolina—but he did identify for the White House Gore's "position on the Supreme Court nominees and RN's VN policies as major factors" in Brock's victory. David Broder saw it in a more complex light: "the cultural issues were very clear and the contrast in the way in which they were attempting to communicate their messages to the voters were very clear. That sticks out in my mind much more than the racial component." Race was one, but not the only, part of a white backlash against the federal government's interference in traditional local values in schools, law and order, and religion.[39]

Coda

Albert Gore was the only victim of Nixon's Southern Strategy. At the same time as he was defeated, a new generation of southern Democrats got elected to governorships: John West in South Carolina, Reubin Askew in Florida, and Jimmy Carter in Georgia. Albert Brewer almost defeated George Wallace in Alabama. They had put together a biracial, cross-class alliance of affluent whites, committed to economic growth and racial moderation, and blacks. As Randy Sanders has shown, successful Democrats in 1970 campaigned for the governorships as new faces who, in a rather fuzzy and indeterminate way, were racial moderates. Gore was neither a new face nor fuzzy. He was unlikely to appeal to affluent whites because of business opposition to his economic policies. In addition, gubernatorial candidates were not encumbered by clear policy stances on either the War or on the Supreme Court candidates.[40] They could appeal to upper-income southern whites anxious for racial and economic progress and to African Americans anxious for symbolic and practical recognition of their newfound voting rights. Albert Gore found himself too distant from the social and cultural conservatism of his former white supporters and could not persuade them that economics trumped race.

Gore had gone to Washington when civil rights were not part and parcel of national liberalism. He had been driven by a faith that the federal government could solve the problems of a poor region like the South. Through the end of the Depression, World War II, and the unbroken years of unprecedented economic growth he never lost faith in the power of the federal government to sustain economic growth, to transform the South's infrastructure and to raise the income of poor Tennesseans. As his longtime friend and political ally, Martha Ragland, critically noted, Gore regretted that he could not find an alternative to the race issue. Whatever he may have desired, African American activism in the 1960s foreclosed any alternative. What the 1970 election revealed was that too many white Tennesseans no longer shared his faith in a beneficent federal government. Gore's brand of unapologetic economic liberalism would rarely be seen again in white politicians either in Tennessee or the South.[41]

Notes

I am very grateful to Lisa Pruitt, Betty Rowland, and Jim Williams of the Gore Research Center for their enormous help; to Michael S. Martin and Sean Smith for their admirable research assistance; to Catherine Maddison and Liz Lundeen, my former students in Cambridge, and to Fleming Wilt and the Samuel Fleming Foundation and to Middle Tennessee State University for their generous financial support for the research for this essay.

1. "Gore Joins Receiving Line for Agnew," *New York Times*, September 23, 1970, 21.
2. Robert D. Novak, *The Prince of Darkness* (New York: Crown Forum, 2007), 70.
3. *Chattanooga News*, August 13, 1970.
4. Ted Kennedy interview with the author, December 2003.
5. Winfield Dunn, *From a Standing Start: My Tennessee Political Odyssey* (Brentwood, Tenn.: Magellan Press, 2007). Winfield Dunn interview with the author, April 2008.
6. Thad Stem Jr. to Jonathan Daniels, October 27, 1970; Daniels to Stem, November 11, 1970, Papers of Jonathan Worth Daniels, Southern Historical Collection, Chapel Hill, N.C.
7. *Tennessean*, December 26, 1992. Al Gore interview with the author, April 9, 2005.
8. Gore's weighting of the regional benefit of economic growth against the environmental costs was illustrated when, after his defeat, he became the chair of Armand

Hammer's Island Creek Coal, a company whose headquarters were in Lexington, close to Gore's Carthage home, and whose specialism was deep mine drilling.

9. Ira Katznelson, Kim Geiger, and Daniel Kryder, "Limiting Liberalism: The Southern Vote in Congress," *Political Science Quarterly* 108 (1993): 283–306. The authors note this liberalism did not extend to prolabor votes. Gore, like most southern congressmen, but unlike Estes Kefauver, did not oppose Taft-Hartley. Alan Brinkley, *The End of Reform: New Deal Liberalism in Recession and War* (New York: Knopf, 1995), 265–271. For persistent social democratic trends in Congress in the 1950s see Roger Biles, *Crusading Liberal: Paul H. Douglas of Illinois* (DeKalb: Northern Illinois University Press, 2002) and Meg Jacobs, *Pocketbook Politics: Economic Citizenship in Twentieth-Century America* (Princeton: Princeton University Press, 2006).

10. Eugene McCarthy, interview, Democrats 2000 (video held by the Gore Research Center, Middle Tennessee State University, Murfreesboro, Tenn.). Remarks before the American Road Builders Association, March 6, 1961, Albert Gore Senate Papers, Gore Research Center, Albert Gore Sr., *Let the Glory Out: My South and Its Politics* (New York: Viking, 1972), 221–229. Albert Gore to John F. Kennedy, November 22, 1960, John Kenneth Galbraith to Albert Gore, November 30, 1960, Albert Gore and Paul Douglas to Galbraith, August 15, 1963, Galbraith to Gore, January 14, 1964, Series 3 General Correspondence, 1932–2006, Box 32m, Folder G—General 12/1/63–1/31/1964, Personal Papers of John Kenneth Galbraith, John F. Kennedy Library, Boston, Mass.

11. Lawrence O'Brien Memo to President, September 24, 1964, White House Central File Name File, Lyndon Baines Johnson Library, Austin, Tex. Albert Gore to Mrs. Alex Shell, September 11, 1964, C15, Capitol Commentary July 12, 1965 C44. Gore Senate Papers. Gore, *Let the Glory Out*, 177–182.

12. Albert Gore Oral History Interviews John F. Kennedy Library and Southern Historical Collection, Chapel Hill, N.C. John Kenneth Galbraith, *A Life in Our Times: Memoirs* (London: Deutsch, 1981), 144. John Kenneth Galbraith *Name-dropping: From FDR On* (New York: Houghton Mifflin, 1999). Katherine Graham, *A Personal History* (New York: Knopf, 1997).

13. Nick Bryant has very effectively shown how, because of Kennedy's caution on civil rights, which was designed to allow southerners to support his domestic social programs, he also failed to achieve his economic priorities. Most southern senators saw no reason to respond positively. They accepted the concessions on civil rights but continued to vote conservatively on economic issues. See Bryant, *The Bystander: John F. Kennedy and the Struggle for Black Equality* (New York: Basic Books, 2006). Liberals like Hill and Sparkman believed that their own constituency pressures also dictated a rightward shift in votes on economic and social issues.

14. Don Oberdorfer interview with the author, September 17, 2007.

15. Interview with Jack Robinson Sr., January 23, 2003. Interview with David Halberstam, December 12, 2006. I have written on Gore's early attitude to civil rights in "'No shining knight': Albert Gore Sr., White Moderation and Black Activism in Tennessee, 1938–1956," copy in the author's possession.

16. John Seigenthaler interview with the author, February 27, 2003. James Sasser interview with the author, December 10, 2003.

17. Jack Robinson Sr. interview with the author, January 26, 2003. Jim Wright interview with the author, November 18, 1996. Dante Fascell interview with the author February 27, 1997. Tony Badger, "Southerners Who Refused to Sign the Southern Manifesto," in *New Deal/New South: An Anthony J. Badger Reader* (Fayetteville: University of Arkansas Press, 2007), 87.

18. Albert Gore to Larry McHee, March 16, 1965, to Mrs. Curtis E. Fort, March 24, 1965, to Mary Walton Collier, March 12, 1965, C 17 Legis. J. R. Philyaw to Gore, April 16, 1965, Mrs. H. R. Parotte to Gore, April 10, 1965, A47 Issue Mail, Gore Senate Papers. Tony Badger, "Albert Gore Sr. and Civil Rights." Paper at the Gore Research Center, November 8, 1997.

19. Badger, "Albert Gore Sr. and Civil Rights."

20. David Halberstam, "The End of a Populist," *Harpers* (February 1971). Robinson interview. Gore, *Let the Glory Out*, 276.

21. Gore, *Let the Glory Out*, 211. Memphis *Press-Scimitar*, August 20, 1968. *Tennessean*, August 29, September 1, 1968. Seigenthaler interview. George Barrett interview with the author, January 10, 2006. Buford Ellington interview, Oral History Interviews, Lyndon B. Johnson Library. The Tennessee Democratic party organizational difficulties also reflect Lyndon Johnson's lack of interest in party political organization, Lewis Gould, "Never a Deep Partisan: Lyndon Johnson and the Democratic Party, 1963–69," in Robert Divine, ed., *The Johnson Years: LBJ at Home and Abroad* (Lawrence: University of Kansas Press, 1994), 21–52.

22. Howard H. Baker Jr. interview with the author, April 2008.

23. Gore, *Let the Glory Out*, 214. Interview with Al Gore, April 9, 2005. Interview with Jim Sasser, December 10, 2003.

24. Jack Robinson, interview with the author, January 23, 2003. Gore, *Let the Glory Out*, 247. Seigenthaler interview with the author, February 27, 2003, Gilbert Merritt interview with the author, February 24, 2003. Numan V. Bartley and Hugh Davis Graham, *Southern Politics and the Second Reconstruction* (Baltimore: Johns Hopkins University Press, 1975), 153–154.

25. Hudley Crockett interviews with the author, July 2004, November 2006.

26. Crockett 2004 interview. *Tennessean*, August 9, 1970. *Memphis Commercial Appeal*, July 12, 1970, *Chattanooga News*, August 9, 1970. *New York Times*, August 10, 1970.

27. Harry Dent Memo to John Erlichman, July 15, 1969, White House Series, Box 1, File 20; Harry Dent Memos; Tennessee Politics, November–December 1969; White House Series, Box 3, File 93, Papers of Harry S. Dent, Special Collections, Clemson University.

28. Interview with William E. Brock 1979, Former Members of Congress Inc. Oral History Collection, Manuscript Division, Library of Congress, Washington D.C. William E. Brock, interview with author, December 5, 2006. Interviews with William E.

Brock, William C. Cater, and William L. Carter, Southern Oral History Project, Southern Historical Collection, Chapel Hill. Jack Bass and William DeVries, *The Transformation of Southern Politics: Social Change and Political Consequence since 1945* (New York: Basic Books, 1976), 292–295. Press Releases and clippings, Box 12, Brock Papers.

29. William E. Brock interview with the author, December 5, 2006.

30. Interview with William E. Brock, 1979 Former Members of Congress Inc. Oral History Collection. Interviews with William E. Brock, William C. Cater, and William L. Carter, Southern Oral History Project, Southern Historical Collection, Chapel Hill. Jack Bass and William DeVries, *The Transformation of Southern Politics*, 292–295. Press Releases and clippings, Box 12, Papers of William E. Brock, Special Collections, University of Tennessee, Knoxville. Brock 2006 interview.

31. Brock 2006 interview, Jim Allison to Harry Dent, October 9, 1969, John Stuckey to Bill Brock, nd, Box 31, Brock Papers. Brock was unexpectedly challenged in the Republican primary by the erudite country singer, Tex Ritter, who was encouraged to run by friends of Howard Baker. But, as with Roy Acuff in 1948, more Tennesseans flocked to campaign rallies featuring a galaxy of country stars than were prepared to vote for Ritter.

32. Polls and Strategy, Box 14, Kenneth Rietz to staff, November 24, 1969, Box 31, Brock Papers. Al Gore 2005 interview. A complete set of Brock TV commercials is held at the Julian P. Kanter Political Commercials Archive, University of Oklahoma, Norman, Okla.

33. *Tennessean*, April 5, 1970.

34. The Gore ads are in the Julian P. Kanter collection. "Electronic Politics: The Image Game," *Time*, September 21, 1970.

35. Brock 2006 interview. Norman Ferris interview with the author, April 2004. Gene Graham, "Gore's Lost Cause," *New South* (1971): 26–34.

36. Ferris interview. David S. Broder interview with the author, April 6, 2006.

37. J. Lee Annis Jr., *Howard Baker: Conciliator in an Age of Crisis* (New York: Madison Books, 1995), 55–56. *Nashville Banner*, October 19 and 22, 1970.

38. Al Gore interview with the author, March 20, 2007. Karenna Gore-Schiff interview with the author, December 11, 2006.

39. David Halberstam, "The End of a Populist." Halberstam 2006 interview. Graham, "Gore's Lost Cause." C. Vann Woodward to Willie Morris, January 11, 1971, Papers of C. Vann Woodward, Special Collections, Yale University. (I am grateful to Michael O'Brien for drawing this letter to my attention.)

40. Randy Sanders, *Mighty Peculiar Elections: The New South Gubernatorial Campaigns of 1970 and the Changing Politics of Race* (Gainesville: University of Florida Press, 2002), 1–10. White House Special Files: Staff Member and Office Files: John D. Erlichman, Alphabetical Subject Files, 1963–1973, Box 23, 1970, Postelection analysis, Nixon Presidential Materials Project.

41. File 125 Scrap/fragment in Martha Ragland's hand, Martha Ragland Papers, Schlesinger Library, Harvard University.

8

Forgotten Architects of the Second Reconstruction
Republicans and Civil Rights, 1945–1972

TIMOTHY N. THURBER

Historians of twentieth-century liberalism have written scores of books and articles on the politics and policy of the Democratic Party and its most prominent figures. A generation of scholars coming of age soon after World War II largely credited liberalism for notable achievements to make American society more just on behalf of previously marginalized groups. New Left scholars writing during and soon after the 1960s, (as well as some historians writing since then) tended to write off liberalism as little more than token reforms that upheld the existing social, political, and economic order. Wondering why America never adopted a social welfare state similar to what arose across Europe after the war, they tended to blame liberals' political timidity, their role in furthering the Cold War, or their insufficient understanding of problems such as race and poverty. More recently, a long overdue wave of scholarship on post-1945 conservatism directly or implicitly raises the question of whether liberalism ever had much influence at all. Each collection of scholars raises some trenchant criticisms and persuasive insights about the influence, or lack thereof, of postwar liberalism.

Though liberalism did not accomplish as much as its most ardent followers or admiring scholars believed, historians must not lose sight of liberalism's achievements and its staying power. Scholars typically identify the 1964 Civil Rights Act and the Voting Rights Act as seminal achievements of Lyndon Johnson's presidency and, more broadly, postwar liberalism. Democrats take center stage in the histories of these important policy developments, with Johnson and Senator Hubert Humphrey (Minn.) cast as leading proponents of reform and southerners such as Senator Richard Russell (Ga.) or Governor George Wallace (Ala.) appearing as the faces of opposition. In this essay I will explore how the Republican Party dealt with two of the core goals of the civil rights movement—economic equality and voting rights—between the 1940s and the early 1970s by looking at its approach to proposals to create (and then strengthen) the Equal Employment Opportunity Commission (EEOC) and the enactment and renewal of the Voting Rights Act. There was a broad wave of policy proposals and reforms from the 1940s to the 1970s in each of these areas. Looking at the history of the Republican Party's role in these policy battles helps explain the timing and content of liberal reform, because the GOP favored some approaches but staunchly rejected others. Liberal Democrats in Congress and the White House had to acknowledge the power of the GOP if they wanted to pass any reform at all. Republican influence was stronger than many at the time or since then have acknowledged. At the same time, looking at these battles reinforces historians Bruce Schulman and Julian Zelizer's point that the turn toward conservatism in the Republican Party and, more broadly, in American politics and culture since the 1960s "involved . . . crucial compromises in which the accomplishments of twentieth-century liberalism remained strong." During the 1960s and 1970s the GOP helped bring to fruition civil rights policy proposals that earlier generations of Republicans easily dismissed out of lack of interest or abiding commitments to a minimal or nonexistent role for the state in racial matters. By the 1970s, policies once considered by most Republicans to be too liberal, or even radical, had become widely accepted. Liberalism was indeed on the defensive politically by the late 1960s, but it retained enough strength among Republicans in Congress, especially in the Senate, and the Nixon administration so that important civil rights policies were preserved and even advanced. None of this is to suggest that liberal policies solved America's racial problems or that there was some steady, inevitable march of liberal triumphalism as the twentieth century advanced. Policy changes came in fits and starts and were dependent upon the confluence of numerous structural forces as well as contingency. Rather, it is to say that much of the popular, and some of the scholarly, talk about the death of liberalism, or its ineffectiveness, is exaggerated.[1]

Equal Employment Opportunity

As World War II ended, prominent civil rights groups, such as the National Association for the Advancement of Colored People (NAACP) and union leader A. Philip Randolph's March on Washington Movement, viewed a permanent Fair Employment Practices Commission (FEPC) as critical to their efforts to preserve hard-won economic gains made by African Americans during the conflict and build a broad social welfare state that would offer workers a measure of economic security. Under pressure from Randolph, President Franklin Roosevelt had created an FEPC in 1941 to ensure equal opportunity in wartime industries. Two years later, FDR broadened its scope to cover all firms and unions working on government contracts. The FEPC did not have enforcement powers, however. Known as a "voluntary" FEPC, the body could only investigate, advise, and educate on employment discrimination. In contrast, reformers wanted a "compulsory" agency, one that had its own enforcement powers. Indeed, the NAACP's Roy Wilkins had objected to a voluntary FEPC bill in 1945 by commenting that the existence of employment discrimination was "too obvious to require argument" and that even illiterate blacks knew that to rely only on persuasion to change employment practices "is of no avail." Wilkins and other civil rights proponents considered the federal government, despite its long and extensive history of neglect and discrimination regarding African Americans, to be a potential ally. Modeled after the National Labor Relations Board, a compulsory FEPC, reflected liberals' faith that government intervention in the marketplace to protect labor rights, rather than more substantial overhaul of basic economic structures, would lead to a more just and prosperous society. Reliance upon the private sector and state and local officials to change the racial status quo, liberals contended, had yielded far too little progress. Black income had jumped significantly in the early 1940s; yet as World War II, ended African American workers still suffered from widespread discrimination in hiring, firing, promotion, wages, working conditions, and union membership. The war, black migration to the North, the international situation, and heightened African American activism made race a more prominent political issue than in the past; where a politician stood on FEPC and other racial matters became a defining test for the degree of his/her liberalism.[2]

The NAACP and other prominent civil rights groups took a bipartisan approach to legislation, for they correctly posited that no civil rights bill could pass without considerable Republican support. Institutional procedures and rules, such as the Senate filibuster rule, as well as command of important committees in both houses of Congress, had enabled southern Democrats to thwart civil rights measures for decades. Southern Democrats had, moreover, allied with Republicans since the late 1930s to thwart social welfare legislation. Civil rights groups plowed forward anyway, hoping to change legislators' minds by appealing to morality, connecting civil rights reforms as essential to Cold War foreign policy, and claiming that winning the surging black vote in the North would provide the key to control of the White House and Congress.[3]

Most Republicans, however, staunchly opposed FEPC bills of any type, and as a result Congress did nothing in this area for nearly twenty years. They offered several core objections during the 1946 Senate FEPC debate that have remained, to varying degrees, part of Republican thinking about employment and race ever since. Proclaiming the racial innocence of their white constituents, some Republicans argued that job discrimination largely did not exist or had been greatly exaggerated by FEPC proponents. Such a stance ignored considerable evidence to the contrary, but it was sincerely held. Many Republicans, especially in the House of Representatives, came from small towns in the Midwest or West where few African Americans resided, and in the late 1940s direct action protests were negligible compared to what they would become twenty years later. Major national media outlets provided scant coverage to racial problems. Few Republicans, then, had much knowledge of racial conditions.[4]

Republicans also insisted that FEPC constituted a misguided attempt at social engineering. It would allegedly force white and black workers to work alongside one another before they were ready to do so. State action could not hasten social change, they insisted. Instead, education and time would bring transformation in individuals' hearts, and in turn that would change the racial status quo. Senator Albert Hawkes (N.J.) recalled that when he discovered that some black workers in his factory made ten cents an hour less than whites despite performing at the same level he met with supervisors to equalize pay rates. "That shows what can be done by education and being on the ground," he boasted. Most important, Republicans resented what they saw as another unconstitutional intrusion into property rights, especially regarding labor-management relations. They considered that relationship to be a harmonious, cross-class alliance that benefited each party. Federal interference, they worried, had already grown too extensive during the New Deal era. More federal meddling would bring greater conflict and rob corporate leaders of their freedom to hire and fire at will. Senator Eugene Millikin (Colo.), for example, condemned bigotry and defended the right of an employer "to give or withhold the use of his enterprise or his premises to those of another faith or race." Should FEPC become law the only way an employer could keep federal regulators at bay would be to engage in proportional hiring; yet this would, according to Republicans, foster racial animosity and turn white workers and managers into victims of unjust quotas. This approach would also supposedly undermine African Americans' work ethic, for they would be hired without having to prove their merit. To Republicans, the knowledge that one could not count on a job spurred ambition. They also insisted that FEPC was not needed because ambition would find ample reward in a nation where upward mobility was guaranteed for the industrious.[5]

FEPC legislation went nowhere in Congress during the 1940s and 1950s. Some Republicans at the state and local level helped FEPC proposals become law across the North and West, but here, too, the more important party legacy, as sociologist Anthony Chen has shown, was obstruction, delay, and softening of bills that did pass. Civil rights organizations worked throughout the 1950s for federal FEPC laws, too, but the legislative situation began to thaw only when the racial crisis escalated in 1963 and 1964. Direct action protests coupled with closer media attention brought the horrors of racial oppression in the South to greater public consciousness. Demonstrations in the North intensified as African Americans there grew angrier over the slow pace, or lack, of improvement in their lives. Politicians in both parties increasingly worried about social disorder and America's image abroad. Finally, by the 1960s racial attitudes among whites, including some politicians, were showing some signs of transformation. Jobs were on the reform agenda of African Americans in both the South and the North. This was evident not only in direct action protests in both regions, but also in the efforts of lobbyists such as the NAACP and others to add an FEPC provision to the civil rights legislation submitted by President John F. Kennedy in the summer of 1963. Worried about congressional opposition, Kennedy had left FEPC out of his proposal.[6]

By the following summer, the vast majority of Republicans in both houses of Congress had voted for a civil rights bill with an FEPC provision, now known as the Equal Employment Opportunity Commission (EEOC). Civil rights organizations worried that Kennedy, and then Lyndon Johnson, would bargain away FEPC or some other core part of the bill, as had been the case in 1957 and 1960, but what emerged in the end was legislation that has rightly been regarded as one of the most important, and influential, laws of the twentieth century. Republican votes were essential to passing any bill at all, but to get them the strongest supporters of civil rights in both parties had to accept compromises to the EEOC provisions (and other sections) that weakened the bill. Republican influence on the final product was considerable. On the one hand, Republicans in the House, led by William McCulloch (Oh.) joined northern Democrats to defeat several amendments from southern Democrats to remove or weaken the EEOC. At the same time, however, Republican concern over federal oversight of employers sparked a successful effort by McCulloch and others to remove compulsory FEPC provisions, which had been approved by a subcommittee of the Judiciary Committee, and replace them with language limiting the power of the attorney general to intervene in employment suits and basing enforcement in the courts. Republicans had helped defeat compulsory FEPC in the 1940s, and they did so again. The resulting bill was thus stronger than what Kennedy had originally proposed but weaker than what many liberal groups hoped for. Some Republicans found even these milder employment provisions worrisome, prompting McCulluch and other GOP leaders to reassure them that the bill would not force employers to hire anyone on the basis of race to correct "imbalance" in their workforces and that the presence of state or local employment laws would obviate the need for federal interference. The section of the bill outlawing segregation in public accommodations was aimed squarely at Dixie, but Republicans believed the employment section was, too. The compromise on employment (as well as a few other areas) proved sufficient to rally enough Republican votes for the bill itself to ensure enactment in February 1964. Roughly 80 percent of House Republicans voted to pass the measure.[7]

Senate Republicans also backed the bill. Minority Leader Everett Dirksen (Ill.) further weakened the EEOC section (Title VII) by securing changes that limited the federal role in enforcement. Whereas the House-passed bill would have allowed the EEOC to file lawsuits on behalf of individuals, the final measure gave that right to the attorney general. Even then, the attorney general could sue only after state and local remedies had been exhausted and where a "pattern or practice" of discrimination existed. Dirksen's changes meant that individuals, not groups like the NAACP or the federal government, would file most employment suits. They also set a high legal threshold by requiring proof of intent to discriminate. Civil rights organizations rightly noted that these and other provisions would make challenging employment discrimination a long and arduous road for most victims. Republicans who opposed the law, meanwhile, revived arguments made in the 1940s as they inveighed against quotas and feared federal bureaucrats harassing honorable business owners. Senator Barry Goldwater (Ariz.), denounced the bill as an ominous federal power grab over social and economic life, but the politics of civil rights had shifted significantly over two decades. Public opinion was firmly behind the bill. Those who argued that the federal government had no role to play on employment matters, or that time and education would be sufficient to solve the problem of discrimination, were now on the defensive. The direct action protests of 1963 in the North and the South, and firm commitment to a strong bill from President Johnson and northern Democrats, had helped change the situation on Capitol Hill. Republican senators from midwestern and western states, who previously voted against civil rights legislation without facing political repercussions back home, were now being lobbied by religious groups and others who had been galvanized into action by media reports of white southern violence against peaceful demonstrators. All but six Republican senators allied with northern Democrats to break the southern Democrats' filibuster and then to pass the bill. The climate of protest, coupled with the determination and better organization of Johnson and civil rights advocates in Congress, made some sort of civil rights bill likely. Republicans' best bet was to vote for the measure but limit the reach of the EEOC, which they did. Nevertheless, the inclusion and survival of Title VII, even its weakened form, signaled an important shift toward liberal ideas and policy that was impossible in the 1940s. Employers would henceforth have to contend with federal authority in a way they had not before; even the presence of the EEOC sparked changes in corporate employment practices independent of direct federal intervention.[8]

Civil rights activists in the NAACP and other organizations wasted little time in seeking to augment the enforcement power of the EEOC. They hoped to shift enforcement authority from the courts to the EEOC itself, also known as "cease and desist." This was essentially the same as a compulsory FEPC. Many state and federal regulatory agencies had such powers. Reformers also sought to expand its investigatory capabilities, broaden coverage to employees not included in the original law, and give it authority to order employee training programs. Republican Senator Jacob Javits (N.Y.) and a few other Republicans from the Northeast worked closely with civil rights groups, President Johnson, and liberal Democrats in Congress on these matters, but their proposals found few allies. As civil rights demonstrators over matters such as housing, poverty, and school integration in the North became more vocal, numerous, and sometimes violent, public and politicians' support for any type of civil rights legislation waned. White Americans increasingly felt that integration was proceeding too fast. Civil rights leaders' talk about special outreach efforts to African Americans, or some other type of compensatory policies regarding employment, had also bestirred intense white opposition. A bill to grant cease and desist and other powers to the EEOC passed the House in 1966 with 75 percent of Republicans backing it, but the measure died in the Senate. Repeated efforts for cease and desist and expanded coverage stalled in each house of Congress each of the remaining years of Lyndon Johnson's presidency. Instead of expanding the EEOC, Dirksen led a fight against it. Claiming that the agency had been "harassing employers," the Illinois Republican was instrumental in persuading President Richard Nixon to oust EEOC Chairman Clifford Alexander in 1969.[9]

The logjam broke during Nixon's first term. Civil rights groups and their congressional allies continued to press for cease and desist, while staunch conservatives, encouraged by many business groups, opposed any change to Title VII whatsoever. The Nixon administration crafted a bill that fell between these two poles; the White House plan sought to empower the EEOC to file pattern or practice lawsuits directly but would keep enforcement in the courts. The Senate passed a bill in the fall of 1970 to give the EEOC cease and desist authority, broaden coverage of Title VII to include employees of firms or unions with eight workers or more (down from twenty-five workers), state and local government employees, and workers at educational institutions. Twenty-one Republicans voted for this bill, with just eleven opposed. The support of several liberal Republicans, such as Edward Brooke (Mass.), Clifford Case (N.J.), and Robert Packwood (Ore.), among others, was essential in passing the bill but also in defeating attempts by North Carolina Democrat Sam Ervin to strip the provisions extending coverage to government and education workers. The bill met its demise in the House, however, as William Colmer, a Democrat from Mississippi and head of the Rules Committee, worked with allies in both parties as well as labor unions to run out the legislative clock. The House narrowly passed the Nixon plan in the fall of 1971. Early the following year the Senate plunged into a vigorous debate over reforming the EEOC. Liberal Republicans sided with liberal Democrats initially to defeat the administration's bill, but failure to invoke cloture against a filibuster by southern Democrats opposed to cease and desist meant that this coalition had to accept the White House's more moderate plan for court enforcement. Business leaders, administration officials privately noted, were relieved at the White House's successful efforts to torpedo cease and desist. Court enforcement would ensure a long backlog of cases in the years to come. Nevertheless, this was far from a complete victory for conservatives as reformers correctly saw this as a substantial improvement over the status quo. Title VII was broadened to include millions of employees of state and local governments and educational institutions, as well as workers at smaller firms. Once again liberal Republicans, including northeasterners such as Javits as well as northwesterners such as Robert Packwood (Ore.), provided critical margins in turning back efforts by Ervin and other southern Democrats to prevent or limit federal protection in those cases. The House quickly concurred with the Senate bill, and in March Nixon signed the Equal Employment Opportunity Act of 1972. As in 1964, civil rights groups fell short of their goals thanks in part to Republican opposition, but the GOP had once again helped them achieve some of their aims. Employers still wielded substantial advantages in legal conflicts over job discrimination, but the landscape had nonetheless changed significantly since the 1940s.[10]

Voting Rights

Civil rights activists simultaneously fought for equality on several fronts. Their agenda included access to better jobs and equal treatment in the workplace, but they also demanded full citizenship. Freedom had a political dimension, as reformers put great faith in the power of the ballot to produce better lives for African Americans. Blacks knew all too well that the ability to make the rules under which society operated carried enormous potential for opportunity or oppression. Political inequality was most pronounced in the South, where whites had, since the late 1800s, used violence, threats of violence, economic intimidation, and a wide variety of legal schemes to lock African Americans out of the democratic process. The number of black voters in Dixie had risen by the end of World War II, but the overall totals masked grossly uneven patterns across the region. Black registration had climbed in the Upper South and border states, but in Mississippi and other parts of the Deep South it remained minuscule.

In the 1940s, prominent organizations such as the NAACP centered their legislative efforts on removing the poll tax. The poll tax had never been the main obstacle to black political participation and a few states had abolished it since the 1920s, but civil rights and labor reformers nonetheless urged federal action as part of their drive to broaden the electorate. Ensuring black voting rights was not simply a moral imperative; reformers considered it an essential step toward expanding education and other social welfare provisions in the South and reforming the region's oppressive penal system. White supremacists defended the status quo by pointing to constitutional provisions empowering states to set election laws. As with FEPC, the fight centered on how prominent a role the federal government would play. In 1941, reformers created the National Committee to Abolish the Poll Tax, an umbrella organization consisting of civil rights, labor, religious, and other groups. The key question was what type of federal action would be pursued. In their 1944 platform, Republicans had endorsed a constitutional amendment to abolish the poll tax. This stand, however, put the GOP at odds with the NAACP, which viewed legislation as a quicker, more efficient means to bring change. It also put the GOP in agreement with some southern Democrats who favored this approach as a way to delay or avoid deeper changes to electoral laws in the region. Other southern Democrats firmly opposed any change whatsoever out of fear that any reform, no matter how mild, would open the door to more significant transformations.[11]

As with FEPC, prospects for voting rights reform were nonexistent without Republican assistance. The House passed anti–poll tax bills three times between 1941 and 1945. In each case, Republicans lined up overwhelmingly behind the legislation. The poll tax was not nearly as controversial as FEPC. Whereas the Constitution contained no explicit reference to employment matters, it did clearly forbid discrimination in voting. Republicans were more likely to favor the federal government taking a more prominent role in protecting the freedom to vote than in protecting the right of workers to be free from discrimination. Indeed, favoring voting rights over economic reforms in the South had been the Party's stance since Reconstruction. The poll tax affected only the South, moreover, and thus Republicans could support repeal without risking backlash from northern voters or various interest groups. Southern Democrats successfully filibustered anti–poll tax legislation to death in the Senate in 1942 and 1944. Perhaps with an eye on the upcoming midterm elections, Senate leaders brought up an anti–poll tax bill late in July 1946. President Harry Truman, however, had no desire to fight over civil rights, and, with the end of the session nearing, neither did Republicans. Another southern filibuster succeeded as cloture went down to defeat 39–33. Fifteen Republicans voted to shut off the talkathon; six opposed. More important, sixteen Republicans did not vote. NAACP chief Walter White noted that this poor showing meant that Republicans could not, as they had in the past, blame Democrats for lack of a bill. An irate Wayne Morse, a Republican from Oregon and one of the staunchest supporters of civil rights in the Senate, described the whole affair as "a farce." Anti–poll tax legislation remained stuck throughout the remainder of Truman's presidency.[12]

Republicans moved in a slightly more progressive direction regarding voting rights under Dwight Eisenhower. The former general had no interest in civil rights legislation of any sort during most of his first term. Like many Republicans, Eisenhower placed great faith in the power of education and time to erode racial hatred. He harbored grave doubts about the efficacy of law as an instrument of reform and had considerable sympathy for southern whites as they wrestled with the implications of ending legal school segregation in the wake of the Supreme Court's 1954 decision in *Brown v. Board of Education*. By 1956 the terrain had shifted, however. African American groups were becoming more vocal and better organized, and increasing numbers of African Americans in the South were filing lawsuits to bring about school integration and trying to register to vote. Tensions across Dixie were escalating as whites struggled fiercely to maintain the status quo. Thanks in part to prodding by Attorney General Herbert Brownell, a strong believer in civil rights, the president had become more worried about social chaos in the region escalating to the point where he would have to use federal troops to preserve order and enforce the law. That prospect deeply disturbed Eisenhower. The president was also sincerely troubled by reports of how whites were denying qualified African Americans the franchise. He, too, was becoming better educated about how race operated in Dixie. In 1956 Eisenhower proposed a legislative package that he hoped would bring peace and measured progress to the South by offering expanded federal protection for African American voting rights. Though the overall number of African American voters in the South continued to climb, registration was actually falling in several Deep South states.[13]

The bill failed, but it became law a year later as congressional Republicans, influenced by Eisenhower's commitment to the voting provisions in his bill as well as the (apparently) sharp increase in black support for the president in the 1956 election, voted overwhelmingly to pass the first civil rights law in more than eighty years. As usual, the chief battleground was the Senate. On several key procedural votes Senate Republicans sided with pro–civil rights Democrats to move the bill forward. However, when controversy erupted over how the bill would enable the federal government to enforce school integration (Title III), much of the initial Republican desire to back all of the president's plan evaporated. Even Eisenhower publicly waffled about his intentions. Eighteen Republicans voted to eliminate Title III; many, including the president, argued that what they really wanted to do was protect voting rights. Even here, however, the Party's commitment was less than firm. A small group of twelve Republicans, most of whom were from midwestern states with few African American residents, played a critical role in helping Democrats, some southern and others not from the South, add a jury trial amendment that weakened enforcement of voting and other civil rights. The jury fight, however, demonstrated how Republican views on voting rights protections had developed since the 1940s. A majority of Republicans denounced the amendment and rightly viewed its inclusion as a serious setback. One administration aide described Eisenhower as angrier than at any other time of his presidency. Eisenhower told his Cabinet on August 2 that the jury vote was one of the most serious losses of his presidency and that there was "not much forgiveness in [his] soul" for those who supported the amendment. Nixon testily told reporters that the addition of the amendment was "a vote against the right to vote." Just as civil rights leaders had predicted, the bill led to few new registered voters. Nevertheless, that any legislation passed signaled that the politics of civil rights had shifted. Heightened black assertiveness and closer media scrutiny weakened southern Democrats' claims that election matters were best left to the states. Republicans had now shown that they would, under certain conditions, abandon their longstanding alliance with southern Democrats and vote for increased federal oversight of electoral practices. Southern Democrats knew that though they remained strong their hand had grown weaker since the 1940s. This was evident in their decision not to filibuster, lest deployment of that traditionally effective weapon stir public anger as well as drive Republicans further into alliance with pro–civil rights Democrats, with the result being a stronger federal intervention in Dixie.[14]

Meaningful progress in securing franchise rights for southern African Americans did not occur for another eight years. Eisenhower and Republicans in Congress backed a voting bill in 1960, but this too was largely ineffective. A few liberal Republicans tried to ally with pro–civil rights Democrats in the early 1960s to remedy the ongoing problems, but President Kennedy and most members of Congress in both parties showed little interest in fighting for a strong bill. Javits and other pro–civil rights Republicans on Capitol Hill regularly blasted Kennedy for failing to address this problem. In 1961, for example, Javits echoed the complaints of King and other civil rights leaders when he accused the president of waging a "campaign of appeasement" toward the South and displaying a "striking dereliction of responsibility" on civil rights. Senator Kenneth Keating (N.Y.) similarly commented, "I am filled with wonder as to how so many who criticized President Eisenhower for not going far enough in this field can sit by silently accepting every excuse for this administration's glaring failure to move forward one inch toward the goal of fair treatment for all Americans." Meanwhile, African Americans' direct action protests were expanding across the South; jails were filling with individuals who were determined to resist Jim Crow laws and other forms of white supremacy. Media scrutiny of southern resistance intensified. U.S. Cold War propaganda efforts regarding the virtues of democracy looked increasingly hypocritical, and the Soviet Union seized upon racial oppression to try to woo non-Caucasian allies around the globe.[15]

By 1965, President Lyndon Johnson was ready to advance a far more sweeping voting rights proposal. Black voter registration had continued to climb in the South overall, but much of that progress occurred in urban areas and the Upper South. Little had changed in rural locales; registration remained abysmally low in the Deep South. Only about 7 percent of eligible African Americans in Mississippi were registered in 1964. Blacks in the Magnolia State and other parts of the South were subject to economic reprisals, capricious enforcement of ostensibly "race neutral" literacy tests, and violence when they tried to register. In drafting his bill, the president met with Dirksen and other Senate Republicans. Johnson unveiled a tough new voting bill in March in the wake of brutal violence directed at peaceful demonstrators in Selma, Alabama. Selma epitomized the problem—African Americans comprised 57 percent of the town's population, but just 2 percent were registered. Johnson's bill greatly expanded federal power over elections, mostly in the Deep South, by containing an automatic trigger formula that suspended literacy tests and allowed for registration of voters supervised by federal officials in areas with low black registration. Six southern states, as well as dozens of counties in North Carolina, were most directly affected. Dirksen had lobbied for judicial oversight rather than this type of administrative approach, but the White House held firm. Moreover, the areas where the bill applied had to request approval from federal authorities before changing any of their voting laws; this was known as *preclearance*. The most important element here was that Johnson's plan took the burden of securing voting rights off the shoulders of individuals and empowered the executive branch, in particular the Justice Department, to boost black registration; the 1957 and 1960 laws had required individuals to go to court, a lengthy and cumbersome process that had clearly failed.[16]

To be sure, a few hard-core conservatives, such as Barry Goldwater, claimed that existing laws were sufficient and often sided with southern Democrats, but the vast majority of Republicans in both houses voted for the president's bill. That southern Democrats could not count on their traditional allies across the aisle was evident on March 18, when the Senate voted 67–13 to send the administration's proposal to the Judiciary Committee with instructions that the Committee report it back by early April. Twenty-five Republicans backed this move; just two opposed. Southern Democrats, who had used control of the Committee to crush civil rights bills for decades, were outraged but powerless. Dirksen replied that the South had spent long enough "trying to catch up with the Fifteenth Amendment." Similarly, Republicans voted 22–8 to defeat an amendment from North Carolina Democrat Sam Ervin that would have deleted the automatic trigger formula and allowed for the appointment of federal examiners only after a *local* federal court, as opposed to the federal bench in the District of Columbia (typically a more liberal court) had ruled that discrimination existed. A few Republicans criticized the White House plan as too weak, for it did not address low levels of African American registration in parts of several southern states that did not use literacy tests (including Johnson's home of Texas). They offered an alternative model that based the automatic trigger on different data, but this effort failed to gain traction, especially with Democrats who remained loyal to the president. House Republicans, typically more conservative than those in the Senate, initially rallied to an alternative bill, crafted by McCulloch and GOP leader Gerald Ford (Mich.) that rejected any trigger formula whatsoever. These Republicans argued that the trigger represented an assumption of guilt without firm evidence of discrimination. This, too, stalled quickly. Javits and a few liberal Republicans joined Edward Kennedy (Mass.) and other liberal Democrats to push for inclusion of a ban on the poll tax, but this failed over doubts about its constitutionality. Dirksen was able to secure language that once again directed the bill at the South; he led a successful effort to permit a state with a literacy test and low voter turnout to escape the automatic trigger if less than 20 percent of its voting age population were nonwhite. Southern Republicans appealed to GOP lawmakers and Party officials across the nation to oppose a bill that would, according to Mississippi GOP chief Wirt Yeager Jr., "be harmful to the growing Republican Party in the South." Republicans firmly supported cloture against the southern Democrats' filibuster and the bill itself. House Republicans tried to revive their plan that summer, but it became unpalatable to a critical group of northern GOP lawmakers when a southern Democrat endorsed it. The House essentially went along with the strong Senate bill. The Voting Rights Act, which the Leadership Conference on Civil Rights described as "altogether a superior piece of legislation," constituted a bold, far-reaching federal effort to make the franchise a reality for millions of southern African Americans. Black registration in many parts of the Deep South rose substantially soon thereafter; by 1967, nearly 60 percent of African Americans in Mississippi were registered.[17]

The rapid and substantial success of the Voting Rights Act led southern Democrats, as well as some Nixon administration officials such as Attorney General John Mitchell, to argue that the law was no longer needed when it came up for renewal in 1970. If outright repeal failed, their fallback position was to try to curtail enforcement mechanisms. Civil rights organizations favored a five-year extension with no changes; they welcomed the progress that had indeed occurred but remained adamant about maintaining federal protections. The preclearance provisions drew the most anger and fire from white southerners, who typically pointed to rising levels of black registration as evidence that discrimination was a thing of the past. Preclearance, they also claimed, unfairly presumed guilt and singled out the South when voting abuses occurred nationwide. Southern Democrats allied with the Nixon administration on proposals to ban literacy tests nationwide, eliminate preclearance, shift the burden of proof in voting cases from states and localities to the federal government, and move jurisdiction out of the liberal District of Columbia federal court. Speaking for the Nixon administration proposal, House Republican leader Gerald Ford called the Voting Rights Act "discriminatory in spirit and in practice," and maintained that reform was needed because four "eventful" years had occurred.[18]

Once again, however, Republicans, especially those in the Senate, played a critical role in fending off the alliance of the administration and southern Democrats. The outcome of this fight was far from certain and showed sharp divisions within the GOP. Many northern Republicans in the House denounced the Nixon plan as a retreat from what they had voted for in 1965. William McCulloch commented, "The administration creates a remedy for which there is no wrong and leaves general wrongs without adequate remedy." Strong White House pressure on Republicans nevertheless helped the administration's bill narrowly pass the House. The Senate then exerted its customarily moderating influence. There, Sam Ervin led southern Democrats in a tenacious battle for amendments to end preclearance, shift the burden of proof to the federal government, and move legal proceedings to local federal courts. Ervin also sponsored an amendment to change the date by which the trigger formula was calculated from 1964 to 1968; because many black voters had been registered during that time, the effect of such a plan would have left only Georgia and South Carolina under the trigger provision. Another Ervin plan would have enabled any state that had abolished a literacy test after 1964 to escape coverage of the Voting Rights altogether. Similarly, James Allen of Alabama sought to have the preclearance and automatic trigger parts of the bill expire in 1975. (By then, it had become clear that the surge in black voters in the South, nearly all of whom voted Democratic, had, as Wirt Yeager Jr. had feared in 1965, helped block the growth of the GOP across Dixie as southern whites continued to vote for Democratic incumbents in congressional and state and local races. The South would not become solidly Republican at those levels until the 1990s, when whites largely abandoned the Democrats.) The Senate, with Republican Hugh Scott (Pa.) taking a prominent role, overwhelmingly voted down each of these proposals. Republicans did not help the southern Democrats on procedural matters, and they did not vote with them on the amendments or the legislation itself. The Senate easily adopted a bill that extended the Voting Rights Act for five years, maintained the 1965 law's provisions that affected the South, lowered the voting age to eighteen, and broadened coverage to other parts of the nation. House Republicans attempted to resist the stronger Senate bill, but their efforts failed and the House easily passed the Senate version. Nixon reluctantly signed it over objections from his attorney general and chief political aides. The president informed John Ehrlichman that he saw no political gains regarding youth or African Americans, but he confessed that he had some "obligation not to have the god damn country blow up."[19]

These were uplifting times for civil rights organizations. Though the NAACP and other groups rightly worried about some of Nixon's civil rights policies and rhetoric, they had recently worked with a bipartisan coalition in the Senate to defeat the president's nominations of conservatives Clement Haynsworth and Harold Carswell to the Supreme Court, and now they had secured renewal of one of the most important laws of the twentieth century. In contrast, a frustrated Strom Thurmond wrote Nixon reminding him of a meeting in 1968 when, as a candidate for the GOP nomination, Nixon had gathered with southern leaders in Atlanta and affirmed his opposition to legislation that singled out the region. Some of those in attendance, Thurmond noted, were now calling him wondering what had gone wrong. A bewildered Thurmond wanted to know what to tell them.[20]

Thurmond's reaction suggests that the history of civil rights policy since World War II contains many surprising twists and turns. Important changes came to the South (and to the North), changes that Republicans had shaped to a considerable extent. At times they helped obstruct, but at other times they helped enact and preserve. Their beliefs about race, the role of the state, and their political calculations shaped the content of liberal policy reforms, often in ways that limited the reach of the federal government into racial affairs. For much of the 1940s and 1950s, most Republicans in Congress sided with southern Democrats or demonstrated indifference to racial equality. Opposition to federal policies to advance or protect African Americans' rights and interests did not suddenly materialize in the late 1960s. By the 1960s and early 1970s, however, Republicans, especially in the Senate, were playing critical roles in achieving and then securing notable policy victories. Large numbers of Republicans eventually backed policy proposals that would have been anathema to nearly every GOP lawmaker in the 1940s. Motivated by foreign policy concerns, a desire for black votes, and sincere commitment to a stronger federal role in racial matters, a pro–civil rights Republican bloc of senators from the Northeast, Midwest, and Northwest remained influential into the mid-1970s.

That policy history would have long-term implications not only for policy but also for politics. Though the nomination of Barry Goldwater as the GOP presidential nominee in 1964 was indeed a substantial victory for conservatives, their gains were far from complete in the Party and the nation. Many of those who initially opposed the 1964 Civil Rights Act when it was being debated, such as George H. W. Bush, later reversed their stance in part due to changed convictions but also due to the undeniable political reality that holding to their original views would be politically suicidal. Goldwater was a conservative because he opposed the 1964 Civil Rights Act, especially Title VII and provisions to outlaw Jim Crow laws in public places. A generation later, few if any of the conservatives who dominate the GOP openly take such a position. On the contrary, they try to prove their racial bona fides by repeatedly noting that a higher percentage of Republicans than Democrats voted for the 1964 Civil Rights Act. Some conservative Republicans continue to denounce federal interference in southern voting rights laws more than three decades after the enactment of the Voting Rights Act, but they have long been on the losing end. As the historian Gareth Davies has argued, once they are enacted policies are difficult at best to uproot entirely. The history of liberalism and conservatism, then, is deeply intertwined. Republicans helped define liberalism, but liberalism would also alter the meaning of conservatism and in the process demonstrate its enduring strength.[21]

Notes

1. Bruce J. Schulman and Julian E. Zelizer, eds. *Rightward Bound: Making America Conservative in the 1970s* (Cambridge: Harvard University Press, 2008), 3–5.

2. Roy Wilkins to Robert Taft, March 29, 1945, Box 606, Robert Taft Papers, Library of Congress, Washington, D.C.; Statement of Roy Wilkins, March 14, 1945, Series II, Box A255, NAACP Papers, Library of Congress, Washington, D.C.; Paula Pfeffer, *A. Philip Randolph: Pioneer of the Civil Rights Movement* (Baton Rouge: Louisiana State University Press, 1990), 90–98; Risa Goluboff, *The Lost Promise of Civil Rights* (Cambridge: Harvard University Press, 2007), 18–22, 35–39, 81–100; Robert Norrell, *The House I Live In: Race in the American Century* (New York: Oxford University Press, 2005), 117–127; Ira Katznelson, *When Affirmative Action Was White: An Untold History of Racial Inequality in Twentieth-Century America* (New York: W. W. Norton, 2005); Desmond King, *Separate and Unequal: Black Americans and the U. S. Federal Government* (Oxford: Clarendon Press, 1995); Donna Hamilton and Charles Hamilton, *The Dual Agenda: The African American Struggle for Civil and Economic Equality*

(New York: Columbia University Press, 1997), 43–66; Kevin Schultz, "The FEPC and the Legacy of the Labor-Based Civil Rights Movement of the 1940s," *Labor History* 49 (February 2008): 71–92; Jacquelyn Hall, "The Long Civil Rights Movement and the Political Uses of the Past," *Journal of American History* 91 (March 2005): 1,233–1,252; Thomas Sugrue, *Sweet Land of Liberty: The Forgotten Struggle for Civil Rights in the North* (New York: Random House, 2008), 32–40; Rayford W. Logan, ed. *What the Negro Wants* (Notre Dame: University of Notre Dame Press, 2001), 124–125, 133–162.

3. Sugrue, *Sweet Land of Liberty*, 88–129. On the relationship between civil rights and foreign policy, see Thomas Borstelmann, *The Cold War and the Color Line: American Race Relations in the Global Arena* (Cambridge: Harvard University Press, 2001); Mary Dudziak, *Cold War, Civil Rights: Race and the Image of American Democracy* (Princeton: Princeton University Press, 2000).

4. *Congressional Record*, 79th Congress, 2nd Session, 1,130–1,131; Gene Roberts and Hank Klibanoff, *The Race Beat: The Press, the Civil Rights Struggle, and the Awakening of a Nation* (New York: Knopf, 2006), 3–11.

5. *Congressional Record*, 79th Congress, 2nd Session, 186, 496, 711–713, 1,037–1,038, 1,211–1,212, 1,239; Donald Critchlow, *The Conservative Ascendancy: How the GOP Right Made Political History* (Cambridge: Harvard University Press, 2007), 8–9.

6. Anthony Chen, "The Party of Lincoln and the Politics of State Fair Employment Practices Legislation in the North, 1945–1964," *American Journal of Sociology* 112 (May 2007): 1,713–1,774; Sugrue, *Sweet Land of Liberty*, 286–305; Jonathan Rosenberg and Zachary Karabell, *Kennedy, Johnson, and the Quest for Justice: The Civil Rights Tapes* (New York: Norton, 2003), 118–119, 130–133.

7. Herman Edelsberg and David Brody, "Civil Rights in the 88th Congress, 1st Session, nd, Box 11, Legislative Files, ADA Papers, Madison; David Filvaroff and Raymond E. Wolfinger, "The Origin and Enactment of the Civil Rights Act of 1964," in *Legacies of the 1964 Civil Rights Act*, ed. Bernard Grofman (Charlottesville: University of Virginia Press, 2000), 17–22; Anthony Chen, *The Fifth Freedom: Jobs, Politics, and Civil Rights in the United States, 1941–1972* (Princeton: Princeton University Press, 2009), 185–187; *Congressional Quarterly*, July 26, 1963; *Congressional Quarterly*, November 1, 1963; *Congressional Record*, 88th Congress, 2nd Session, 2,541–2,542.

8. Daniel B. Rodriguez and Barry R. Weingast, "The Positive Political Theory of Legislative History: New Perspectives on the 1964 Civil Right Act and Its Interpretation," *University of Pennsylvania Law Review* 151 (April 2003): 1,417–1,542; Memorandum of Reasons for Opposing the Civil Rights Bill, As Amended in the House, February 11, 1964, William Cramer Files, University of Tampa, Tampa, Fla.; *Congressional Quarterly*, February 14, 1964; Charles and Barbara Whalen, *The Longest Debate; A Legislative History of the 1964 Civil Rights Act* (Cabin John, Md.: Seven Locks Press, 1985), 122; Newsletter, February 19, 1964, Box 37, Committee Files, Charles Goodell Papers, New York City Public Library, New York, N.Y.; Analysis of the Civil Rights Bill, April 20, 1964, Box 43, William McCulloch Papers, Ohio Northern University, Ada, Ohio; The Civil Rights Bill—Some Observations by Senator Everett McKinley

Dirksen, February 26, 1964, Working Papers F.256, Everett Dirksen Center, Pekin, Ill.; James Finlay, "Religion and Politics in the Sixties: The Churches and the Civil Rights Act of 1964," *Journal of American History* 77 (June 1990): 66–92; Jennifer Delton, *Racial Integration in Corporate America* (Cambridge: Cambridge University Press, 2009), 194–224.

9. *Congressional Record*, 89th Congress, 2nd Session, 6,093–6,094; *Congressional Quarterly*, April 29, 1966; *Congressional Quarterly*, May 17, 1968; *1969 CQ Almanac*; Herbert Hill, "The Equal Employment Opportunity Acts of 1964 and 1972: A Critical Analysis of the Legislative History and Administration of the Law," *Industrial Relations Law Journal* 2 (Spring 1977): 75–76; The Afro-American Voter, March–April 1969, Box 38, William Workman Papers, University of South Carolina, Columbia, S.C.

10. *1970 CQ Almanac*; Leonard Garment to John Ehrlichman, January 16, 1971, Box 4, Leonard Garment Papers, Library of Congress, Washington, D.C.; Hugh Graham, *The Civil Rights Era: Origins and Development of National Policy, 1960–1972* (New York: Oxford University Press, 1990), 433–434; Peter Flanigan to David Parker, March 17, 1972, Box 17, White House Central Files, Ex HU 2-2, Richard Nixon Papers Project, National Archives and Records Administration, College Park, Md.; *1972 CQ Almanac*; Nina Moore, *Governing Race: Policy, Process, and the Politics of Race* (Westport, Conn,: Praeger, 2000), 105.

11. David J. Garrow, *Protest at Selma: Martin Luther King, Jr. and the Voting Rights Act of 1965* (New Haven: Yale University Press, 1985), 7–9; Steven Lawson, *Black Ballots: Voting Rights in the South, 1944–1969* (New York: Columbia University Press, 1976), 55–85; Manfred Berg, *The Ticket to Freedom: The NAACP and the Struggle for Black Political Integration* (Gainesville: University Press of Florida, 2005), 105; Glenda Gilmore, *Defying Dixie: The Radical Origins of Civil Rights, 1919–1950* (New York: Norton, 2008), 338–339; Norrell, *The House I Live In*, 116–119; John T. Elifff, "The United States Department of Justice and Individual Rights, 1937–1962," (PhD dissertation, Harvard University, 1967), 222; Frederic Odgen, *The Poll Tax in the South* (Tuscaloosa: University of Alabama Press, 1958), 57, 77, 176, 242–252; NAACP Press Release, April 1, 1946, Series II, Box A509, NAACP Papers; Finlay, 100–102.

12. Lawson, *Black Ballots*, 67–78; Senate Votes on Civil Rights, 1944–1946, Box 40, Stephen Spingarn Papers, Harry S. Truman Library, Independence, Mo.; *New York Times*, July 30, 1946; *New York Times*, August 1, 1946; Walter White newspaper column, October 31, 1946, Box 34, Roy Wilkins Papers, Library of Congress, Washington, D.C.

13. David Nichols, *A Matter of Justice: Eisenhower and the Beginning of the Civil Rights Revolution* (New York: Simon and Schuster, 2007), 115–134; Michael Klarman, *From Jim Crow to Civil Rights: The Supreme Court and the Struggle for Racial Equality* (New York: Oxford University Press, 2004), 392.

14. Nichols, *A Matter of Justice*, 143–168; *New York Times*, July 24, 1957; Gayle Montgomery and James Johnson, *One Step from the White House: The Rise and Fall of Senator William F. Knowland* (Berkeley: University of California Press, 1998), 213;

Washington Star, June 24, 1967; *Christian Science Monitor*, June 29, 1957; Roy Wilkins to C. B. Powell, August 22, 1957, Series III, Box A73, NAACP Papers; Robert Caro, *Master of the Senate: The Years of Lyndon Johnson, Volume III* (New York: Knopf, 2002), 912–920, 970–978; Notes of Legislative Leadership Meeting, 7-30-57, Box 2, Legislative Meeting Series, Ann Whitman File, Dwight D. Eisenhower Papers, Dwight D. Eisenhower Library (DDEL), Abilene, Kans.; *New York Times*, August 2, 1957; *New York Times*, August 3, 1957; Minutes of Cabinet Meeting, August 2, 1957, Box 26, Ann Whitman File, Dwight D. Eisenhower Diary Series, DDEL; *Congressional Quarterly*, May 6, 1960; Paul Douglas, "The 1960 Voting Rights Bill: The Struggle, The Final Results, and the Reasons," *Journal of Intergroup Relations* 1 (Summer 1960): 83.

15. Nichols, *A Matter of Justice*, 252–256; *Congressional Record*, 87th Congress, 1st Session, 855–856, 875; Press Release, April 10, 1961, Series II, Box 999, Kenneth Keating Papers, University of Rochester, Rochester, New York; Press Release, May 4, 1961, Series 9, Box 19, Keating Papers; Press Release, August 21, 1961, Series II, Box 471, Keating Papers.

16. Garrow, *Protest at Selma*, 19–30, 94–95; Graham, *The Civil Rights Era*, 165; Richard Vallely, *The Two Reconstructions: The Struggle for Black Enfranchisement* (Chicago: University of Chicago Press, 2004), 188–189; *New York Times*, February 24, 1965; Jacob Javits et al. to Nicholas Katzenbach, February 26, 1965, Box 102, Hugh Scott Papers, University of Virginia, Charlottesville, Va.; *Congressional Quarterly*, March 19, 1965; *New York Times*, March 12, 1965.

17. *New York Times*, March 10, 1965; *New York Times*, March 18, 1965; *Congressional Quarterly*, March 19, 1965; *Congressional Quarterly*, March 26, 1965; *New York Times*, March 25, 1965; *Congressional Quarterly*, April 9, 1965; Joint Statement by Gerald Ford and William McCulloch, April 5, 1965, Series 4.1, Box 2, Charles McC. Mathias Papers, Johns Hopkins University, Baltimore, Md.; *New York Times*, April 18, 1965; Wirt Yeager Jr. to Walter Wittoff, April 16, 1965, Charlton Lyons to Everett Dirksen, March 31, 1965, both in Box 26, Raymond Bliss Papers, Ohio Historical Society, Columbus, Ohio; *Congressional Quarterly*, May 14, 1965; *Congressional Quarterly*, May 28, 1965; *Congressional Quarterly*, July 9, 1965; *Roanoke Times*, July 9, 1965; *Congressional Quarterly*, August 6, 1965; Chandler Davidson, "The Voting Rights Act: A Brief History," in *Controversies in Minority Voting: The Voting Rights Act in Perspective*, eds. Bernard Grofman and Chandler Davidson (Washington, D.C.: Brookings Institution, 1992), 21. The two Republicans who voted against the move to send the bill to the Judiciary Committee with instructions to report it back soon were Strom Thurmond (S.C.) and Margaret Chase Smith (Me.). Smith had supported civil rights proposals in the past, so her vote was likely due to procedural concerns or some other matter not related to the substance of the bill. Thurmond, of course, had long opposed civil rights legislation.

18. Abigail Thernstrom, *Whose Votes Count? Affirmative Action and Minority Voting Rights* (Cambridge: Harvard University Press, 1987), 30–33; Press Release, no date, Box 105, Robert Hartmann Files, Gerald R. Ford Library, Ann Arbor, Mich.

19. Thernstrom, *Whose Votes Count?*, 33; John Anderson et al. to Colleague, April 7, 1970, Box 60, Edward Hutchinson Papers, Ford Library; *1970 Congressional Quarterly Almanac*; Garrow, *Potest at Selma*, 196–197; Vallely, *The Two Reconstructions*, 233; Roland Evans Jr. and Robert Novak, *Nixon in the White House: The Frustration of Power* (New York: Random House, 1971), 128–131; Ehrlichman Notes, June 19, 1970, Box 3, White House Special Files, Staff Member and Office Files—John Ehrlichman, Nixon Papers Project.

20. *1970 Congressional Quarterly Almanac*; Strom Thurmond to Richard Nixon, June 23, 1970, Box 1, W. House Correspondence Series, Strom Thurmond Papers, Clemson University, Clemson, S.C.

21. Gareth Davies, *See Government Grow: Education Politics from Johnson to Reagan* (Lawrence: University Press of Kansas, 2007).

9

Liberal Feminism and the Reshaping of the New Deal Order

SUSAN M. HARTMANN

In 1970, Mrs. Frank Hallonquist wrote from Waco, Texas, to Michigan Congresswoman Martha Griffiths about the unfairness of her retirement situation. "My working days were during the depression," she recalled, "5½ to 6 days working week, no coffee breaks, no additional benefits, other than a check at the end of the month. I worked hard and have EARNED every penny of my SS [Social Security] retirement." Yet, as a married woman she would not receive the full value of her payments to a system that she had been required to contribute to. Hallonquist noted that she had no company pension to mitigate her family's financial need. "We don't want any guaranteed family income nonsense," she concluded, "all we want is ALL THAT WE HAVE WORKED AND PAID FOR."[1]

In imploring Griffiths to act against the discrimination embedded in the Social Security system, Hallonquist implicitly identified the gender bias of New Deal programs that contemporaries and later scholars erroneously described as "universal." In addition, Hallonquist's sense of injustice challenges those who dichotomize twentieth-century liberalism as class-oriented or rights-oriented. Indeed, her claim for rights, which Griffiths incorporated into her feminist agenda in Congress, was firmly based in her own and her family's material needs and interests.

This essay examines the policy goals and activism of the "mainstream" wing of second-wave feminism to understand how this movement both sustained and redefined liberalism and the New Deal order after World War II. It challenges the argument that liberalism fell into disarray when it turned away from a universal economic agenda laid down in the New Deal to one promoting the rights and interests of particular groups.² To be sure, incorporation of gender issues into the liberal agenda contributed to the rise of a conservative countermovement, but without equal rights, the universal promise of New Deal economics would remain empty. Feminists allied with the Democratic Party did not abandon economic issues, but, like Mrs. Hallonquist, sought to ensure that the New Deal programs offered equal benefits to women. Theirs was a "rights" liberalism, but it was so because they were seeking the same right to economic security that the New Deal granted to white men. Rather than deviating from the New Deal policy order, liberal feminists sought to include women within its benefits and to expand its regulatory and social provision powers to accommodate women's dual roles as workers and mothers.³ Moreover, in their focus on material security, mainstream feminists coalesced across divides of race, ethnicity, and class on behalf of policies that would expand economic justice for a broad range of disadvantaged groups.⁴ And, while the conservative countermovement that arose in the 1970s certainly objected to what its participants considered feminist threats to traditional values, material interests also motivated antifeminists.

In the 1990s, scholars began to deconstruct the understanding of New Deal liberalism as a set of universalist policies. First, building on the work of political scientist Barbara Nelson, Linda Gordon articulated the two-tiered nature of the Social Security Act. White men gained social insurance against unemployment and old age, entitlements based on their status as workers.⁵ Some women gained benefits through their status as wives and daughters of male workers, but most employed women and minority men were left out because their jobs lay beyond the coverage of these programs. By contrast, women gained public assistance, the Aid to Dependent Children program, based on their status as dependent and needy. Alice Kessler-Harris extended this analysis of what she calls the "gendered habits of the mind" embedded in New Deal legislation; they privileged white men not only in Social Security, but also in tax policy and the Fair Labor Standards Act.⁶

The white male–breadwinner orientation of these liberal programs gave those who were left out no alternative but to argue for their rights to inclusion. Scholars have demonstrated this inseparability of rights and material interests in a number of settings. For example, studies of black tobacco workers and steelworkers show that their struggles joined civil rights to industrial democracy.⁷ Other scholars, such as Dorothy Sue Cobble, Dennis A. Deslippe, and Nancy Gabin, have described how union women actually prefigured second-wave feminism in seeking the right to equal economic opportunity within the context of industrial unionism.⁸ More recently, Nancy MacLean demonstrated that the demand for economic security through the right to be free from employment discrimination was central to the civil rights movement, while the National Organization for Women—known primarily for its goals of an Equal Rights Amendment and abortion rights—devoted intense energies to ending sex discrimination in employment.[9] Even Donald Mathews and Jane De Hart, who centered their analysis of the defeat of the Equal Rights Amendment around battles over values and the cultural meanings of womanhood, acknowledged that "Equality and work were closely identified in resurgent feminism."[10]

As a whole, however, historians of second-wave feminism as well as scholars and writers in general have emphasized how that movement challenged traditional social and cultural values rather than its attention to women's economic disadvantage.[11] They have tended to focus on radical feminists, whose dramatic protests captured the media limelight, and whose theoretical insights revealed how thoroughly gender shaped institutions and everyday life. Radical feminists' distrust of established, male-dominated institutions, expressed in Audre Lorde's contention that "The master's tools will never dismantle the master's house," and their fruitful attention to personal relationships have contributed to the tendency of feminist historians to neglect the impact of the second wave on mainstream politics and policies. Both the media coverage of second-wave feminism, with its emphasis on the bizarre and outrageous, and the interest of historians of women in women's liberation rather than liberal feminism have left unappreciated the ways in which feminists reconfigured liberal policies and politics in the 1960s and 1970s.[12]

This reshaping of the New Deal welfare state began before the emergence of a visible women's movement, as a handful of Congresswomen began to compel attention to women's stake in government measures to promote economic security. At the forefront were Edith Green and Martha Wright Griffiths. Both women defeated Republican incumbents to win House seats in 1954, contributing to the Democrats' recapture of that body and joining the windfall of sixteen women in Congress, the most up to that time. Joined by Patsy Takemoto Mink from Hawaii a decade later, these New Deal liberals sought to make the welfare state work for women, leaving their marks on policies in four key areas: equal employment opportunities; Social Security benefits and taxes; equity in education; and inclusion in antipoverty programs and minimum wage protections.

Edith Green, representing Oregon's 3rd district located in and around Portland, headed her state delegation at the national Democratic convention in 1960, where she seconded the nomination of John F. Kennedy; and she ran Robert F. Kennedy's presidential primary campaign in Oregon in 1968. A respected, independent, and plainspoken legislator and skillful floor manager, Green served for eighteen years on the Committee on Labor and Education, exerting her greatest influence in the areas of education and women's rights. Throughout her House career, Green worked for measures to ban sex discrimination. She leveraged her early support for Kennedy in 1960 to solidify his backing of the Equal Pay Act of 1963, which she had cosponsored since first setting foot in the House in 1955. The law reflected women's steadily growing importance to the economy; by 1961 some 24 million women constituted more than one-third of the workforce, and 30 percent of all married women were employed. Although opposition required compromises that limited the force and reach of Green's original bill, the Equal Pay Act marked a significant extension of the New Deal's Fair Labor Standards Act on behalf of women.[13] This first in what would be a series of laws affirming women's right to be free from sex discrimination, stood squarely in the New Deal tradition of securing workers' material well-being.

Like other liberals, Green hesitated at the next opportunity to implement economic justice for women. Although "very keenly and very painfully aware" of sex discrimination, Green was the only congresswoman to oppose the amendment to Title VII of the Civil Rights Act of 1964 banning sex discrimination in all areas of employment. Considering racial discrimination "10 times maybe 100 times" worse than sex discrimination, she feared with fellow liberals that the amendment would "clutter up" the civil rights bill with a provision that was bound—and probably intended by its sponsor Virginia Democrat Howard Smith—to increase opposition.[14] Once the sex provision was approved, however, she supported the amended bill.

Although in concert with Green on most women's issues, Martha Griffiths had no such qualms about adding sex to Title VII's ban on discrimination in employment. Having earned a law degree from the University of Michigan, Griffiths negotiated contracts for the Army Ordnance Department during World War II and thereafter practiced law in Detroit with her husband. At the center of a group of reform Democrats in Michigan, she served in the state legislature from 1949 to 1953 and in 1954 won election to the House of Representatives from Michigan's 17th district, incorporating part of Detroit and its suburbs.

Griffiths led the fight for the addition of sex discrimination to Title VII in the House, arguing inconsistently that, on the one hand, without the amendment white women would be the only group left unprotected, and on the other, that the amendment was necessary to secure the bill's benefits for African American women.¹⁵ Although labor—along with liberals in general—formally opposed the inclusion of sex discrimination, Griffiths won applause from some women wage earners.¹⁶ Once the civil rights bill passed with the ban on sex discrimination included in Title VII, Griffiths worked closely with the emerging feminist movement to make sure that it was enforced. For the first few years of its life, the law's enforcement agency, the Equal Employment Opportunity Commission (EEOC), seemed unable to comprehend the injuries of sex discrimination, leading Griffiths to charge that it had "failed to perform its statutory duty."¹⁷ Her fiery speech in Congress in June 1966, castigating the EEOC for having "reached the peak of contempt for women's rights," helped galvanize the group of feminists who months later founded the National Organization for Women.¹⁸

After 1966, Congressional feminists both encouraged and benefited from the support of a budding movement that evinced a comparable dedication to amending the gender exclusiveness of New Deal liberalism. The National Organization for Women (NOW) held its first formal meeting in October 1966 and immediately began pressuring the administration and Congress for equal opportunity in employment. Although the public and scholars alike associate NOW, the principal organization of second-wave feminism, with the Equal Rights Amendment and abortion rights, from its beginning NOW gave high priority to improving women's material status. It was created in the first place to compel the Equal Employment Opportunity Commission to act aggressively on employment discrimination against women. Betty Friedan drafted NOW's founding "Statement of Purpose" and that document reprised key themes of her 1963 book, *The Feminine Mystique*. Yet in addition to asserting the grievances of white suburban middle-class women trapped in domesticity, protesting the media images of women and claiming women's right to "dignity, self-fulfillment, self-determination," the founding statement emphasized the income disparity between men and women, the double economic discrimination against black women, and the need for public provision of child care.¹⁹

NOW's early attention to the material bases of women's subordination was consistent with Betty Friedan's radical past and with the makeup of the organization's founding leadership. As Daniel Horowitz has demonstrated, Friedan spent the late 1930s and early 1940s in the American Left and worked as a writer for the radical United Electrical Workers, one of the few unions committed to representing fully the interests of their female members.²⁰ Moreover, women of color and union women—including Pauli Murray, Anna Arnold Hedgeman, Aileen Hernandez, Caroline Davis, and Dorothy

Haener—were among the founders and early officers of NOW.[21] Their presence most likely explains the difference between Friedan's draft of the Statement of Purpose, with its focus on the middle-class suburban housewife, and the final version's attention to working-class and African American women.[22]

At its second national conference, in November 1967, NOW more specifically sought remedies for women's material disadvantage. Occupying the first and last place on an eight-point Bill of Rights, the two hotly contested issues were an Equal Rights Amendment to the Constitution and the right to contraception and abortion. Although the ERA and abortion became the women's movement's signature issues in the 1970s and gained the lion's share of media attention, they should not obscure the considerable attention that feminists paid to economic issues. Of the remaining six points in the NOW's Bill of Rights, one dealt with equal educational opportunities, and the rest called for government action to end job discrimination, guarantee maternity leave rights to employed women, provide public child-care facilities, and afford women equal treatment with men in job training and other poverty programs. NOW claimed the right of poor women to be treated in welfare programs with "dignity, privacy and self-respect" and the right of welfare mothers to choose "whether to work or stay home with their children."[23]

Two separate resolutions emphasized NOW's appreciation of impoverished women's concerns. One addressed discrimination against women within the Job Corps and other poverty programs. The second referred to Social Security revisions that had passed the House and were under consideration in the Senate. NOW strongly objected to provisions requiring women receiving welfare payments to be forced to take jobs or training, insisting that it was "punitive, undemocratic and un-American to deny welfare mothers of the option of choosing whether to work or stay home with their children."[24] As Marisa Chappell has shown, NOW's antipoverty activism did not match its rhetoric and in fact paled in comparison with that of more traditional women's groups like the League of Women Voters. Yet, economic security was on NOW's agenda from the beginning, and its attention to poverty and welfare intensified in the late 1970s.[25]

Before second-wave feminism took organizational form, Edith Green and Patsy Mink had already forced the Johnson administration to provide for women in its war on poverty. In hearings on the administration's first formal presentation of its antipoverty initiatives, Green noted that the war on poverty, like the New Deal, rested on the assumption that men were the breadwinners and that, consequently, male earning ability was the key to ending poverty. On this point Green specifically challenged administration representatives Sargent Shriver, whom Johnson had tapped to head the antipoverty program, and Defense Secretary Robert McNamara. She demanded to know why women were not included in the proposed Job Corps, a residential program designed to train men in the 16–21 age group for employment. When Shriver and McNamara explained that the program intended to help "young men, who we hope will be heads of family and wage earners," Green pointed out that women comprised one-third of the labor force. Moreover, she maintained, "there are millions of women who are heads of families, yet they are paid less and they are given fewer opportunities."[26]

Green's importance on the House Education and Labor Committee made her support for the antipoverty program necessary, and the administration agreed to include women. By January 1966, five Job Corps centers for women had opened, and women constituted 18 percent of all Job Corps enrollees.[27] Green had understood that at least one-third of the enrollments would go to women, and she continued to push Shriver in this direction, with help from Congresswoman Patsy Mink, several traditional women's organizations whose members helped to recruit women to the Job Corps, and, as we have seen, the infant NOW.[28] Green relentlessly cited statistics that girls constituted half of all school dropouts and that minority women in the 16–25 age bracket bore the highest unemployment rate in the country.[29] "Young girls," she insisted in 1967, "need it as desperately as young boys."[30] Green's amendment to eliminate completely discrimination in Job Corps enrollments failed, and she became increasingly critical of what she considered the waste and disorganization in antipoverty programs.[31]

In 1972, Green looked back on her efforts for women in a speech to the Portland City Club. While taking heat from some feminists for speaking to an organization that refused to admit women, Green used the occasion to deliver a stinging attack on sex discrimination. Reciting the statistics of women's labor force participation, the sharp disparity between median incomes of men and women working full time, and the disproportionate numbers of women in the poverty population, she concluded, "May I suggest that the female rebellion of these years had sound economic grounds."[32] In centering her feminism on women's material disadvantages, Green allowed no distinction between rights and economic security—women's right to equal pay and their right to inclusion in job training programs were inseparable if liberalism was to live up to its promise of a decent livelihood for all Americans.

While Green took the lead in protecting women's interests in the emerging Great Society, Griffiths worked to incorporate gender justice into the New Deal welfare state, most actively as a member of the House Ways and Means

Committee, which had jurisdiction over tax and Social Security legislation. Like Green, Griffiths was responding to the march of married women into the labor force and the consequent disjuncture with the male-breadwinner assumptions that underlay the welfare state. She routinely explained her support for an Equal Rights Amendment to the Constitution, which she sponsored in the House beginning in 1959, in terms of the need to eliminate such injustices as disparate treatment of women "in employment and particular pension benefit programs."[33] Even Griffiths's support for repeal of restrictive abortion laws reflected her sense of economic injustice. Recognizing the greater opportunities for financially secure women to get abortions when they remained illegal in most states, she asked in 1970, "Why should a safe abortion be limited to women with money?"[34]

Throughout the 1960s Griffiths waged a battle against the "gendered habits of the mind" that anchored the Social Security program. As Griffiths pointed out, "the social security laws were simply not written with working couples in mind," even though some 15 percent of married women were in the labor force in the 1930s.[35] By the 1960s, two-earner couples were twice as common and growing. And as women who had worked in the early years of Social Security reached retirement age, they became concretely aware of how inequitably their contributions translated into benefits. Like Mrs. Hallonquist, women and men appealed to Griffiths from across the country. "As one of the too few women legislators," Ruth Crothers wrote, "you represent all the women.... If you do not represent the interests of all of us, then we are without representation on a committee made up principally of married men, who are naturally interested in the welfare of their wives."[36] In fact, Griffiths was the only woman on Ways and Means, where she recalled, her arguments often fell on "mighty deaf ears."[37]

At the root of the gender injustice embedded in Social Security was that women as workers paid into the system just as men did, but when it came time to collect their pensions or other benefits, as wives they suffered inequities. For example, until Griffiths got the law amended in 1967, a mother's survivor benefits were denied to her children if she had been out of the labor force for more than eighteen months when she died. When a wife died, her husband could not claim his wife's survivor benefits if he was not dependent on her, although a wife could claim her deceased husband's benefits regardless of whether she was self-sufficient or not.

Most egregious to Griffiths and to the women and men who asked for her assistance was the stipulation that a woman who had paid into the Social Security system had to choose between claiming the benefits to which she had contributed as a worker or the benefits to which she was entitled as the wife of Social Security beneficiary. Ethel Oros wrote Griffiths from Schenectady, New York, about the effects of this requirement on low-income families. Oros compared the woman "who works [for wages] and cares for her family, usually not by choice" with the homemaker who "never paid a cent to the Social Security fund; never had to divide herself and her time into two people, a worker and a housewife." She suggested that the working wife's "life was much harder in order to gain the same living standard of the non-worker whose husband probably earned enough to be the sole support of the family." Oros concluded, "We are only asking for full credit for our contributions."[38]

Griffiths echoed Oros's dismay that the Social Security system used women workers' contributions to subsidize benefits for wives who had never been employed outside the home. "Under current law," she wrote to another constituent, "retired working couples can—and often do—draw lower benefits than couples with identical earnings in which only the husband has worked."[39] Griffiths and the women who relied on her as their best hope for policy reform were clearly indignant about the government's indifference to their right to the contributions their labor had made to the Social Security fund. "Why DISCRIMINATE against the married women, forced to contribute to something that she will not realize anything from?" inquired Mrs. Hallonquist.[40] More than equality for its own sake, however, they wanted the concrete benefits that equal treatment would confer on lower-income women and their families.

Feminist congresswomen continued their efforts into the 1970s to incorporate gender justice into New Deal programs. Even before the Equal Pay Act of 1963 went into effect, Green was pushing to expand the Fair Labor Standards Act (FLSA) so that it would "have meaning to women at the lowest rung of the economic ladder." She pointed out that only 7.4 million out of the 25 million women employed were covered under the FLSA; left out were women who worked in hotels, restaurants, laundries, retail stores, on farms, and in other people's homes.[41] By the early 1970s Green, Griffiths, and Mink found allies among several new Democratic congresswomen, who owed their elections in part to the new politics of the 1960s and whose concern for the most disadvantaged groups was part and parcel of their feminism. In 1968 New York assemblywoman and civil rights activist Shirley Chisholm was elected to Congress, followed two years later by antiwar Democrat Bella Abzug (New York). And in 1972, civil rights lawyer Yvonne Braithwaite Burke moved from the California Assembly to the House; Elizabeth Holtzman unseated one of the staunchest opponents of the Equal Rights Amendment, Emanuel

Cellar; Barbara Jordan won election in a newly created district in Houston; and Patricia Schroeder defeated a conservative Colorado incumbent.

During the second Nixon administration, these women formed a nucleus of support for an extensive revision of the Fair Labor Standards Act, which since 1963 had banned sex discrimination in wages. Their bill, which provided for increasing the minimum wage and extending coverage to include some five million government and professional workers as well as domestic workers, offered benefits to two groups of women. The poorest of wage earners, domestic servants, would be covered under the minimum wage provisions, while more privileged women would benefit from the extension of its equal pay provisions to professional and government employees. Congresswoman Chisholm provided leadership for a coalition of pressure groups in support of the bill. These included organized labor, longstanding women's organizations such as the Federation of Business and Professional Women's clubs and religious groups, and feminist groups including NOW, the more conservative Women's Equity Action League, and the National Women's Political Caucus, which had been founded in 1971 by Chisholm, Abzug, Friedan, and others to advance women and their interests in the political system and work for "sweeping social change" by combating sexism, racism, institutional violence, and poverty.[42] In 1973, Chisholm enlisted support from interest group organizations, used her Congressional office's resources to train lobbyists and coordinate efforts, and mobilized her fellow Congresswomen as well as the Congressional Black Caucus.

Although representatives of various interest groups were understandably committed to the provisions that would benefit their particular members, Chisholm's coalition insisted on approval of all of the bill's provisions. On behalf of NOW, for example, Dorothy Haener testified before the House Education and Labor General Subcommittee on Labor that women constituted nearly half of workers currently excluded from minimum wage coverage. The minimum wage was a women's issue, she said, "because poverty in this country is mainly the poverty of women and children."[43] Representing the largely middle-class membership of WEAL, Bernice Sandler insisted that her organization "strongly supports the extension downward" of the FLSA "as well as upward."[44] Representatives of the American Association of University Women and the National Federation of Business and Professional Women likewise pushed for the extension of minimum wage provisions to domestic workers.[45] United Auto Workers representative, William Callison, in return, urged the extension of equal pay provisions for administrative, executive, and professional women workers, as did representatives of the American

Federation of State, County, and Municipal Employees and the International Ladies' Garment Workers' Union.[46]

The coalition held together against efforts to limit the bill's scope. When Chisholm learned of pressures on the House subcommittee to eliminate the expansion of coverage to domestic workers, she got thirteen of the fifteen women in the House to sign a letter to the subcommittee chair. The letter was filled with statistics about the income gaps between white men, black men, white women, and black women, women's need to work to support their families, and the pitiful wages of domestic workers.[47] Coverage of domestic workers stayed in the bill, and while the measure fell to Nixon's veto in 1973, Congress passed a similar bill in 1974, which he signed. The long battle over the FLSA amendments testified to mainstream feminism's commitment to economic security for all women and the ability of women activists to coalesce across class and racial lines, while it resulted in the closing of one more gender gap in the welfare state.

If mainstream feminists largely succeeded in eliminating gender inequities from the New Deal welfare state, they faced more substantial obstacles as their claims expanded beyond measures instituting formal equality to government action that would alleviate women's double burden of employment and traditional care-giving responsibilities. Just as the initial Social Security system stood on the assumption that men were breadwinners, so were all public institutions—from schools to factories to government—shaped around the norm that men would populate the public arena while women would take care of housework and children. Lacking such domestic support, women were disadvantaged in the labor force not just by sex discrimination but also by their dual responsibilities. Recognizing that simple equal economic opportunities would not solve women's burden of combining family responsibilities with employment outside the home, NOW's founding Statement of Purpose asserted that "true equality of opportunity requires . . . a nationwide network of child-care centers;" and its 1967 Bill of Rights called for "child care facilities [to] be established by law on the same basis as parks, libraries, and public schools."

Since 1954 lower-income families had been eligible for income tax deductions for child-care expenses; and in the 1960s Congress authorized modest funds for child care services attached to welfare or antipoverty programs, primarily as a means to encourage or require welfare mothers to seek job training or employment.[48] Universal child care would be especially beneficial to lower-income women who did not qualify for services available to welfare recipients but who could not afford private day-care services.

Feminists in and outside of Congress became part of another broad coalition, which included labor, child welfare professionals, civil rights groups, and other liberals who sought to make child care a welfare state social provision as it was in many European countries. After two years of hearings in House and Senate committees, in 1971 Congress passed a comprehensive child development bill, which, for the first time since the federally supported child-care centers of World War II, authorized services for middle-class families as well as the poor. The measure provided $2 billion to be allocated to local councils to establish services for the first year of the program. Child-care programs for low-income families would be free; other families would be charged on a sliding scale linked to their ability to pay.[49]

Unlike the FLSA amendments, which increased the regulatory functions of the state, the child-care bill provided for the expansion of government's role in social provision. Thus conservatives attacked the measure not only for threatening traditional gender roles by encouraging mothers to work outside the home but also for expanding federal government power and expenditures. Although conservatives in Congress failed to stop the measure, Nixon did. His veto message echoed the sentiments of right-wing opponents, insisting that the government should do no more than help parents "purchase needed day care services in the private, open market." He found the costs of universal child care too great, an unwarranted intrusion into the prerogatives of the states, and likely to create "a new army of bureaucrats." Nixon did not overtly connect the child-care provision with women's opportunities for employment, except to point out that the government was already providing child care for welfare recipients. More subtly, he alluded to the potential of such a program to change gender roles in his assertion that it "would lead to altering the family relationship," and align the government "to the side of communal approaches to child rearing over the family-centered approach," views that reflected an emerging antifeminist strain within the conservative movement.[50]

The breadth and economic focus of liberal feminism's agenda was best illustrated at the National Women's Conference held in Houston in 1977. Responding to the United Nations designation of 1975 as International Women's Year, Congress authorized $5 million for a national women's conference. More than 2,000 women elected at special meetings in their localities—and including a minority of women organized by conservative antifeminists—gathered at Houston to produce a twenty-five–plank National Plan of Action. The document called for equal "opportunities, rights, privileges and responsibilities," but it stressed the "daily reality of discrimination, limited opportunities and economic hardship [faced by] millions of women." Ratification of the ERA and defense of abortion rights were two of the proposals; the rest covered a wide field with attention to needs of specific groups of women, such as those who are disabled or older, racial minorities, lesbians, and homemakers. The most extensive items in the plan were the ones that concerned disabled women, employment, international affairs, minority women, and welfare and poverty.[51] Calling for an expanded welfare state, Bella Abzug delivered the official report of the conference to President Carter in March 1978, insisting that "Women suffer because we lack a national health security system and a full employment policy."[52]

Widespread support to end discrimination against pregnant workers manifested liberal feminism's continuing concern with women's economic needs, and it secured an early victory for one item on the National Plan of Action. In the 1970s more than one-fourth of women workers had no right to even unpaid maternity leave or to reemployment after childbirth; and a large majority of companies' benefits programs excluded pregnancy and childbirth from sick leave policies and medical coverage. Before the Houston conference, a group of women assisted by their union, the International Union of Electrical Workers, filed suit against General Electric on the grounds that such practices violated Title VII's prohibition of sex discrimination. The plaintiffs won at the district and circuit court level, but in 1976 the Supreme Court ruled against them. Making what seemed to many a ludicrous distinction, Justice William Rehnquist explained that denial of benefits did not constitute sex discrimination because such policies excluded pregnancy, not pregnant women, from coverage.[53]

NOW, the National Women's Action League, the National Women's Political Caucus and other feminist groups joined labor unions and church and civil rights groups in a three-hundred–member coalition seeking relief from Congress. In less than two years, they won passage of the Pregnancy Discrimination Act, which banned discrimination against pregnant women in every aspect of employment, required companies that offered health insurance to cover pregnancy and childbirth, and protected a woman's job while she was on maternity leave. The importance of the legislation to the material well-being of working-class women was evident in the strong efforts of unions behind its passage.

Carter signed the pregnancy bill, but other elements of the National Plan of Action set feminists on a collision course with his administration, as women's groups defended the welfare state and pushed for its expansion against an increasingly reluctant president. Carter had recognized the growing clout of feminists within the Democratic Party during his presidential campaign, appointing a committee to advise his campaign on policy and strategy concerning women and urging feminist leaders to "be as tough, as militant and as eloquent as you can be."[54] Yet the administration and feminists were soon at odds. Women's movement leaders felt (unrealistically) that he did not do enough to gain ratification of the ERA; and they condemned his agreement with Congress's ban on the use of Medicaid funds for abortion. But the most dramatic and visible break came over feminists' determination to defend the welfare state.

Following a recommendation from the Houston conference, Carter appointed representatives of diverse feminist and other women's organizations to a National Advisory Committee for Women (NACW) to follow up on the National Plan of Action. As chair he appointed Bella Abzug, who had given up her House seat in an unsuccessful attempt to win election to the Senate in 1976. Abzug saw the NACW as a voice of the women's movement rather than an instrument of the administration. As Carter responded to a heightening economic crisis by adjusting budget proposals to attack inflation and strengthen the military, the committee took issue with his economic and defense policies. It distributed a statement to the press criticizing administration plans to hike military spending by 10 percent, while cutting social welfare programs that would hurt poor, working-class, and minority women. When Abzug was dismissed after a heated exchange with the president, more than half the committee members resigned in protest. Even those who disliked Abzug's aggressiveness objected to the abrupt firing.[55]

The agenda of the women's movement that triggered the controversy over Abzug and the NACW went far beyond the goal of equal rights, reflecting attention to women's material security that had informed second-wave feminism from the beginning. Political columnist David Broder noted in 1978 that feminism was beginning to "intersect with the traditional main concerns of American politics . . . the central political-economic-social questions of the cities and the poor."[56] But that intersection had begun much earlier, and it grew more visible as threats to the welfare state intensified in the 1970s. In 1975, for example, NOW identified women's issues as "employment and income maintenance, the price and quality of food, housing, medical care, childcare and education," asserting that none of these issues could "be intelligently addressed outside the context of recent long term changes in our economy."[57] Similarly, the lead article in WEAL's October 1976 newsletter linked proposed full employment legislation with women's economic security.[58] Early in Carter's administration, representatives of more than fifty women's organizations criticized Carter's economic stimulus plan. As Edith

Green had challenged Johnson's war on poverty, these leaders protested that Carter's plan lacked any mention of women or their particular needs for employment and job training, noting that minority women faced "double discrimination."[59] Several months later feminist and Democratic Party activist Gloria Steinem and others pressed White House staff to consider in their planning for welfare reform whether there were sufficient decently paid jobs available for women.[60]

Left-liberals, such as Abzug and Steinem, and explicitly feminist organizations did not stand alone. Abzug's temporary replacement as chair of the NACW was Marjorie Bell Chambers, president of the American Association of University Women. Within two months at her new post, she was expressing some of the same concerns. Using more diplomatic language and acknowledging the administration's efforts on behalf of women, Chambers insisted that Carter's anti-inflation program would hurt women because of their concentration in low-paying jobs both in the private economy and government, their low rate of union membership, and the wage gap between men and women.[61]

Even after Carter reconstituted the committee as the President's Advisory Committee for Women, which emphasized its responsibility to the president rather than to women, it continued to press him with concerns about his economic priorities. In March 1980, the new committee's chair, Linda Johnson Robb, expressed appreciation that leaders of women's groups had participated in budget consultations. Yet she insisted that trimming the budget to combat inflation should not come at women's expense. Cutting "vital programs," such as food stamps, assistance to poor women and their infants, job training for displaced homemakers, domestic violence prevention, and educational equity, she wrote, would be a "serious disappointment to the women of this country." Although Robb was even more conciliatory than Chambers, she made clear how central economic security was to the agenda of liberal feminism. That point was made much more forcefully by a diverse group of women's professional, religious, welfare, and explicitly feminist organizations. Making domestic programs bear the brunt of budget cuts, they argued, was "incredibly shortsighted and outrageous:" "one-sided slashes ... strangle our most vulnerable citizens."[62]

Moreover, mainstream feminists joined other coalitions to fulfill liberalism's promise of economic security. For example, the Full Employment Action Council, organized to push for full employment legislation and codirected by Coretta Scott King and labor leader Murray H. Finley, counted among its board members representatives from the National Organization for Women and the League of Women Voters as well as individual feminists such as Karen DeCrow, LaDonna Harris, and Gloria Steinem.[63] Feminists in this broad-based coalition focused on ensuring that Carter's full employment legislation did not neglect women. And, in the end, they gained little, as the watered-down Humphrey Hawkins bill failed to staunch unemployment for any group. Yet, like the activists who campaigned for extension of minimum wage coverage and the ban on pregnancy discrimination, they crossed divides of race and class, contributing to a campaign not just for women's rights but for a genuinely universal program that would address the material needs of disadvantaged groups across the board.

The women's movement, then, shouldered a liberal agenda based on economic justice while Carter and other leaders moved the Democratic Party increasingly to the right. Feminists' inability to prevail on most of this program had multiple causes. Certainly ratification of the ERA was the highest priority for liberal women's movement groups in the 1970s and consumed large amounts of energy and resources. They worked to get Congress to extend the time limit for ratification in 1978 but then failed to win approval in three more states before falling to the new deadline in 1982. Even more critically, the economic reverses of the 1970s—signaled by oil shortages, growing unemployment, and inflation—along with intensification of the Cold War not only consumed policy makers' attention but also put pressures on the federal budget that virtually foreclosed increased spending for social provision.

The greatest brake on the feminist engine was the powerful countermovement that it provoked and that the economic crisis aided, a movement that opposed both the rights goals as well as the bread-and-butter agenda of the women's movement and pushed the Democratic leadership to the right. Feminism threatened conservatives not just because it promoted changes in sex roles and the family, but also because feminists and their allies among most women's organizations favored expansion of the welfare state.

The antigovernment strain of traditional conservatism had always formed an obstacle to state intervention for economic justice. Moreover, the Old Right venerated the conventional family, which was, according to leading postwar conservative intellectual Russell Kirk, "the natural source and core of any good society." Although conservatism paid no more attention than did liberalism to gender roles or women's rights before the 1970s, Kirk in 1957 foreshadowed themes that the New Right would elevate less than two decades later. Discussing the family in *The Intelligent Woman's Guide to Conservatism*, Kirk decried, "planned encouragement of divorce, 'sexual freedom,' and 'deprivatization of women,' through legislation or official propaganda."

Freedoms that ended up "converting man and woman into a mere blur, with identical functions and tasks" were the opposite of the "ordered liberty" cherished by conservatives.[64]

In the 1970s Phyllis Schlafly helped to politicize new groups of women and to make antifeminism an integral part of the conservative agenda. She did so by deftly entwining the antigovernment strands of traditional conservatism with a heightened emphasis on preserving traditional family roles. A devoted Republican conservative since the 1950s, Schlafly gained national prominence in 1964 with her book, *A Choice Not an Echo*, a million-copy seller that pushed Barry Goldwater for the Republican presidential nomination. In 1967 she began publication of her monthly newsletter, *The Phyllis Schlafly Report*. At first the newsletter concentrated on the three cardinal principles of postwar conservatism—the Communist threat, the need for a strong national defense, and the dangers of big government—with only occasional mention of the social or moral issues that would galvanize the Christian right in the 1970s and 1980s. By 1972, however, Schlafly began to organize STOP ERA, the movement that ultimately crushed the Equal Rights Amendment; from that time on, she blended the old laissez faire, anti-Communist right with the new social conservatism.[65]

A devout Catholic who believed that traditional gender roles were God-given and that abortion was a sin, Schlafly helped to mitigate (though not entirely successfully) the dissonance between religious conservatives' determination to control private behavior and the older secular right's devotion to laissez faire. For example, she merged the anti-Communism of the Old Right with the new antifeminism by derogating the Soviet version of equal rights for women; American women, she declared, were the most privileged in the world because the free enterprise system had liberated them from drudgery. Like Nixon, she attacked day care and other feminist projects as Communist-inspired and deadly threats to American institutions. Schlafly held up the ERA, which empowered Congress to enforce sexual equality throughout the nation, as an extreme example of big government overriding states' rights.[66] In depicting the amendment as a tool for feminists to "carry out a radical and destructive assault on the family, on marriage, on parenthood, on the private enterprise system," Schlafly hit the hot buttons of both the new social conservatism and a cardinal principle of the traditional right.[67]

While Martha Griffiths and other ERA advocates linked the amendment with women's ability to improve their material conditions, antifeminists in the New Right not only charged that it violated God-given or natural differences between men and women but also that it threatened the material interests of the traditional male-breadwinner/female-homemaker family that was the foundation of social stability. Appealing to the economic interests of her supporters, Schlafly relentlessly insisted that the ERA would take away the right of wives to be supported by their husbands, and she devoted two entire issues of her newsletter in 1973 to the various ways that the ERA would reshape traditional marriage.[68] She characterized the women's movement as "women's libbers," or "radicals who are waging a total assault on the family, on marriage, and on children."[69] ERA opponents shrewdly linked the amendment to several already highly charged issues, insisting that it would place mothers on the front lines of combat, legalize homosexual marriages, solidify forever women's right to abortions, and force the integration of public toilets.[70]

Antifeminists' skill in spinning the feminist agenda so as to suggest extreme challenges to morals and values has made it easy to overlook the economic themes embedded in antifeminism. Profamily advocates did not publicly object to women's employment or to equal pay for equal work; one of their arguments was that the ERA was unnecessary because women were already protected from employment discrimination through Title VII and from bias in education through Title IX. Conservatives did object to measures that would encourage women with children to leave the home for the marketplace, and their economic arguments centered on the material interests of women who were full-time homemakers with a huge stake in the breadwinning capabilities of their husbands.

In the 1970s economic stagnation and a decline in real wages intensified the forces pushing more and more women into the labor force; median family income stood still, and one paycheck became ever less sufficient for families to participate in the consumer economy.[71] Profamily ideas proved attractive to women who were attached to conventional family roles and feared losing economic security if deprived of an adequate livelihood from their husbands. Thus, full-time homemakers disproportionately filled the ranks of Schlafly's anti-ERA movement.[72] Antifeminism also appealed to men and women who saw husbands' economic prospects constrained by new competition from women entering the labor force. As Barbara Ehrenreich and others have pointed out, women on both sides of the divide over feminism sought economic security; but while feminists tried to make women self-sufficient, antifeminists wanted to ensure that they could rely on men to support their families.[73]

Schlafly capitalized on economic frustrations and class resentments and linked them to feminism. Although in reality most new women workers did not compete with men because they continued to occupy traditionally female areas of employment, she charged that sex discrimination laws preventing employers from favoring a married man with children over a single woman constituted "clear and cruel discrimination (especially in a time of high unemployment) . . . against a man's right and ability to fulfill his role as a provider, and against the right of his wife to be a full-time homemaker."[74] Affirmative action, she insisted, prevented skilled male workers from supporting their families, "because the government has forced the employer to hire an artificial quota of women."[75] Veterans were warned that if ERA were ratified their economic security would be jeopardized because, "the women's libbers will push to invalidate veterans' preferences." Schlafly also connected antifeminism to the growing taxpayers' revolt, opposing tax credits for child care because they forced "the working father . . . to pay additional taxes in order to subsidize career mothers who obviously don't need employment if their family income is in the neighborhood of $35,000 [the limit for child-care tax deductions]."[76]

Unable to ignore the massive presence of women in the labor force, Schlafly sought to align her anti-ERA position with working-class women. She framed the ERA and the entire feminist agenda as "an elitist upper-middle class cause" undertaken by selfish privileged women who "neither understand nor represent the needs or desires of women who work in industry or in manual labor jobs."[77] When feminists proposed requiring employers to provide family and medical leave as a way to mitigate women workers' dual burdens, she argued that such measures would benefit only "highly paid, two-earner yuppie couples" who had the means to take advantage of unpaid leave.[78] Ignoring the considerable involvement of union women in feminist projects and the cross-class alliances that won such measures as equal pay legislation, extension of the minimum wage, and the ban on pregnancy discrimination, Schlafly contributed to the public image of feminism as a middle-class movement for privileged women narrowly focused on their rights—an image that continues to misrepresent liberal feminism.

To be sure, intense religion-infused feelings about such "social issues" as abortion and traditional gender roles drew lower-income voters to the New Right, and the racial backlash formed a vigorous element of the new conservatism.[79] Too often overlooked in the Right's success was the ability of antifeminists to frame feminism in ways that responded to the plummeting incomes of working-class families during the 1970s and resonated with class resentments. Such emphases enabled Reagan Democrats to vote in ways that seemed not entirely incompatible with their material interests.[80]

It would be misguided to discount the profound challenges to values posed by second-wave feminism. The momentous transformations in traditional family and gender roles promoted both by powerful economic and social developments that swept postwar America and by the women's movement itself delivered a strong shock to women and men whose identities had been shaped in the framework of conventional norms of femininity and masculinity. It would be similarly mistaken to disregard the claims for individual rights, autonomy, and opportunity for self-fulfillment that informed liberal feminism. The culture wars that ate into the decades-long dominance of the Democratic Party were indeed about morals and values.

Nonetheless, culture wars and social issues do not provide adequate frameworks to capture fully the liberal wing of second-wave feminism, the ways in which it sustained New Deal liberalism in electoral politics and sought to make that liberalism more inclusive, or the political conflicts of the last four decades of the twentieth century.[81] Alongside and often embedded within the divide over social issues was a debate over material interests. As we have seen, many of the goals and achievements of mainstream feminists—equal pay and employment opportunities, equity in Social Security, minimum wage protections and other welfare state programs, a more generous economic safety net, and accommodations to ameliorate women's dual responsibilities of wage earning and child care—were critical to women's material security. Such policies, moreover, lay squarely in the New Deal tradition of economic justice achieved through government regulation, redistribution, and social provision. Understanding how much the women's movement's claims for rights involved using the state for these social welfare purposes helps to explain as well both the power and the nature of the movement that rose to resist feminism and to reshape American politics.

Notes

1. Mrs. Frank Hallonquist to Martha Griffiths, August 3, 1970, Martha Wright Griffiths Papers, Box 34, Folder: L/Soc. Sec. Comb. Earnings, Bentley Historical Library, University of Michigan, Ann Arbor, Michigan (hereafter Griffiths Papers). When a married woman retired from employment, she could claim either her own benefit or 50 percent of her husband's. Because of low wages and intermittent earnings, married women often found that they received more drawing the benefit through their husband. This meant, as was the case for Hallonquist, that they received nothing for all the contributions they had made to Social Security during their working years.

2. See, for example, Steve Fraser and Gary Gerstle, eds., *The Rise and Fall of the New Deal Order, 1930–1980* (Princeton: Princeton University Press, 1989); Thomas Byrd Edsall with Mary D. Edsall, *Chain Reaction: The Impact of Race, Rights and Taxes on American Politics* (New York: W. W. Norton and Company, 1991); Alan

Brinkley, *The End of Reform: New Deal Liberalism in Recession and War* (New York: Vintage Books, 1995); Nelson Lichtenstein, *The Most Dangerous Man in Detroit: Walter Reuther and the Fate of American Labor* (New York: Basic Books, 1995); Cheryl Greenberg, "Twentieth Century Liberalisms: Transformations of an Ideology," in Harvard Sitkoff, ed., *Perspectives on Modern America: Making Sense of the Twentieth Century* (New York: Oxford University Press, 2001), 55–79; William H. Chafe, ed., *The Achievement of American Liberalism: The New Deal and Its Legacies* (New York: Columbia University Press, 2003).

3. By examining the activities of women's movement groups on behalf of specific legislation, this essay challenges the conclusions of Kristin A. Goss and Theda Skocpol, "Changing Agendas: The Impact of Feminism on American Politics," 323–357, in Brenda O'Neill and Elisabeth Gidengil, eds., *Gender and Social Capital* (New York: Routledge, 2006), who also lament activists' focus on rights. Goss and Skocpol draw on a large data set of women's organizations to argue that these women's organizations have narrowed their long-standing agenda of broad social reforms to one focusing on special women's interests. The evidence that I draw from specific policy campaigns suggests that, at least through the 1970s, feminists promoted a broad reform agenda; the kinds of advances for women that feminists sought would have materially benefited the most disadvantaged Americans.

4. Sara Evans, *Tidal Wave: How Women Changed America at Century's End* (New York: The Free Press, 2003) and Nancy MacLean, *Freedom Is Not Enough: The Opening of the American Workplace* (Cambridge: Harvard University Press, with the Russell Sage Foundation, New York, 2006) both comment on the active participation of women of color with white women in liberal feminist projects. See also Susan M. Hartmann, *The Other Feminists: Activists in the Liberal Establishment* (New Haven: Yale University Press, 1998).

5. Linda Gordon, *Pitied but Not Entitled: Single Mothers and the History of Welfare* (New York: The Free Press, 1994).

6. Alice Kessler-Harris, *In Pursuit of Equity: Women, Men and the Quest for Economic Citizenship in 20th-Century America* (New York: Oxford University Press, 2001). See also Suzanne Mettler, *Dividing Citizens: Gender and Federalism in New Deal Public Policy* (Ithaca: Cornell University Press, 1998) and *Soldiers to Citizens: The G.I. Bill and the Making of the Greatest Generation* (New York: Oxford University Press, 2005). For a study of the racial exclusiveness of liberal policies from the New Deal to the GI Bill, see Ira Katznelson, *When Affirmative Action Was White: An Untold History of Racial Inequality in Twentieth-Century America* (New York, W. W. Norton, 2005).

7. Robert Rodgers Korstad, *Civil Rights Unionism: Tobacco Workers and the Struggle for Democracy in the Mid-Twentieth Century South* (Chapel Hill: University of North Carolina Press, 2003); Ruth Needleman, *Black Freedom Fighters in Steel: The Struggle for Democratic Unionism* (Ithaca: ILR, 2003).

8. Dorothy Sue Cobble, *The Other Women's Movement: Workplace Justice and So-*

cial Rights in Modern America (Princeton: Princeton University Press, 2004); Dennis A. Deslippe, *"Rights, Not Roses": Unions and the Rise of Working-Class Feminism, 1945–1980* (Urbana: University of Illinois Press, 2000); Nancy F. Gabin, *Feminism in the Labor Movement: Women and the United Auto Workers, 1935–1975* (Ithaca: Cornell University Press, 1990).

9. Nancy MacLean, *Freedom Is Not Enough: The Opening of the American Workplace* (Cambridge: Harvard University Press, with the Russell Sage Foundation, New York, 2006).

10. Donald G. Mathews and Jane Sherron De Hart, *Sex, Gender, and the Politics of ERA* (New York: Oxford University Press, 1990), 169.

11. Important exceptions to the preoccupation with radical feminism are Sara Evans, *Tidal Wave: How Women Changed America at Century's End* (New York: The Free Press, 2003); and Cynthia Harrison, *On Account of Sex: The Politics of Women's Issues, 1945–1968* (Berkeley: University of California Press, 1988), an early work that focuses on mainstream politics. Both Evans and MacLean comment on the significant presence of women of color and union women in liberal feminist projects.

12. For historians' focus on radical feminism, see Alice Echols, *Daring to Be Bad: Radical Feminism in America, 1967–1975* (Minneapolis: University of Minnesota Press, 1989); Ruth Rosen, *The World Split Open: How the Modern Women's Movement Changed America* (New York: Viking, 2000); Lauri Umansky, *Motherhood Reconceived: Feminism and the Legacies of the Sixties* (New York: New York University Press, 1996); Anne M. Valk, *Radical Sisters: Second-Wave Feminism and Black Liberation in Washington, D.C.* (Urbana: University of Illinois Press, 2008). For media coverage of the second wave, see Patricia Bradley, *Mass Media and the Shaping of American Feminism, 1963–1975* (Jackson: University Press of Mississippi, 2003).

13. Patricia G. Zelman, *Women, Work, and National Policy: The Kennedy-Johnson Years* (Ann Arbor, Mich.: UMI Research Press, 1980), 24–28, 30–32. Harrison, *On Account of Sex*, 89–105. The Equal Pay Act affected only those already covered by the FLSA, i.e., only about one-third of the female work force, and it regulated only those situations where men and women did the same—not comparable—work, leaving unprotected the majority of women, who labored in sex-segregated jobs .

14. *Congressional Record-House*, 88th Congress, 2nd Session, February 8, 1964, 2591.

15. Kessler-Harris, *In Pursuit of Equity*, 242.

16. Caroline Davis to Martha W. Griffiths, February 10, 1964, Griffiths Papers, Box 47, Folder: Civil Rights Bill.

17. Statement by Congresswoman Martha W. Griffiths at Hearing of the Equal Employment Opportunity Commission, May 3, 1967, Griffiths Papers, Box 31, Folder: C/Statements of Martha Griffiths, 7.

18. Inka O'Hanrahan to Martha Griffiths, May 9, 1967, Griffiths Papers, Box 31, Folder: C/NOW.

19. "The National Organization for Women (NOW) Statement of Purpose," in

Betty Friedan, *It Changed My Life: Writings on the Women's Movement* (New York: Random House, 1976), 84, 87–91.

20. Daniel Horowitz, *Betty Friedan and the Making of the Feminine Mystique: The American Left, the Cold War, and Modern Feminism* (Amherst: University of Massachusetts Press, 1998).

21. NOW, Minutes of the Organizing Conference, October 29–30, 1966, Papers of Pauli Murray, Box 51, Folder: 898, Schlesinger Library, Radcliffe College, Cambridge, Massachusetts.

22. Horowitz, *Betty Friedan and the Making of the Feminine Mystique*, 227–228.

23. NOW Press Release, nd [November 1967], Griffiths Papers, Box 31, Folder: National Organization for Women.

24. NOW Press Release, November 20 [1967], Griffiths Papers, Box 31, Folder: C/NOW.

25. Marisa Chappell, "Rethinking Women's Politics in the 1970s: The League of Women Voters and the National Organization for Women Confront Poverty," *Journal of Women's History* 13 (Winter 2002): 158–160, 167. See also Marisa Chappell, *The War on Welfare: Family, Poverty, and Politics in Modern America* (Philadelphia: University of Pennsylvania Press, 2010).

26. U.S. Congress, House Committee on Education and Labor, Subcommittee on the War on Poverty Program, *Hearings on H.R. 10440*, 88th Congress, 2nd Session (April 7–14, 1964), 64–65, 114–115.

27. Sargent Shriver to Edith Green, January 18, 1966, Edith Green Papers, Box 8 (22.2.5), Folder: Economic Opportunity Act, Title I, Part A, Job Corps, MSS 1424, Oregon Historical Society Research Library, Portland, Oregon [hereafter Green Papers].

28. Zelman, 83–84; Patsy T. Mink to Sargent Shriver, February 28, 1966, Green Papers, Box 8 (22.2.5), Folder: Economic Opportunity Act, Title I, Part A, Job Corps. The women's organizations included the National Council of Catholic Women, the National Council of Jewish Women, the National Council of Negro Women, and United Church Women.

29. See, for example, Green to Mrs. Robert Mariana, February 7, 1966, and similar letters in the file, Green Papers, Box 8 (22.2.5), Folder: Economic Opportunity Act, Title I, Part A, Job Corps.

30. *Oregonian*, November 11, 1967, 33.

31. With her lifelong ties to public education, it is not surprising that Green looked to the public school system as potentially the best antipoverty program. She often noted that it cost more than ten times as much to support a Job Corps enrollee for a year than it did to educate a student in a public school; smaller classrooms, she believed, would reduce dropouts; and putting more money into public education, and especially vocational education, she argued, would be more efficient than the Job Corps program. See, for example, Green to the Reverend Robert A. Hutchinson, DD, February 10, 1966, Green Papers, Box 8 (22.2.5), Folder: Economic Opportunity Act, Title I, Part A, Job Corps.

32. "Green Rips Sex Bias in City Club Address," *Oregon Journal*, January 29, 1972, 3.

33. Martha Griffiths to Mrs. Lee Sturtevant, 2/9/71, Griffiths Papers, Box 1, Folder: Office—MG Biog.

34. "Mrs. Griffiths Champions Women's Rights," *Detroit News*, May 14, 1970, 6.

35. Martha Griffiths to Mrs. Clifford H. Brown, August 5, 1966, Griffiths Papers, Box 26, Folder: 89th Soc. Security—Women.

36. Ruth Crothers to Martha Griffiths, October 25, 1966, Griffiths Papers, Box 22, Folder: 89th Ways and Means—Taxes.

37. Griffiths quoted in Emily George, *Martha W. Griffiths* (Washington. D.C.: University Press of America, 1982), 166.

38. Mrs. Ethel Oros to Martha Griffiths, August 24, 1970, Griffiths Papers, Box 34, Folder: L/Soc. Sec. Comb. Earnings.

39. Martha Griffiths to Anne Galbraith, November 7, 1967, Griffiths Papers, Box 28, Folder: Security Women.

40. Hallonquist to Griffiths, August 3, 1970.

41. "Effective Date of the Equal Pay Legislation," White House, June 11, 1964, Green Papers, Sub 2C, Box 1, Folder: Articles—Mrs. Green Speeches.

42. Rona F. Feit, "Organizing for Political Power: The National Women's Political Caucus," in Bernice Cummings and Victoria Schuck, eds., *Women Organizing: An Anthology* (Metuchen, N.J.: The Scarecrow Press, 1979), 185, 191–193.

43. Haener quoted in *Congressional Quarterly Almanac, 1973* (Washington, D.C.: Congressional Quarterly, Inc., 1972), 331.

44. *To Amend the Fair Labor Standards Act*, Hearings before the General Subcommittee on Labor of the Committee on Education and Labor, House of Representatives, 91st Congress, 2nd Session, on H.R. 10948 and H.R. 17596, June 17–July 23, 1970, Part 1; July 29–September 17, 1970, Part 2, 551.

45. Ibid., 793, 858–863.

46. Ibid., 788, 863; *Fair Labor Standards Amendments of 1971*. Hearings before Subcommittee on Labor of the Committee on Labor and Public Welfare, U.S. Senate 92nd Cong., 1st Session, on S. 1861 and S. 2259, May 26–September 30, 1971 (GPO, 1971), 369–375.

47. Shirley Chisholm to Chairman Dent, March 28, 1973, Shirley Chisholm to Bella Abzug, March 28, 1973, Bella Abzug Papers, Catalogued Correspondence, Box C-G, Rare Book and Manuscript Library, Columbia University, New York (hereafter Abzug Papers).

48. Susan M. Hartmann, "Women's Employment and the Domestic Ideal in the Early Cold War Years," in Joanne Meyerowitz, *Not June Cleaver: Women and Gender in Postwar America, 1945–1960* (Philadelphia: Temple University Press, 1994), 94–97; Sonya Michel, *Children's Interests/Mothers' Rights: The Shaping of America's Child Care Policy* (New Haven: Yale University Press, 1999), 243–247.

49. *Congressional Quarterly Almanac, 1971*, 504.

50. Veto of the Economic Opportunity Amendments of 1971, *Public Papers of the*

Presidents of the United States: Richard M. Nixon, 1971 (Washington, D.C.: Government Printing Office, 1972), 1176–1177.

51. U.S. National Commission on the Observance of National Women's Year, *National Plan of Action Adopted at National Women's Conference, November 18–21, 1977, Houston Tex.* (Washington, D.C.: Government Printing Office, 1978).

52. National Commission on the Observance of International Women's Year, Remarks by Presiding Officer Bella Abzug, Official Presentation of "Spirit of Houston" Report to President Carter, March 22, 1978, Gloria Steinem Papers, Box 142, Folder: 5, Sophia Smith Collection, Smith College, Northampton, Massachusetts.

53. See Joyce Gelb and Marian Lief Palley, *Women and Public Policies* (Princeton: Princeton University Press, 1982), 154–166, and Susan M. Hartmann, *The Other Feminists: Activists in the Liberal Establishment* (New Haven: Yale University Press, 1998), 43–46, for fuller treatments of the pregnancy discrimination issue.

54. Peter G. Bourne, *Jimmy Carter: A Comprehensive Biography from Plains to Post-presidency* (New York: Scribner, 1997), 345; *Washington Post*, October 3, 1976, A1, A3.

55. Rhodri Jeffreys-Jones, *Changing Differences: Women and the Shaping of American Foreign Policy, 1917–1994* (New Brunswick: Rutgers University Press, 1995), 151–153; Bella Abzug with Mim Kelber, *Gender Gap: Bella Abzug's Guide to Political Power for American Women* (Boston: Houghton Mifflin, 1984), 63, 77–79; Bella Abzug and Carmen Delgado Votaw, cochairs, National Advisory Committee for Women, Statement to President Carter, January 12, 1979, Sarah Weddington Files, Box 14, Jimmy Carter Presidential Library, Atlanta Georgia; Catherine East to Rosalynn Carter, January 29, 1979, Weddington Files, Box 13; National Advisory Committee for Women Press Release, January 12, 1979, NACW Source Material, Abzug Papers, Box 987.

56. *Washington Post*, February 8, 1978, A19.

57. *National Women's Conference.* Hearing before the Subcommittee on Government Information and Individual Rights of the Committee on Government Operations, House, 94th, 1st Session, on H.R. 8903, September 30, 1975 (GPO, 1975), 34.

58. *WEAL Washington Report*, 5:4 (October 1976), Abzug Papers, Subject Files, Box 18, Folder: Labor and Employment, Women—General.

59. Ad Hoc Coalition for Women, Summary of Priority Requests Made by Coalition in Meeting with President Carter and Vice President Mondale at White House Meeting, March 10, 1977, Martha Mitchell Files, Box 25, Carter Library.

60. Beth Abramowitz to Stuart Eizenstat, September 12, 1977, Domestic Policy Staff Records (DPS)—Eizenstat, Box 323, Carter Library.

61. Marjorie Bell Chambers to Jimmy Carter, March 30, 1979, White House Central Files, Box FG-221, Carter Library.

62. Linda Johnson Robb to Jimmy Carter, March 5, 1980, and March 21, 1980, White House Central Files Box F1–11; Statement on Women and the Federal Budget, March 12, 1980, Weddington Files, Box 20, Carter Library.

63. Statement of Coretta Scott King and Murray Finley, Full Employment Action

Council, November 22, 1977, Steinem Papers, Box 190, Folder: 13. For a more extensive and complicated analysis of liberal feminism and the issue of poverty, see Chappell, *The War on Welfare*.

64. Russell Kirk, *The Intelligent Woman's Guide to Conservatism* (New York: Devin-Adair, 1957), 46–49.

65. Donald T. Critchlow, *Phyllis Schlafly and Grassroots Conservatism: A Woman's Crusade* (Princeton: Princeton University Press, 2005).

66. *The Phyllis Schlafly Report* 5:7 (February 1972): 2, 3; 6:10 (May 1973), 1–2.

67. "Will E.R.A. Make Child-Care the State's Job?" *The Phyllis Schlafly Report* 9:5 (November 1975): 1.

68. *The Phyllis Schlafly Report* 7:1 (August 1973), 7:2 (November 1973).

69. *The Phyllis Schlafly Report* 5:7 (February 1972): 3.

70. Jane Dehart Mathews and Donald Mathews, "The Cultural Politics of the ERA's Defeat," in Joan Hoff Wilson, ed., *Rights of Passage: The Past and Future of the ERA* (Bloomington: Indiana University Press, 1986), 58–59; "The Hypocrisy of ERA Proponents," *The Phyllis Schlafly Report* 8:12 (July 1975): 3.

71. Frank Levy, *The New Dollars and Dreams: American Incomes and Economic Change* (New York: Russell Sage Foundation, rev. ed. 1998), 36–53.

72. Susan Marshall, "Keep Us on the Pedestal: Women against Feminism in Twentieth-Century America," in Jo Freeman, ed., *Women: A Feminist Perspective* (Mountain View, Calif.: Mayfield Publishing Company, 4th ed., 1989), 576; Christina Wolbrecht, *The Politics of Women's Rights: Parties, Positions, and Change* (Princeton: Princeton University Press, 2000), 170; Val Burris, "Who Opposed the ERA? An Analysis of the Social Bases of Antifeminism" *Social Science Quarterly* 64 (June 1983): 306, 310; Kent L. Tedin et al., "Social Background and Political Differences between Pro- and Anti-ERA Activists," *American Politics Quarterly* 5 (July 1977): 402–405; Theodore S. Arrington and Patricia A. Kyle, "Equal Rights Amendment Activists in North Carolina," *Signs: Journal of Women in Culture and Society* 3 (Spring 1978): 667–669, 673–675; Janet K. Boles, *The Politics of the Equal Rights Amendment: Conflict and the Decision Process* (New York: Longman, 1979), 82–87.

73. Barbara Ehrenreich, *The Hearts of Men: American Dreams and the Flight from Commitment* (Garden City, N.Y.: Anchor Press, 1983), 144–149.

74. "How ERA Will Hurt Men," *The Phyllis Schlafly Report* 8:10 (May 1975): 3.

75. "Do Women Get Equal Pay for Equal Work?" *The Phyllis Schlafly Report* 14:10 (May 1981): 1.

76. "Child-Care Responsibility—Family or State?" *The Phyllis Schlafly Report* 9:3 (October 1975): 2.

77. *The Phyllis Schlafly Report* 6:12 (July 1973): 3.

78. Schlafly quoted in Marshall, "Rattle on the Right: Bridge Labor in Antifeminist Organizations," in Kathleen M. Blee, ed., *No Middle Ground: Women and Radical Protest* (New York: New York University Press, 1998), 162.

79. Dan T. Carter argues that race was the central element in national politics'

move to the right, although he, too, recognizes the connections between rights and material needs. See *From George Wallace to Newt Gingrich: Race in the Conservative Counterrevolution, 1963–1994* (Baton Rouge: Louisiana State University Press, 1996).

80. Although he focuses on a later period, Mark A. Smith likewise argues for the important force of economic issues in the Republican resurgence and the ability of conservatives to frame issues to appeal to working-class Americans. See Mark A. Smith, "Economic Insecurity, Party Reputations, and the Republican Ascendance," 135–159, in Paul Pierson and Theda Skocpol, eds., *The Transformation of American Politics: Activist Government and the Rise of Conservatism* (Princeton: Princeton University Press, 2007).

81. Women voters as well as feminist activists reflected a continuing commitment to New Deal liberalism. The gender gap in voting that opened in the 1980s and persists to this day saw women supporting Democratic candidates by as many as twelve percentage points over men. In 2008, just 1 percentage point separated men's preference for Obama over McCain, while women favored Obama over McCain 56 percent to 43 percent. Unmarried women, who constitute a quarter of all voters and who especially depend on a safety net and government action for their material security, favored Obama by an enormous 70 to 29 percent.

10

Labor, Liberalism, and the Democratic Party
A Fruitful but Vexed Alliance

NELSON LICHTENSTEIN

When Barack Obama was swept into office in 2008, a labor-liberal revival seemed a tangible possibility. For the first time in nearly half a century, a liberal, Democratic president, both urban and northern, occupied the White House. A new New Deal was on the agenda, a legislative and political initiative that promised a cavalcade of long-sought social legislation, an invigorated liberal movement and a revitalization of American labor, whose organizations now represented a smaller proportion of the workforce than at any time since Calvin Coolidge took the oath of presidential office.[1]

American trade union leaders were pleased and hopeful. They had played a decisive role in putting Obama over the top in battleground states like Ohio, Nevada, Pennsylvania, and Virginia, where the key campaign issue revolved around the extent to which the white working class would vote for a black liberal when, and if, they entered the voting booth. And during the bruising legislative battles that preceded enactment of Obama's New Dealish agenda, the labor movement was a steadfast ally even when it felt the President and many Democratic legislators were far too cautious. "We know we haven't achieved everything we worked for. But we've made progress—and we have to keep it going," AFL-CIO president Richard Trumka told unionists on the eve of the 2010 elections. "We have to save our anger for the corporate lapdogs who made this mess and the Republicans in the Senate who are determined to keep us in it."[2]

But Trumka's dutiful loyalty to Obama and his party could not forestall defeats suffered by labor-backed Democrats during the midterm elections;

nor could it mask the failure of the labor movement to win for itself legislation that would enable the unions to once again begin organizing within the private sector of the American economy, where employer hostility was both fierce and near universal. Indeed, conservatives of all stripes made enactment of the Employee Free Choice Act (EFCA), which was designed to advance the institutional strength of the trade unions by curbing a number of antiunion tactics routinely deployed by such employers, a rallying point for opponents of both the Obama administration and the labor movement. EFCA's details—majority sign-up (card check), larger penalties on labor law violators, first contract arbitration after impasse—were far less important than the organizational consequence of its passage. It had the potential to create a more robust and expansive labor movement, indeed a rescue of private sector trade unionism—now representing about 7.5 percent of the workforce—from virtual extinction.[3]

Labor-liberal politics repeated an old story. For more than half a century the trade unions have been the backbone of American liberalism and a key electoral element making possible those moments of progressive legislative reform, be they massive as in the mid-1960s or far more modest, exemplified by the Clinton agenda of the early 1990s. But regardless of the extent of liberal legislative success, one outcome remains constant: neither the trade unions nor their ostensible Democratic allies have been able to muster the political muscle or ideological persuasiveness to enact the kind of legislation that would actually enable the unions themselves to increase their size, power, and legitimacy at the bargaining table or in the political arena. Indeed, for more than half a century the trade union movement has almost always emerged from eras of liberal legislative reform in a weaker and more tenuous political shape than when such moments began.

To understand the dynamic that made labor so important to the Obama victory, but which produced such a paltry political and legislative payoff for the unions, we need to recognize the character of the contemporary industrial relations regime in which labor now functions and why this is so different from those that have gone before. Indeed, three regimes have governed trade union "bargaining"—with employers, with the Democrats, and with the state—during the era since the New Deal. They are the era of the New Deal itself (1933–1947) during which a corporatist politicization of all wage, price, and production issues achieved some purchase; the years of classic industrial pluralism and collective bargaining (1947–1980), in which industrial relations was reprivatized to a large extent; and finally, our current moment, (1980s forward) in which the labor movement exists and holds the possibility of growth largely in government and the service sector. A highly politicized form of tripartite bargaining, between companies, unions, and government (mainly state and local), has provided the chief avenue for raising the social wage and building nodes of trade union influence in key government-dependent sectors of the economy. With the arrival of the Obama era, this third system is becoming the only game in town, regardless of the fate that has befallen EFCA.

In the New Deal–era trade union growth was rapid, political engagement took place at multiple levels, and industrial actions were frequent and not always contained by the law. Most importantly, this was an era of corporatist bargaining in which virtually every important economic or organizational initiative put forward by the unions had a political dimension. This was obvious in the strikes of the mid-1930s, during which the legality and legitimacy of trade unionism itself was on the bargaining agenda; and not just in Detroit and Pittsburgh, but in Lansing, Michigan; Washington, D.C.; and in every other capital where legislators, jurists, and government administrators considered the meaning of trade unionism and the functions it might perform. During World War II and shortly thereafter, such politicized bargaining arrangements covered virtually the entire working population. Key decisions—on wages for war workers and the price of steel, a yard of cloth, or a pound of meat—were made in either the White House itself or in a Federal Triangle building where tripartite panels representing business, labor, and the government had assumed something close to a new normality.[4] Under such circumstances the alliance between the labor movement and the Democrats was both intimate and tempestuous, and not only because the American South and its congressional representatives were so hostile to the union impulse. The effort to inject a consistent social democratic ethos into the northern Democratic Party generated much tension. As Jack Kroll of the CIO-PAC put it in the early 1950s, the unions were bargaining with the Democratic Party "much as it would with an employer."[5]

But the white South was the main problem. As Ira Katznelson and his coauthors established in their now-classic 1993 essay, "Limiting Liberalism: the Southern Veto in Congress," southern determination to maintain control of the labor market in the South proved the driving force that first fractured the New Deal congressional majority and then reshaped the meaning of what constituted a viable liberalism in the postwar era. As these political scientists make clear, for most of the 1930s the South had been supportive of a New Deal agenda, but once a mass labor movement sought to nationalize the labor market and open the door to African American economic citizenship, the white South went into opposition. But this did not mean that in the 1940s or even later, the Democratic South completely eviscerated all policies and programs that constituted a liberal agenda. The GOP-Dixiecrat alliance staunched an expansion of the welfare state and any legislation that furthered labor's institutional strength, but that alliance faltered when it came to other initiatives considered part of the liberal agenda, including Keynesian fiscal policies, free trade and foreign aid, farm subsidies, and infrastructure spending. Liberalism was limited and distorted. It lost most of its social democratic cast, and it consigned labor largely to an industrial archipelago that did not directly threaten southern, later Sun Belt, political-economic arrangements.[6]

Summing up, Katznelson and his coauthors quote the British historian D. W. Brogan, who in 1957 observed, "The American liberal today is confronted first of all by the memory of something that did not happen": the development of coherent social democratic programs and organizations. Elsewhere in the West, wrote Brogan, the Democratic Left created parties committed to strong political control over capitalist development, labor movements insistent on being recognized on a par with business, and coalitions of workers and farmers as the basis for political mobilizations. In the United States, on the other hand, the southern veto reduced the scope of labor's national political ambitions and instead gave priority to aggressive collective bargaining in core industries. "The large unions have largely contracted out of the state system," observed Brogan.[7]

Indeed, this well describes a key feature of the second industrial relations regime, a high noon of American industrial pluralism, when private sector collective bargaining stood center stage. Bargaining with stable companies and industries in the North and West, strong unions in transport, manufacturing, and mining generated a set of wage and benefit patterns that effectively set the template for a majority of workers, union or not, in the economy's core industries. While unions and their corporate adversaries remained engaged during each election season, this was an era of relative depoliticization, in which the bargaining regime functioned somewhat independent of the world of political contestation. Management and the political right favored this ghettoizing of the bargaining function, which is why Barry Goldwater could praise an industrial militant like Jimmy Hoffa but condemn the corporatist Walter Reuther during the high-profile McClellan Committee hearings of 1957 and 1958.[8]

This was not an era of consensus or of a labor-management accord—strikes were frequent and organizing increasingly difficult—but for that portion of the working population enrolled in strong trade unions, the political system, including the Democratic Party, was an increasingly detached "other." Therefore, a shift to the right on social or racial issues seemed to carry few costs for many rank and file unionists and the local union leaders who represented them. In the building trades and in trucking, airlines, and communications, the bargaining regime was remarkably insulated from outside political pressures. This suited conservative union leaders and their employer adversaries just fine. And even in a trade union like the UAW, with a highly politicized and liberal leadership, it became increasingly difficult to mobilize anything but a thin slice of the membership in support of the organization's larger social democratic goals.[9]

But the unions did not abandon their larger vision entirely: they did not become the parochial interest group that so many conservatives wanted and so many pluralist academics seemed to celebrate. Most union leaders looked for ways to break out of the bargaining ghetto to which they had been consigned, and this ambition even extended to figures such as cigar-smoking George Meany, the AFL-CIO chief who seemingly embodied caution, bureaucracy, and organizational parochialism. Indeed, it was a set of politics put forward by Meany that socialist Michael Harrington celebrated when he described the American labor movement as an invisible social democracy standing on the center left of the Democratic Party, even in the tumultuous 1960s.[10]

Case in point: in 1965 labor thought that the time had finally arrived to repeal Section 14B of the Taft-Hartley Act, which gave individual states the authority to proscribe the union shop. To most unionists at that time, 14B seemed the chief obstacle to organization of the South and the Mountain West. Congress itself had a genuinely liberal majority, if not a filibuster-proof supermajority, for the first time since the 1930s. And this was the liberal hour in which a progressive/civil rights agenda was pushed through the legislature and signed by the president. In the photograph taken at virtually every signing ceremony, George Meany stands somewhere not far behind President Lyndon Johnson, a signifier of the key role organized labor played in pushing through Medicare, Immigration Reform, Aid to Education, Model Cities, and the two great civil rights statutes of 1964 and 1965.

But when it came to the repeal of 14B, President Johnson put the labor reform at the end of the legislative line and failed to use his famous "treatment" on the Senate barons. To the public and too many in Congress, the repeal of 14B was a parochial, special-interest proposal. This was certainly the view of the Senate Minority leader Everett McKinley Dirksen, who offered George Meany a deal. Just as Dirksen had gone along with the civil rights bills, the Republican leader would cease his opposition to repeal of 14B if

Meany would agree not to resist a constitutional amendment overturning the Supreme Court's 1962 ruling, *Baker v. Carr*, that mandated one person, one vote reapportionment of state legislatures, a boon to liberals and minorities in the South and California. But Meany told Dirksen, no deal! "As badly as I want 14b repealed," Meany told his biographer, "I do not want it that badly. And the Senate Minority Leader and all his anti-labor stooges can filibuster until hell freezes over before I will agree to sell the people short for that kind of a deal."[11]

This was an incident that Michael Harrington deployed to assert that organized labor did not play the role of a self-serving interest group, despite the gravitational pull in that direction exerted by the privatized collective bargaining system of that era. "If the unions have been acting as an interest group they would have snapped up Dirksen's offer," wrote Harrington, "since it would have guaranteed passage of a law that was explicitly in their favor. But they chose to maximize a much more long-term perspective and to stick to their support for reapportionment. Labor's orientation toward playing a role in the center of American politics, where one-man/one-vote was so important, had prevailed over narrow organizational concerns. The unions, in short, had created a social democratic party, with its own apparatus and program, within the Democratic Party."[12]

Of course, that social democracy had a rough road before it. In two more instances, in 1978 and again in 1994, labor pushed forward legislation that would have sustained the institutional strength of the unions. During the Carter administration the unions settled upon an exceedingly modest piece of reform legislation—after realizing that repeal of 14B was simply off the agenda—which would have expanded the NLRB, insured timely certification of elections, and imposed penalties on labor law violators. And during the second year of the Clinton administration, the industrial unions backed a bill that would have made it more difficult for companies to replace striking workers during the course of a work stoppage, a maneuver that had become a commonplace management tactic in the years since Ronald Reagan fired eleven thousand members of the Professional Air Traffic Controllers Organization during a 1981 strike.[13]

In both instances, labor lost because the President and the Democrats in Congress followed a well-worn script. Although Carter and Clinton were both Democrats who had enjoyed much labor support during the campaign and although both briefly enjoyed large Democratic majorities in the Congress, these presidents saw labor law reform as a grudging tribute owed to their labor allies rather than a core part of their legislative agenda. Because the labor movement had more than two-thirds of all its members in just ten states, any legislation the AFL-CIO hoped to pass required either a full court press by the President and the Democrats or a division within conservative ranks. But in both 1978 and 1994, as in 1965, labor faced opposition from the business community and from the Republicans that was practically unanimous. Within Democratic Party ranks, a significant contingent from the South remained coy but essentially hostile.

Neither Carter nor Clinton put labor law reform high on his administration's agenda. Carter expended what little political capital he had in a bruising, bitter, but ultimately successful effort to cajole the Senate into passing a treaty that transferred ownership of the Panama Canal to the government of the country that it traversed. Thus by the time labor law reform reached Senate debate in the Spring of 1978, it faced a fully mobilized opposition—what two of the president's aides later described as "the most expensive and powerful lobby ever mounted against a bill in the nation's history."[14] In contrast. Carter's backing of the labor law reform bill, which would have sped up NLRB procedures and given union supporters and organizers a bit more protection from employer reprisal, proved tepid and uninspired. He rarely spoke in favor of the proposed law and when asked about it, he usually emphasized its limited impact. "I don't think that the legislation would lead to more rapid establishment of union workers in the South," he told a questioner on a presidential visit to Yazoo City.[15]

The same dynamic was at work in the early years of the Clinton administration. The president first spent political capital on a controversial foreign trade initiative, the North American Free Trade Agreement, which many liberals and almost all laborites opposed outright. Then came the all-consuming battle over health care reform, as well as an ultimately futile effort to reach common ground with the business community on a series of labor law reforms exhaustively debated by a high-profile commission presided over by former Secretary of Labor John Dunlop. By the time the Senate did debate a Workplace Fairness Bill that would have prevented employers from permanently replacing strikers after a work stoppage, President Clinton, like Carter before him, had pretty much exhausted his political capital, putting a cloture vote in the Senate just out of reach. Clinton's labor bill, editorialized the *New York Times*, "never inspired the midnight phone calls and political arm twisting the White House had lavished on other difficult political issues, like the North American Free Trade Agreement or last year's budget."[16]

In 1994 as well as 1978, legislative defeat came when a handful of southern Democratic Senators—with Arkansas "moderates" playing a key role in each instance—voted with opponents of the institutional reform.[17]

To understand these failures it is not enough to fault the legislative tactics of the congressional leadership or the timing of the presidential agenda, although in both instances mistakes were clearly made on both counts. Instead, we have to look to the interplay of ideology and interest, which had robbed labor of so much of its legitimacy and which had made Harrington's social democratic claims hard to credit for anyone not then a subscriber to *Dissent*.

Two issues are paramount: trade and civil rights. By the 1970s, American unions were already engaged in a fierce battle to defend themselves from a global trading regime that seemed to eat away at the foundations of labor strength in the most important industrial sectors of the economy. Labor's presumptive, parochial "protectionism" put it at odds with both Carter and Clinton, not to mention the GOP. But as historian Andrew Cohen has pointed out, labor and business had once seen protectionism as the essence of modernity. In the half century ending in 1930, Republicans had courted both labor and the most technologically advanced representatives of capital by linking high tariffs, high wages, and entrepreneurial innovation as the very essence of a progressive modernism. "Protectionists," writes Cohen, "viewed the customhouse as the guardian of an egalitarian society endangered by America's new affluence and global trade." Indeed, the same conservative jurists and politicians who enforced Lochner-era free markets during the early twentieth century, sustained the constitutionality of the protective tariff, despite intense opposition from the Democrats, both Tammany and Bourbon.[18]

This formula collapsed in the Great Depression when a new definition of progressive, democratic modernity took its place, linking direct welfare-state protections for labor with free trade and an internationalist engagement. This was an equation sustained by the enormous productivity of the American industrial economy after 1940 and by the Cold War posture of the American establishment. Within labor's ranks the greatest champions of the free trade regime came from those unions most sensitive to ethnic and racial discrimination, especially the needle trades, who linked trade, higher levels of immigration, and ethnic pluralism as foundational to the New Deal ethos. Indeed, one of the complex strands that kept southern segregationists and northern labor-liberals within the same party was a commitment to this free trade regime, backstopped—outside the South—by government enforcement of a high social wage and the gradual easing of immigration restrictions.[19]

That arrangement eroded rapidly in the 1970s, not only because of a greater level of global trade competition, but because labor lost any hope for a protectionist partner within either party. Except for some congressmen and women from rustbelt districts, there were no prominent Democratic figures who championed import restrictions to protect American jobs or sustain wages in the manufacturing sector; and among the Republicans the high-tariff wing, even if remnants of it still existed, was in no mood to reconstruct the social bargain it had once proffered to American labor in the pre–New Deal era. As a consequence, writes Cohen, virtually all critiques of free trade are viewed as an "archaic form of false consciousness."[20] This was a view that reached a symbiosis of sorts in Thomas Friedman's now (in)famous denunciation of the 1999 World Trade Organization protesters in Seattle as a "Noah's ark of flat-earth advocates, protectionist trade unions and yuppies looking for their 1960's fix."[21]

A second and even more important development also eroded a sense that trade unionism was a modernist phenomenon that meshed with Democratic Party interests and liberal goals. In the heyday of the collective bargaining regime, a cautious, pluralist understanding of how democracy functioned, certainly in contrast to the cataclysm that had engulfed Europe and Asia during the first half of the twentieth century, provided a sturdy foundation for interest-group politics and big-time collective bargaining. "Collective bargaining is the great social invention that has institutionalized industrial conflict," wrote the labor economist Robert Dublin in 1954. "In much the same way that the electoral process and majority rule have institutionalized political conflict in a democracy, collective bargaining has created a stable means for resolving industrial conflict."[22] Six years later theologian Reinhold Niebuhr, who had once denounced Henry Ford from a Detroit pulpit in the 1920s, summed up the wishful yet cautious ethos into which the organization of the Western working class had been consigned by America's most respected liberals. "Collective bargaining has come to be regarded as almost as basic as the right to vote," Niebuhr told the labor-liberals who read the staunchly anti-Communist *New Leader*. "The equilibrium of power achieved between management and labor . . . is one of the instruments used by a highly technical society, with ever larger aggregates of power, to achieve that tolerable justice which has rendered Western Civilization immune to the Communist virus."[23]

The rights revolution that reached fruition in the 1960s soon supplanted this pluralist understanding of what made liberalism a dynamic and progressive faith, certainly in terms of labor and its role in the larger polity. Labor's relative eclipse during the era of civil rights is not just the story of white working-class racism and a calculating trade union leadership that put its muscle behind the new civil rights laws of the mid-1960s while dragging its feet on their application inside the house of labor. All this is true and no apologia is on offer in this essay. But the real question is why labor could not recapture a sense of momentum once demography and organizational opportunities transformed the trade union movement, in the 1980s and 1990s, into an institution that is both far more multicultural and in many respects more democratic than that which existed on the eve of the civil rights movement.

From a legal perspective the labor movement was battered from two directions in the years after the 1960s. After the passage of the 1964 civil rights law, the nation had two sets of labor laws, one having its origins in the Wagner Act, the other arising out of the judicial reinterpretation of Title VII of the 1964 law. In her *Freedom Is Not Enough: The Opening of the American Workplace*, Nancy MacLean has demonstrated how the struggle to pass and then implement Title VII had a near revolutionary impact on employment opportunities and patterns for tens of millions of workers, even as the American right, in turn southern, corporate, and neoconservative, sought to eviscerate such legal and social transformations.[24]

But as with so many labor-liberal achievements in the postwar era, the genuine breakthrough represented by Title VII had unforeseen and deleterious consequences for the institutional strength and integrity of the trade unions, including those that had long been advocates of racial liberalism in the workplace. Title VII and other similar laws and administrative rulings proved an invitation to judicial activism, argues Paul Frymer in his recent *Black and Blue: African Americans, the Labor Movement and the Decline of the Democratic Party*.[25] Norris-LaGuardia and the Wagner Act had seemingly rid the United States of the intrusive, antilabor judicial policy-making characteristic of the Lochner Era, but now the courts were once again intruding themselves into the interpretation and application of labor and employment law, in part as a result of civil rights litigation on behalf of minorities discriminated against by unions and employers, and in part because of the stalemate in the labor law that Congress could not resolve. To Frymer the "federal courts had in many ways regained their position as the primary overseer of the workplace"[26]

With civil rights and labor rights divided into two different organizational and judicial categories, unions were vulnerable to administrators and judges with little knowledge or sympathy for the particularities of union politics and institutional structures. Although the failure of trade unions to protect their minority members was not the only reason for judicial activism, it set a precedent that was repeatedly used to strip unions of power and legitimacy when other issues involving seniority, strikes, membership, and dues are concerned. AFL-CIO litigation costs doubled between 1966 and 1973, doubled again by 1979, and then quadrupled over the next four years. As Frymer put it "Once courts became involved in labor policy making on matters of race, it is not a far leap to where they extend this involvement to broader questions previously handled by electoral officials. Courts have not only scaled back the NLRA, they have extended their influence to a wide range of employment matters, using tort and contract law to increase individual worker rights independent from legislative involvement."[27]

Frymer's story is one of how a discourse arising from the growth of a rights-conscious liberalism undermined trade unionism, but often in an inadvertent and unforeseen fashion. But a far more cynical and mendacious assault on union power also used a discourse made potent by the civil rights movement, but it emanated from long-standing southern, antiunion business interests, which after 1955 were the chief funders and proponents of the National-Right-to-Work Committee. Passage of right-to-work laws became a cause célèbre in the 1940s even before Taft-Hartley and Section 14B opened the door for state-level Right-to-Work statutes that proscribed the union shop and weakened trade union power, chiefly in the southern and western states. When the Right-to-Work Committee was founded in the 1950s it was funded by the most reactionary textile, oil, and food-processing interests. Its propaganda against the union shop was virtually indistinguishable from a larger antiunion, anti-Communist, states' rights discourse that often evoked McCarthyite and segregationist themes.[28]

In the mid-1960s however, right-to-work advocates began to switch their source of rhetorical authority from natural law to civil rights constitutionalism. Indeed, as the legal historian Sophia Lee has pointed out in an essay on right-to-work litigation, these conservative antiunion lawyers and publicists no longer described their legal struggle as one that ran parallel to that of the civil rights impulse, but rather it was a legal strategy that was actually *part* of the civil rights movement. Soon African American litigants—representing but a tiny minority of that minority, but just enough to cast a creditable cloak over the enterprise—were prominent in right-to-work publicity and court cases. The Right-to-Work Committee promised to represent "workers who are suffering legal injustice as a result of employment discrimination under compulsory union membership arrangements" even as they touted its mission to "Protect Human and Civil Rights for America's Wage Earners."

Through the 1970s and 1980s the Committee's efforts to link this antiunion propaganda and litigation with civil rights themes became more elaborate, institutionalized and sophisticated. Committee membership mushroomed from less than fifty thousand to almost three hundred thousand by 1975 alone, while its network of cooperating attorneys had grown to include one hundred lawyers. By the mid-1980s the foundation was pursuing scores of right-to-work cases in as many venues. Thus, even as Republican politicians were courting southern Democrats and promising race-coded assaults on welfare and crime in the 1970s, the right-to-work movement tested a different approach, which advanced a species of rights talk, originally spawned by the black liberation movement, in order to achieve doctrinal victories in the courts, generate antiunion propaganda, and deploy a potent weapon against its sworn enemy, "big labor," and thereby weaken its implicit foe, the Democratic Party.[29]

The era of intense conflict between the unions and civil rights forces is now over. As the industrial unions and the construction trades have declined in size and influence, the center of gravity of American trade unionism has shifted to the service sector, where a multicultural workforce and a relative deemphasis on traditional collective bargaining have marginalized the job control and seniority issues that were once such lightening rods for racial conflict and litigation. But the legacy of the defeats, political and ideological, suffered by the old union movement live on. The strike weapon is dead, union density drops almost every year, and the administrative/legal regime put in place by the New Deal is dysfunctional, both in rust-belt manufacturing and big-box retail. Strikes and lockouts, precipitated by management, are now a corporate weapon; likewise collective bargaining, especially on health and pension issues, is more likely to generate union givebacks than contract improvement.[30]

But a new, highly politicized, highly public system of "bargaining" has arisen in place of the mid-twentieth-century collective bargaining model. It is a system that has linked the unions ever more closely to the Democrats, at the state level perhaps even more than at the national, and it has transformed the metrics by which we measure the strength and influence of American trade unionism, which is one reason that conservative hostility to organized labor has taken on a very sharp edge, even as labor's numerical ranks have sunk to new lows. In effect, industrial relations in the United States have once again taken on some of the corporatist coloration that was so important to the labor-liberal agenda in the 1930s and 1940s.

The first phenomenon that repoliticized U.S. labor relations was the jump in union membership among government workers. This began in the late

1950s, accelerated all through the 1960s and 1970s, and then reached a plateau in the years after 1980, when union density in public employment stood at about 35 percent. Today more unionists can be found working for a government entity than for a private employer. "This means government is the main playing field for modern unionism," editorialized the *Wall Street Journal* with some alarm.[31] By its very nature, state and municipal trade unionism is highly political. Key decisions are often made not at the bargaining table, but at the ballot box and in the legislative chamber. New York State now has the highest union density in the nation thanks to the adroit, if not always pretty, capacity of the municipal employees, school teachers, and nonprofit hospital workers to bargain with governors of both political parties.[32] In the South, where laws banning public employee unionism still exist, union density is truly minuscule, less than 5 percent in many instances. Thus, U.S. trade unionism, always a regional phenomenon, is even more so today than in decades past. This is one reason for the sharp divide between blue and red states (and why Democratic gains in the upper South are almost always tenuous unless they are backstopped by the organizational weight of unions that have a foothold among local public sector workers).

The second development that has politicized the relationship between the unions and the electoral system has been the growth, or attempted growth, of unionism in the service sector of the economy, especially in the growing hospital, health care, higher education, hotel, retail, and telecommunications sectors of the economy. In all of these industries, government subsidies, regulations, and zoning approvals are crucial, which is why all unions in the service sector maintain outsized research staffs, whose primary function is to figure out at what points the unions and their political allies can leverage government power and money on behalf of the workers and companies they seek to organize or influence. In the 1950s, the UAW maintained a research staff of about half a dozen, whose primary job was to read the General Motors annual report and determine how much the union could safely demand without bankrupting Chrysler and other less profitable companies. Today, UNITE-HERE, a far smaller union, which largely organizes in the hotel sector, has a research staff of almost one hundred, all of whom are experts in the politics of state and city zoning and in the complex arrangements by which new hotels and convention centers are financed. As Harold Meyerson observed in a recent commentary, "HERE's decision to create a cadre of corporate campaigners was based on the grimmest of facts: Traditional private-sector union organizing—signing up workers who want to join a union, winning a certification election conducted by the government, and securing a collective-bargaining agreement in negotiations with the employer—had become a dead-end." Not a single hotel could be organized absent a campaign to bring so much financial, political, and community pressure on the employer that it would agree not to oppose unionization. "The mere desire of workers to form a union no longer sufficed," asserted Meyerson.[33]

For almost two decades such corporate campaigns have been largely worked out at the state and local levels where unions have used their political and lobbying clout to "make a deal" in the state capital or in city hall. This has generated bargains in which employers have agreed to remain neutral and/or accept "card-check" union certification when new hotels, convention centers, shopping malls, and airports were built, or where a new level of government financial aid was necessary to sustain nursing homes, hospitals, and home health care services. In progressive states like California, Maryland, and Illinois, a Democratic Party–labor alliance has become increasingly symbiotic; conversely, the Republicans have sharpened their denunciation of this politicized unionism and through various legal gambits and referenda, including "paycheck protection" laws proscribing union expenditure of member dues for political purses, have sought to curb the trade union capacity to lobby and exercise electoral influence.[34]

With the Democrats now in power at the national level, this kind of labor politics has become a flashpoint for high-level debate. Take the question of part-time work in the service sector, a contentious issue fought out by labor and management for many years. In what was probably the last great union victory in a traditional strike and bargaining situation, the Teamsters in 1997 forced United Parcel Service to transform more than ten thousand part-time jobs into full-time positions with regular pay and benefits. But the overwhelming majority of service sector workers are unorganized, so regardless of the internal difficulties that crippled further Teamster efforts on this front, such strike action was not repeated. Thus, during the Bush era, part-time work flourished, along with the paltry benefits, rapid turnover, and low pay characteristic of these jobs.[35]

But tucked away within the Obama administration's 2009 stimulus package was a provision that promised a substantial impact on the status of part-time work. In exchange for a large increase in the federal government's contribution to state unemployment compensation funds, state officials were required to extend unemployment benefits to thousands of part-time workers who were never before eligible. This had been a long-sought goal of the union movement, because it offers financial and legal incentives to upgrade part-time work, thus reducing turnover, raising take-home pay, and in some instances making unionization easier. Not unexpectedly, such a revision in the law was anathema among labor-intensive employers in the service sector, first among them the big-box retailers who use part-time workers as a reserve army of the semiemployed to put downward pressure on wages and enhance management capacity to deploy labor in the most "flexible" fashion. By including such workers in the unemployment system, more of them can say, "Take this job and shove it." Thus it was hardly surprising, or a political miscalculation, to find that in states like South Carolina, Texas, and Louisiana, where labor is weak and big-box retailing strong, Republican governors rejected Obama's unemployment funds in order to avoid tilting the unemployment compensation law even slightly in a labor's favor.[36] Katznelson's "Southern Veto" thesis still makes its weight felt, albeit under twenty-first–century conditions.

And the fate of the Employee Free Choice Act is even more instructive. President Obama and the rest of the Democratic Party, now purged of much of its southern wing, had a more genuine commitment to labor law reform than either Presidents Carter and Clinton, or the Democratic legislators of their era. But like Carter and Clinton, Obama put other legislative initiatives higher on his agenda, health care reform first and foremost. And on this question, the labor movement heartily endorsed the President's reform priorities, if only because health care reform was a grand corporatist bargain that, whatever its limitations, promised to greatly enhance health care provision for upward of thirty-two million working-class Americans. This was a hugely progressive transfer of income, security, and well-being, but the right-wing mobilization engendered by the yearlong battle necessary to enact health care reform also doomed prospects for a revision of the labor law that would make union organizing a less arduous and dangerous enterprise.

Equally important, this mobilization opened the door to an intense season of antiunion rhetoric and legislation, not only in the South or the agricultural West, where such gambits were routine, but in the very heartland of contemporary union strength: the tier of Northern industrial states from New Jersey westward where a new cohort of conservative Republican governors, many elected in 2010, put the virtual destruction of public sector unionism, and the evisceration of the state-level corporatism that sustained these unions, at the very top of their legislative agenda. Wisconsin was ground zero, where Governor Scott Walker pushed through a conservative state legislature a radical revision of existing law that virtually eliminated collective bargaining in the public sector and stripped unions of much of the monetary resources necessary to engage in effective political action. Conservative Republicans put similar antiunion initiatives on the legislative agenda in Ohio, New Jersey, Michigan, and Indiana. And even in New York, Massachusetts, and California Democratic governors, elected with union support, took a harder line against public sector trade unions.[37]

The fiscal crisis that starved so many state budgets in the aftermath of the 2008–2009 financial crisis was the proximate rationale for this assault. By emphasizing, and in some cases manipulating, the red ink flowing through so many state budgets, the antiunion Right leveraged the crisis to declare the pension benefits and health care standards negotiated by public sector unions, not to mention collective bargaining itself, as fiscally unsustainable. Unionists were quick to point out that neither pensions nor wage standards contributed decisively to state and local budget deficits; indeed, in Madison, Columbus and elsewhere, they mounted large and spirited demonstrations that blunted for a time the conservative onslaught.[38]

But if unionists remained steadfast, organized labor had greater difficulty in winning to their side those private sector workers whose own wage and benefit standards had either stagnated or declined in recent years. Under such economically fraught circumstances, even the limited bargaining success enjoyed by public sector trade unions often generated an intense, pseudo-populist resentment among millions of others that Republican officeholders were all too skillful in projecting against the organizations that sustained the living standards and relatively secure jobs of so many teachers, clerks, firemen, social workers, and other state and local employees.[39] Corporatism within one economic sector could not long sustain itself within a world of growing inequality and insecurity.

In conclusion, let's return to the conundrum with which we began this survey of post–New Deal labor-liberalism. Today, as in the 1930s and 1940s, the labor movement composes a liberal, even a social democratic wing within the Democratic Party. Issues of foreign policy, immigration, cultural politics, and racial parochialism, which once pushed labor toward the neoconservative right, have faded. Though shrunken in size, the unions are a backbone of the Democratic Party electoral effort, even in states where membership is small. Likewise, the Democratic Party itself has become more liberal, largely because of the withering away of the conservative, white southern contingent. So why has the passage of legislation that seeks to strengthen the institutional integrity and assure the potential growth of the unions so problematic, even when Carter, Clinton, or Obama and their legislative cadres had the political wind at their back?

First, business hostility is near universal—far greater, for example, than during the abortive labor law reform efforts of the Johnson administration.

This is because the corporations recognize that any additional organization clout won by the unions will generate not just more leverage at the bargaining table, but more ideological and political influence on the far broader party/political terrain that today constitutes America's social policy battlefield. If a handful of Wal-Mart stores were successfully organized at any point in the foreseeable future, the result would not be higher wages or more benefits in those few, isolated workplaces, but rather an industrywide body blow to the ideology and social praxis that has characterized retail's entire low-wage, low-benefit employment strategy and the cultural politics that sustains it.

Second, the Democratic Party is not united, even with the shrinkage of its southern wing. The culture wars, which drove so many cosmopolitan upscale voters into Democratic ranks, also makes the Party far less homogeneous when it comes to economic policy. Although the trade union impulse that seeks a higher level of purchasing power for the working class now accords with Democratic efforts to redress the income inequalities that have grown so pronounced over the last three decades, the equally important trade union interest in job control issues, including seniority, pensions, work rules, and the like, generate conflict and resentment in all workplaces, including those characteristic of such notably "liberal" industry sectors as the news media, Hollywood, telecommunications, big-city hotels, nonprofit health care, and government service. This has tempered enthusiasm for a rebirth of trade unionism, even in such otherwise liberal locales as Chicago, the Bay Area, and Seattle.[40]

And finally, the union movement itself has failed to infuse the new corporatism that it now propounds with the kind of overarching ideological impulse that once animated the burst of industrial union organizing in the 1930s or the civil rights–inflected growth of the public sector unionism in the 1960s and 1970s. The CIO stood for industrial democracy and cultural pluralism as well as a new organizational form that promised a more efficacious way to represent mass production workers in heavy industry. Likewise, labor's contemporary corporatist initiative requires far more than the "let's make a deal" mentality that has sometimes colored organizing activity and lobbying practice in the health care sector. To rebuild American social democracy, an ideological vision is just as essential as innovations on the organizational front.

Notes

1. Mitchell Rubinstein, "Obama's Big Deal; The 2009 Federal Stimulus; Labor and Employment Law at the Crossroads, " *Rutgers Law Record* 33 (Spring 2009), 1–11, at www.lawrecord.com, accessed September 12, 2011; Peter Dreier, "Will Obama

Inspire a New Generation of Organizers?" *Dissent* (online) (Spring 2008): 1–7, at www.Dissentmagazine.org, accessed September 12, 2011.

2. Christine Bellantoni, "Trumka to Unions: Too Much at Stake to Let Frustration Keep You from Polls" *Talking Point Memo*, August 3, 2010.

3. For a longer discussion of EFCA, see Nelson Lichtenstein, "Despite EFCA's Limitations, Its Demise Is a Profound Defeat for U.S. Labor," in *LABOR: Working-Class History of the Americas* 6 (Fall 2010): 29–32.

4. The literature on labor and the New Deal is rich: for works that discuss the relationship between the unions, the state, and employers, see Steve Fraser, *Labor Will Rule: Sidney Hillman and the Rise of American Labor* (New York: Free Press, 1991), 289–323, 407–494; Colin Gordon, *New Deals: Business, Labor, and Politics in America, 1920–1935* (Cambridge: Cambridge University Press, 1994), 166–239; Melvyn Dubofsky, *The State and Labor in Modern America* (Chapel Hill: University of North Carolina Press, 1994), 107–195; Jennifer Klein, *For All These Rights: Business, Labor, and the Shaping of America's Public-Private Welfare State* (Princeton: Princeton University Press, 2003), 78–161; Meg Jacobs, *Pocketbook Politics: Economic Citizenship in Twentieth-Century America* (Princeton: Princeton University Press, 2005), 136–220; and for a comparative perspective, see Peter A. Swenson, *Capitalists against Markets: The Making of Labor Markets and Welfare States in the United States and Sweden* (New York: Oxford University Press, 2002), 142–220.

5. James C. Foster, *The Union Politic* (Columbia: University of Missouri Press, 1975), 199.

6. Ira Katznelson, Kim Geiger, and Daniel Kryder, "Limiting Liberalism: The Southern Veto in Congress, 1933–1950," *Political Science Quarterly* 108:2 (1993): 283–306.

7. Ibid., 301.

8. Elizabeth Shermer, "Origins of the Conservative Ascendancy: Barry Goldwater's Early Senate Career and the De-legitimization of Organized Labor," *Journal of American History* 95 (December 2008): 700–701; and see Kimberly Phillips-Fein, *Invisible Hands: The Making of the Conservative Movement from the New Deal to Reagan* (New York: W. W. Norton, 2009).

9. Nelson Lichtenstein, *Walter Reuther: The Most Dangerous Man in Detroit* (Urbana: University of Illinois Press, 1997), 299–326. In his *State of the Union* (Princeton: Princeton University Press, 2002), Lichtenstein makes this argument at greater length. See especially "A Labor-Management Accord?" 98–140.

10. Michael Harrington, *Socialism* (New York: Saturday Review Press, 1972); and see Maurice Isserman, *The Other American: The Life of Michael Harrington* (New York: Public Affairs, 2000).

11. Taylor Dark, *The Unions and the Democrats: An Enduring Alliance* (Ithaca: Cornell University Press, 1999), 61.

12. Harrington, *Socialism*, 326.

13. Martin Halpern, *Unions, Radicals, and Democratic Presidents: Seeking Social*

Change in the Twentieth Century (Westport: Praeger, 2003); John Logan, "Labor's Last Stand in National Politics? The Campaign for Striker Replacement Legislation, 1990–1994," in Bruce Kaufman and David Lewin, eds., *Advances in Industrial and Labor Relations* (Ithaca: Cornell University Press, 2004), 197–256.

14. Halpern, *Unions, Radicals, and Democratic Presidents*, 125.

15. Ibid., 124.

16. As quoted in Dark, *The Unions and the Democrats*, 175.

17. Halpern, *Unions, Radicals, and Democratic Presidents*, 167–171.

18. Andrew Wender Cohen, "Unions, Modernity, and the Decline of American Economic Nationalism," paper presented at the conference, "The American Right and U.S. Labor: Politics, Ideology, and Imagination." University of California, Santa Barbara, January 16–17, 2009.

19. Carl Bon Tempo, *American at the Gate: The United States and Refugees during the Cold War* (Princeton: Princeton University Press, 2008).

20. Cohen, "Unions, Modernity, and the Decline of American Economic Nationalism."

21. Thomas Friedman, "Senseless in Seattle," *New York Times*, December 1, 1999.

22. Robert Dublin, "Constructive Aspects of Industrial Conflict," in Arthur Kornhauser, Robert Dublin, and Arthur Ross, eds., *Industrial Conflict* (New York: McGraw-Hill, 1954), 44.

23. Reinhold Niebuhr, "'End of an Era' for Organized Labor," *New Leader*, January 4, 1969, 18. A longer discussion of pluralism as an ideological bulwark for Cold War unionism in found in my *State of the Union: A Century of American Labor* (Princeton: Princeton University Press, 2002), 141–177.

24. Nancy MacLean, *Freedom Is Not Enough: The Opening of the American Workplace* (Cambridge: Harvard University Press, 2006), 333–347.

25. Paul Frymer, *Black and Blue: African Americans, the Labor Movement, and the Decline of the Democratic Party* (Princeton: Princeton University Press, 2008).

26. Paul Frymer, "Race, Labor, and the Twentieth-Century American State," *Politics and Society* 32:4 (December 2004): 477.

27. Ibid., 494. But see Risa Goluboff, *The Lost Promise of Civil Rights* (Cambridge: Harvard University Press, 2007) for an argument that, in a somewhat earlier, era civil rights litigation might well have been advanced in a more judicially harmonious relationship to that of organized labor.

28. Gilbert Gall, *The Politics of Right to Work: The Labor Federations As Special Interests, 1943–1979* (Westport: Greenwood Press, 1988); Elizabeth Tandy Shermer, "Counter-Organizing the Sunbelt: Right-to-Work Campaigns and Anti-Union Conservatism, 1943–1958," *Pacific Historical Review* 78 (February 2009): 81–118.

29. Sophia Lee, "Whose Rights? Litigating the Right to Work, 1950–1980, paper prepared for delivery at the conference, "The American Right and U.S. Labor: Politics, Ideology, and Imagination." University of California, Santa Barbara, January 16–17, 2009.

30. Kim Moody, *US Labor in Trouble and Transition: The Failure of Reform from Above, The Promise of Revival from Below* (New York: Verso, 2007); Steven Greenhouse, *The Big Squeeze: Tough Times for the American Worker* (New York: Alfred A. Knopf, 2008), 71–97; and for a heroic but doomed struggle in the heartland, see Steven Ashby and C. J. Hawking, *Staley: The Fight for a New American Labor Movement* (Urbana: University of Illinois, 2009).

31. "The Public Union Ascendancy," *Wall Street Journal*, February 3, 2010.

32. Joshua Freeman, *Working-Class New York: Life and Labor since World War II* (New York: New Press, 2001), 201–227.

33. Harold Meyerson, "Where Are the Workers? Employees Are Losing Their Central Place in Union Organizing, but Card-Check Legislation Could Turn That Around." *American Prospect* on line, March 4, 2009. For an additional critique of this kind of bargaining, see Moody, *US Labor in Trouble*, 184–197.

34. Steven Malanga, "The Beholden State: How Public-Sector Unions Broke California," *City Journal* 20 (Spring 2010) at www.city-journal.org, accessed September 12, 2011; Marick Masters, Raymond Gibney, and Thomas Zagenczk, "Worker Pay Protection: Implications for Labor's Political Spending and Voice," *Industrial Relations: A Journal of Economy and Society* 48 (October 2009): 557–577.

35. Among other sources, see Nelson Lichtenstein, *The Retail Revolution: How Wal-Mart Created a Brave New World of Business* (New York: Henry Holt, 2009), 85–117.

36. Catherine Rampell, "Stimulus Bill Would Bestow New Aid to Many Workers," *New York Times*, February 14, 2009; David Montgomery and Aman Batheja, "Democrats Will Push to Overturn Perry Move to Reject Some Stimulus Funds," *Austin Star-Telegram*, March 13, 2009.

37. Steven Greenhouse, "A Watershed Moment for Public-Sector Unions," *New York Times*, February 19, 2011, A14.

38. Stanley Aronowitz, "One, Two, Many Madisons: The War on Public Sector Workers" *New Labor Forum* (Spring 2011): 15–21.

39. A. G. Sulzberger and Monica Davey, "Union Bonds in Wisconsin Begin to Fray," *New York Times*, February 22, 2011, A1.

40. John Lippert and Holly Rosenkrantz, "Billionaire Donors Split with Obama on Law That May Hurt Hotels," *Bloomberg News*, May 7, 2009; Enda Brophy, "System Error: Labour Precarity and Collective Organizing at Microsoft," *Canadian Journal of Communication* 31 (2006) at www.cjc-online.ca, accessed September 12, 2011.

Contributors

TONY BADGER has been Paul Mellon Professor of American History since 1992, Fellow of Sidney Sussex College, 1992 to 2003, and Master of Clare College since October 2003. He has written extensively on the New Deal and on the post-1945 American South. His books include *Prosperity Road: The New Deal, Tobacco, and North Carolina* (Chapel Hill: University of North Carolina Press, 1980), *The New Deal: The Depression Years 1933–1940* (London: Macmillan, 1989), *New Deal/New South: The Anthony J. Badger Reader* (Fayetteville: University of Arkansas Press, 2007), and *FDR: The First Hundred Days* (New York: Hill and Wang, 2008). He has edited, with Brian Ward, *The Making of Martin Luther King and the Civil Rights Movement* (New York: Macmillan, 1996), with Walter Edgar and Jan Gretlund, *Southern Landscapes* (Munich: Stauffenburg, 1997) and, with Byron Shafer, *Contesting Democracy: The Substance and Structure of American Political History* (Lawrence: University Press of Kansas, 2001).

JONATHAN BELL is senior lecturer in history and head of history at the University of Reading. He is the author of *The Liberal State on Trial: The Cold War and American Politics in the Truman Years* (New York: Columbia University Press, 2004), *California Crucible: The Forging of Modern American Liberalism* (Philadelphia: University of Pennsylvania Press, 2012), and coeditor with Tim Stanley of *Making Sense of American Liberalism* (Champaign: University of Illinois Press, 2012). He has published numerous journal articles on twentieth-century U.S. history, and is now working on a new project on the American health care system, minority rights, and the state.

LIZABETH COHEN is the Howard Mumford Jones Professor American Studies and currently chair of the History Department of Harvard University. She is the author of *Making a New Deal: Industrial Workers in Chicago, 1919–1939* (Cambridge: Cambridge University Press, 1990, new edition with new introduction 2008), winner of the Bancroft Prize and a finalist for the Pulitzer, and *A Consumers' Republic: The Politics of Mass Consumption in Postwar America* (New York: Alfred A. Knopf, 2003), named an Editor's Choice Selection by *Booklist* and one of the nine best nonfiction books of 2003 by the *Boston Globe*. She is the coauthor, with David Kennedy, of a popular Advanced Placement and College-level U.S. History textbook, *The American Pageant* (Stamford, Conn.: Cengage, 1998, 2002, 2006, 2010). She has also written a number of prize-winning journal articles and contributes book reviews and essays regularly to the popular press. In her current research, she is writing a book entitled *Saving America's Cities: Ed Logue and the Struggle to Renew Urban America in the Suburban Age*. During the academic year 2007–2008 she was the Harold Vyvyan Harmsworth Professor at Oxford University.

SUSAN M. HARTMANN is Arts and Sciences Distinguished Professor of History at Ohio State University, specializing in the political economy of post–World War II U.S. and women's history. She is coauthor of a U.S. history survey and author of four monographs, including *The Other Feminists: Activists in the Liberal Establishment* (Yale, 1998). Her work has been supported by fellowships from the Rockefeller Foundation, the National Endowment for the Humanities, the American Council of Learned Societies, and the Woodrow Wilson International Center for Scholars. She is currently writing a book on gender and the transformation of U.S. politics and policies since World War II.

ELLA HOWARD is assistant professor of history at Armstrong Atlantic State University in Savannah, Georgia. She is the author of the forthcoming book *Homeless: Poverty, Policy, and Place in the Era of Skid Row* (Philadelphia: University of Pennsylvania Press) and of essays on the history of poverty, social and political history, women's history, public history, material culture, and consumerism.

NELSON LICHTENSTEIN is professor of history at the University of California, Santa Barbara, and director of the Center for the Study of Work, Labor, and Democracy. He is the author of numerous books, including *State of the*

Union: A Century of American Labor (New edition, Princeton: Princeton University Press, 2003), *Walter Reuther, The Most Dangerous Man in Detroit* (Champaign: University of Illinois Press, 1997), and *The Retail Revolution: How Wal-Mart Created a Brave New World of Business* (New York: Henry Holt and Company, 2009).

BRUCE MIROFF is professor of political science at the State University of New York, Albany. He received his PhD from the University of California, Berkeley. He has written widely on American politics, focusing on the presidency, political development, and political theory. His books include *Pragmatic Illusions: The Presidential Politics of John F. Kennedy* (Philadelphia: McKay, 1976), *Icons of Democracy: American Leaders as Heroes, Aristocrats, Dissenters, and Democrats* (New York: Basic Books, 1993), and *The Liberals' Moment: The McGovern Insurgency and the Identity Crisis of the Democratic Party* (Lawrence: University Press of Kansas, 2007). He is a former president of the Presidency Research Group of the American Political Science Association.

DOUG ROSSINOW is professor of history and chair of the Department of History at Metropolitan State University in Saint Paul, Minnesota. He is the author of *The Politics of Authenticity: Liberalism, Christianity, and the New Left in America* (New York: Columbia University Press, 1998) and *Visions of Progress: The Left-Liberal Tradition in America* (Philadelphia: University of Pennsylvania Press, 2008), and the coeditor of *The United States since 1945: Historical Interpretations* (Upper Saddle River, N.J.: Pearson, 2007), as well as the author of numerous essays, including "'The Model of a Model Fellow Traveler': Harry F. Ward, The American League for Peace and Democracy, and the 'Russian Question' in American Politics, 1933–1956," *Peace and Change* 29:2 (April 2004), which won the Charles DeBenedetti Prize for the best essay in peace history for 2003–2004. He was vice president of the Peace History Society for 2009–2010. His current book project is *To Begin the World Over: Ronald Reagan and the American 1980s*.

TIMOTHY STANLEY is a Leverhulme Early Career Research Fellow at Royal Holloway College, University of London. He is the author of *Kennedy vs. Carter: The 1980 Battle for the Democratic Party's Soul* (Lawrence: University Press of Kansas, 2008) and *The Crusader: The Life and Turbulent Times of Pat Buchanan* (New York: St. Martin's Press, 2012). He writes a column for the Daily Telegraph on U.S. politics.

TIMOTHY N. THURBER is currently associate professor of history at Virginia Commonwealth University. He is working on a book-length project on the Republican Party and civil rights from 1945 to 1980 and is author of *The Politics of Equality: Hubert H. Humphrey and the African American Freedom Struggle* (New York: Columbia University Press, 1999). He has received research grants from several organizations, including the Everett Dirksen Congressional Leadership Center, the Lyndon B. Johnson Foundation, and the Harry S. Truman Foundation.

Index

abortion rights, 204, 206, 214, 215
Abzug, Bella, 65, 210, 211, 215, 216
Addams, Jane, 22, 115
Affluent Society, The (Galbraith), 151
Afghanistan, invasion by U.S.S.R., 79
Agnew, Spiro, 159
Aid to Dependent Children, 203
alcoholism, 120–21
Alexander, Clifford, 188
Alexander, Lamar, 169
Allen, Bill, 167
Allen, James, 195
Amalgamated Clothing Workers Union (ACWU), 73, 78
American Association of University Women, 211
American Civil Liberties Union (ACLU), 23
American Conservative Thought in the Twentieth Century (Buckley), 150
American Dilemma, An (Myrdal), 28–29
American Federation of Labor and Congress of Industrial Organizations (AFL-CIO), 26, 41, 44, 64, 70, 77, 172–73, 229–45
American Federation of State, County and Municipal Employees (AFSCME), 70, 73, 211–12
American Food for Peace, 96, 97
American Political Science Association (APSA), 92
Americans for Democratic Action (ADA), 29, 49, 64, 70, 93

Americans with Disabilities Act (1990), 144
Andreas, Dwayne, 98
Anson, Robert Sam, 93
Apple, R. W., 171
Arms Control and Disarmament Agency, 95
Arywitz, Sigmund, 44
Asilomar Conference (1952), 45–47
Askew, Reubin, 176

Baker, Ray Stannard, 20
Baker Jr., Howard H., 169, 172, 173, 175
Baker v. Carr (1962), 234
Baldwin, Roger, 24
Banana Kelly Community Improvement Association, 146
Barkan, Al, 170
Barnet, Richard, 93
Barrett, George, 169
Bass, Ross, 169
Bendiner, Elmer, 124
Bingham, Alfred, 27
Black and Blue: African Americans, the Labor Movement and the Decline of the Democratic Party (Fryner), 238
Bolshevik Revolution (1917), 24
Bond, Richard C., 138
Bork, Robert, 19
Boston, urban renewal, 141–43
Boston Redevelopment Authority (BRA), 141–43
Bourne, Randolph, 25

Bowery, the (NYC), 115–16, 121, 123, 125, 126
Bowles, Chester, 139
Brace, Charles Loring, 115
Brewer, Albert, 176
Brinkley, Alan, 163
Brock III, William E., 159, 161, 169, 172, 175
Broder, David, 175, 176, 215
Brooke, Edward, 188
Brooks, Jack, 167
Brown, Pat, 38, 44–45, 46
Brown, Willie, 46
Brownell, Herbert, 191
Brown v. Board of Education (1954), 119, 165, 190
Buckley Jr., William F., 149
Burdick, Thelma, 122
Burgee, John, 144
Burke, Yvonne Braithwaite, 210
Burton, Phil, 46, 55
Bush, George H. W., 197
Bush, George W., 148, 151
Business Week (journal), 77

California: changing dynamics of West Coast liberal politics after WWII, 38–61; club movement and Asilomar Conference (1952), 45–51; political culture in mid-century California, 40–45; relationship between Democratic Party and labor organizations, 44–45; Stevenson campaign (1956), crystallization of Democratic message, and emergence of "the consumers' republic," 52–57
California Democratic Council, 46
Callison, William, 211
Campaign for a Democratic Majority, 64
Campaign for Economic Democracy, 78
Camp Bluefield, 117
Camp Greycourt, 117
Carey, Hugh, 145, 146
Carswell, Harold, 160, 168, 196
Carter, Jimmy, 63, 68, 71–80, 106, 147, 176, 214, 215, 234, 235, 243
Case, Clifford, 188
Cellar, Emanuel, 210–11
Chamberlain, John, 24
Chambers, Marjorie Bell, 216
Chandler, Norman, 43
Charity Organization Society (NYC), 115

child-care provisions, post-WWII feminist campaigns, 212–13
Chisholm, Shirley, 210, 211
Choice Not an Echo, A (Schlafy), 218
Chomsky, Noam, 93
Church, Frank, 18
Citizens' Party, 79
City of New York v. Miln (1837), 119
Civilian Conservation Corps, 117
civil rights, 27–29, 39, 42, 54–57, 64, 94, 104, 139, 159, 165–68, 177, 236; and Republican Party (1945–72), 182–97
Civil Rights Act (1957), 165
Civil Rights Act (1964), 181, 197, 236; Title VII, 205–6, 238
Clayton, Bruce, 167
Clement, Frank, 169, 171
Clifford, Clark, 160
Clinton, Bill, 106, 234, 235, 243
Clinton, Hillary, 76, 106
Coalition for a Democratic Majority (CDM), 105
Cold War, 91, 95, 139, 181, 184, 192, 217, 236
Collins, John, 141
Colmer, William, 188
Columbia Homelessness Project, 123–24
Commission on Law Enforcement and Administration of Justice, 120
Committee Against the NAM Merger, 80
Committee on the Present Danger, 105
Communist Control Act (1954), 30, 95
community development corporations, 146
Congressional Black Caucus, 105, 211
Consumer's Republic, A (Cohen), 136
Conyers, John, 75
Coolidge, Calvin, 229
Cooper, Prentice, 165
Cranston, Alan, 46, 51
Crockett, Hudley, 171
Cuba, 98

Daley, Richard, 101, 104
Daniels, Jonathan, 161
Daughtrey, Larry, 174
Davis, Caroline, 206
Death and Life of Great American Cities (Jacobs), 149
Debs, Eugene, 64
DeCrow, Karen, 217

INDEX · 255

Democracy '76 and Democratic Agenda, 67–76
Democratic Farmer-Labor Party, 74, 93, 99
Democratic Left (journal), 67
Democratic National Committee, 105
Democratic Party: Californian DP after WWII, 38–61; Chicago convention (1968), 101, 168; relationship with socialists in 1970s, 62–89
Democratic Socialist Organizing Committee (DSOC), 63–80
Democratic Socialists of America, 80
Dent, Harry, 172
Dewey, John, 17
Dillon, Douglas, 164
Dirksen, Everett, 175, 186, 187, 193, 194, 233
Dissent (journal), 236
District of Columbia v. Hunt (1947), 119
Douglas, Helen, 51
Douglas, Paul, 29, 160, 163
Driver v. Hinnant (1965), 120
Dunlop, John, 235
Dunn, Winfield, 161, 170

Easter v. District of Columbia (1966), 120
Education of a Public Man, The (Humphrey), 92
Ehrlichman, John, 196
Eisenhower, Dwight D., 95, 139, 163; and voting rights, 190–92
Eizenstat, Stuart E., 76
Ellington, Buford, 169, 171, 172
Employee Free Choice Act, 230–31, 243
Environmentalists for Full Employment, 68, 73
Equal Employment Opportunity Commission (EEOC), 182–89, 206
Equal Opportunity Act (1972), 188–89
Equal Pay Act (1963), 205, 210
Equal Rights Amendment, 175, 204, 206, 207, 209, 218–20
Ervin, Sam, 188, 193, 195
Evins, Eddie, 171
Evins, Joe, 171

Fabian Society, 21
Fair Employment Practices Commission (FEPC), 183, 186
Fair Labor Standards Act (1938) (FLSA), 203, 205, 210, 211

Farewell to Reform (Chamberlain), 25
Farmer-Labor Political Federation, 27
Fascell, Dante, 167
Federal Transient Program (FTP), 116, 129
Feminine Mystique, The (Friedan), 206
feminism, second-wave, policy goals and activism sustaining and redefining liberalism and New Deal order post-WWII, 202–21
Fenster v. Leary (1967), 119
Ferris, Norman, 174
Feuer, Lewis, 30
Fifteenth Amendment, 193
Finley, Murray H., 73, 78, 216
First Amendment, 23
Food for Peace, 94
Ford, Gerald, 194, 195
Ford, Henry, 238
Foster, William Z., 24
Fourteenth Amendment, 120
Fowler, Henry, 164
Fraser, Don, 75, 76
Fraser, Douglas, 65, 70, 76–77, 81
Freedom Is Not Enough: The Opening of the American Workplace (MacLean), 238
Freeman, Joseph, 17
Fried, Joseph, 145
Friedan, Betty, 206, 211
Friedman, Milton, 68
Friedman, Thomas, 237
Fryner, Paul, 238
Fulbright, J. William, 172
Full Employment Action Council, 216
Future of Liberalism, The (Wolfe), 135

Galbraith, John Kenneth, 151, 164
Gideon v. Wainwright (1963), 119
Gigante, Louis, 146
Gingrich, Newt, 18
Ginsburg, Ruth Bader, 18
Gitlin, Todd, 31
Gold Dust Shelter, 117
Goldwater, Barry, 166, 169, 186, 193, 197, 218, 232
Gompers, Samuel, 26
Gordon, Bart, 171
Gore, Pauline, 167
Gore Sr., Albert: defeat in 1970, 168–76; Great Society Liberalism, 161–65; liberal-

ism and the South in 1960s, 159–80; and race, 165–68
Graham, Gene, 174, 176
Graham, Phil, 164
Grapes of Wrath, The (Steinbeck), 116
Grassroots (McGovern autobiography), 92
Great Depression, 24–25, 236
Green, Edith, 204, 207, 210, 215–16
Griffiths, Martha, 202–10, 218
Guggenheim, Charles, 160, 174

Haener, Dorothy, 206–7, 211
Haggerty, C. J., 45
Halbertson, David, 168, 176
Hannity, Sean, 18
Harriman, Averell, 160
Harrington, Michael, 62, 64, 65, 66, 68, 78, 80, 81, 233, 234
Harris, LaDonna, 217
Hart, Gary, 106
Hartford House, 117
Hawkes, Albert, 184
Hayden, Tom, 31, 78
Haynsworth, Clement, 160, 168, 196
health care, 107; Clinton reform, 235; Obama reform, 243
health insurance, 38, 42, 70, 75, 81, 161, 164, 174
Hedgeman, Anna Arnold, 206
Hernandez, Aileen, 206
Hill, Lister, 163, 164
Hobhouse, L. T., 21
Hobson, J. A., 21
Hoffa, Jimmy, 232
Holtzman, Elizabeth, 210
homelessness, policy and programs in NY during Roosevelt and Johnson administrations: background, 113–14; early welfare systems and homelessness, 114–19; midcentury liberal urban policies, 119–30
Hooker, John Jay, 169, 170, 175
House Un-American Activities Committee, 49
Howe, Frederic, 21
Howe, Irving, 65
Howser, Fred, 44
Hull, Cordell, 162
Hull House (settlement house), 22
Humphrey, Hubert, 28, 30, 64, 68, 81, 163, 167, 169, 181; relationship with George McGovern, 90–107

Humphrey-Hawkins (HR50), 68, 69, 72, 75, 76, 81, 105, 217
Hunt Commission, 80
Hurricane Katrina, 136–37

Independent Citizens' Committee of the Arts, Sciences, and Professions (ICCASP), 44
Industrial Workers of the World (IWW), 23
Ingraham, Laura, 18
Inouye, Daniel, 160
Intelligent Women's Guide to Conservatism, The (Kirk), 217
International Association of Machinists (IAM), 70, 73, 160
International Brotherhood of Teamsters (IBT), 160, 242
International Ladies' Garment Workers' Union, 211
International Union of Electrical Workers, 214
International Women's Year (1975), 213
Interstate Highway Act (1956), 162

Jackson, Henry, 64, 102
Jackson, Jesse, 80
Jackson, Scoop, 104, 106
Jacobs, Jane, 138, 148–50
Javits, Jacob, 187, 188, 192, 194
Jellinek, Elvin, 120
Jobs Corps, 207, 208
Johnson, Hiram, 41–42, 47
Johnson, Lyndon B., 94, 98, 102, 114, 145, 169, 170, 181, 187, 192, 233, 244; "war on poverty," 122–25, 207
Johnson, Philip, 144
John Wanamaker of Philadelphia, 138
Joint Committee on National Recovery, 28
Jordan, Barbara, 211
Jordan, Ruth, 73
Jordan, Vernon, 75

Kampelman, Max, 98, 105
Keating, Kenneth, 192
Kefauver, Estes, 52, 54, 167, 169, 173
Kelley, Florence, 17, 22
Kennedy, Anthony, 18
Kennedy, Edward M., 74, 77, 78–80, 81, 160, 161, 194
Kennedy, John F., 94, 97, 100, 160, 166, 185, 192, 204

INDEX · 257

Kennedy, Robert F., 205
Kenny, Robert, 44, 100
Kent, Roger, 46–47, 55
Kerr, Robert, 163
Kerry, John, 18
King, Coretta Scott, 216
King, Martin Luther, 144, 168, 192
Kirk, Russell, 217
Kirkpatrick, Evron, 92
Kirkpatrick, Jeane, 92
Knowland, Joseph, 43
Knowland, William, 43
Koch, Ed, 66, 146
Korean War, 167
Kraft, Tim, 75
Kroll, Jack, 231
Ku Klux Klan, 27
Kuykendall, Dan, 166

labor-liberal politics in the post-New Deal era, 229–45
LaFollette, Robert, 25
LaFon, Whit, 167
League for Independent Political Action, 26–27
League of Women Voters, 207, 217
Lee, Richard, 139
left-liberal tradition in U.S. politics: feminism, 32; influence of trade-union movement, 25–27; influence of WWI, Bolshevik Revolution, and Great Depression, 24–25; interpretation by New Left historians, 19–20; labor-liberal politics in the post-New Deal era, 229–45; liberalism seen as Trojan horse for revolutionary beliefs, or as utterly incompatible with left-wing radicalism, 19; McCarthyism, 18, 30; network of contacts between reformers and radicals, 24; New Left, 30–32; new liberalism and Fabianism, 20–21; Popular Front (1935–48), 26, 28, 29–30; race and civil rights, 27–29; shared belief in transformative social change, 17–23, 25–26; shared political culture, 23–25; use of 'left' and 'liberal' as synonyms, 18–19; Vietnam War, 18, 32
Lehman, Herbert, 163
Lenin, Vladimir, 25
Lerner, Max, 27
liberalism, sustained and redefined post-WWII by mainstream second-wave feminism, 202–21

Lilienthal, David, 161
Lindsay, John, 125, 144
Link, Arthur, 92
Lloyd, Henry Demarest, 21
Logan, Rayford, 28
Logue, Edward J., 138–52
Long, Russell, 163
Looby, Z. Alexander, 167
Lovre, Harold, 96
Lowenstein, Allard, 100

MacLean, Nancy, 238
Manhattan Bowery Project, 126–28
March on Washington Movement, 183
Martin, John Bartlow, 55
McCarthy, Eugene, 100, 101, 163
McCarthy, Joseph, 30
McCarthyism, 95, 239
McClellan Committee hearings (1957 and 1958), 232
McCulloch, William, 185, 194, 195
McDonough, Patrick, 43
McDowell, Mary, 21
McGovern, Eleanor, 96
McGovern, George, 56, 65, 168; relationship with Hubert Humphrey, 90–107
McGovern-Fraser Commission, 69
McGrath, George F., 125
McKeithen, John, 169
McKellar, Kenneth D., 161, 165
McLain, George, 41
McNamara, Robert, 208
Meany, George, 77, 103, 104, 233
Medicare, 161, 164, 174
Melman, Seymour, 95
Merritt, Gill, 170
Mid-Bronx Desperadoes Community Housing Corporation, 146, 147
Miller Jr., George, 46
Millikin, Eugene, 184
Mills, Wilbur, 164
Mink, Patsy Takemoto, 204, 207, 210
Miranda v. Arizona (1966), 119
Mitchell, John, 143, 194
Mondale, Walter, 80
Monroney, Mike, 163, 169
Moore, Dan, 169
Moral Majority, 66, 78
Moreland Act Commission, 145
Morse, Wayne, 190
Moses, Robert, 121

258 · INDEX

Mother Jones (journal), 18
Moynihan, Daniel Patrick, 18
Muni, the (NYC), 125
Muskie, Edmund, 102
Myrdal, Gunnar, 28–29

Nash, George and Patricia, 126
Nation (journal), 18
National Advisory Committee for Women (NACW), 215
National Association for the Advancement of Colored People (NAACP), 27, 70, 167, 182, 185, 186, 189, 196
National Call for Kennedy, 79
National Committee to Abolish the Poll Tax, 189
National Council for Public-Private Partnerships, 151
National Federation of Business and Professional Women, 211
National Labor Relations Board, 183
National Negro Congress, 28
National Organization for Women (NOW), 70, 204, 206, 216–17
National Right-to-Work Committee, 239
National Welfare Rights Organization (NWRO), 66
National Women's Conference (Houston, 1977), 213–14
National Women's Political Caucus, 211
Nazi-Soviet Pact (1939), 29
New American Movement, 80
New Deal, 25–26, 29, 39, 52–53, 91, 92, 113–14, 118, 135–37, 159, 163, 184; and post-WWII labor relations, 230–31; sustained and redefined post-WWII by mainstream second-wave feminism, 202–21
New Haven, urban renewal, 139–41
New Left, 30–31
new liberalism, 20–21
New Republic (journal), 23, 38, 43
New Right, 40, 159, 218, 220
New York, urban renewal, 143–48
New York Charities Directory, 115
New York State Urban Development Corporation (UDC), 143
Niebuhr, Reinhold, 237
Nixon, Richard M., 102, 103, 143, 145, 182, 188, 192, 195, 211, 218; 'Southern Strategy,' 159, 160, 171–73, 176–77

Norris-LaGuardia, 238
North American Free Trade Agreement, 235
Novak, Robert, 159

Obama, Barack, 80, 106, 135–36, 151–52, 229; 2009 stimulus package, 242
Oberdorfer, Don, 165
O'Connor, Sandra, 18
Odegard, Peter, 55
Office for Emergency Planning, 169
Office of Economic Opportunity, 124
Office of Strategic Services, 92
O'Gara, Gerald, 53
Oglesby, Carl, 31
Olson, Culbert, 41
Open Housing Act (1968), 168
Orshansky, Mollie, 122
Outland, George, 41

Packwood, Robert, 188
Palisades Interstate Park, 117
Panama Canal, 235
Panek, Nathalie, 50
Patterson, Ellis, 44
Philadelphia Redevelopment Authority, 122
Phillips, Maxine, 65
Phyllis Schlafy Report, The, 218
Pinchot, Amos, 21
Pollack, Sheldon, 49, 50
poll tax, 189
Popular Front (1935–48), 26, 28, 29–30, 40, 50–51
Powell v. Texas (1968), 120
Pregnancy Discrimination Act (1978), 214
President's Advisory Committee for Women, 216
Professional Air Traffic Controllers Organization, 234
Progressive Citizens of America, 43
Progressive Party, 1948 convention, 94
Proposition 2.5 (Massachusetts), 69, 81
Public (journal), 24
public-private development partnerships, 121, 151

Raglan, Martha, 177
Randolph, A. Philip, 183
Reagan, Ronald, 63, 79, 80, 146, 148, 159, 220, 234

INDEX · 259

Reason (journal), 149
Reconstruction Finance Corporation, 164
Reece, B. Carroll, 172
Rehnquist, William, 214
Reider, Saul, 51
Reitz, Ken, 173, 175
Religion and Socialism Commission, 66
Republican Party and civil rights (1945–72), 182–97
Reuther, Walter, 54, 232
Richards, Richard, 55
right-to-work movement, 239–40
Robb, Linda Johnson, 216
Robinson v. California (1962), 120
Roche, John, 29
Rockefeller, Nelson, 143
Rodgers, Daniel, 21
Roosevelt, Franklin D., 20, 114, 116, 140, 162, 183
Roosevelt, Jimmy, 51
Roosevelt, Theodore, 20
Roosevelt Island, 144–45
Russell, Richard, 166, 182

Sanders, Randy, 176
Sandler, Bernice, 211
Sasser, James, 169
Savage, Michael, 19
Schechter, Hope Mendoza, 44–45
Schlafy, Phyllis, 218–20
Schlesinger Jr., Arthur, 64–65
Schroeder, Patricia, 211
Scopes, John T., 176
Scott, Bob, 169
Scott, Hugh, 195
Scott, James, 150
Seabury, Paul, 50
Seigenthaler, John, 167, 169
settlement houses, 21, 22
Shriver, Sargent, 208
Sinclair, Upton, 41
Slouching towards Gomorrah (Bork), 19
Smith, Al, 175
Smith, Frank, 161
Smith, Howard, 205
Social Democrats USA, 64, 65, 73, 74, 78
social insurance, 118
Socialist Party, 64
Socialist Party USA, 64, 65
socialists and the Democratic Party in the 1970s: Carter administration and the National Call for Kennedy, 72–80; demise of DSOC, 80–82; enlargement of the Democratic coalition, Democracy '76, and Democratic Agenda, 67–76; origins of Democratic Socialist Organizing Committee, 63–67
Social Security Act, gender bias, 203
social security programs, gender bias, 209–21
Sorkin, Martin, 98
South Bronx Development Organization (SBDO), 146
South East Bronx Community Development Corporation, 146
Southern Manifesto, 165, 166
Spargo, John, 20
Sparkman, John J., 163, 164
Stavrianos, Lefton "Lefty," 92
Steel, Ronald, 93
Steffens, Lincoln, 25
Steinbeck, John, 116
Steinem, Gloria, 216, 217
Stern Jr., Thad, 161
Stevenson, Adlai, 51–56, 159
STOP ERA, 218
Strauss, Robert, 105
Students for a Democratic Society (SDS), 30–31
St. Vincent's Hospital (NYC), 125

Taft-Hartley Act, 233, 239
Tanner, John, 171
Tax Justice (pressure group), 70
Tehran hostage-taking (1979), 79
Temporary Emergency Relief Administration (TERA), 117
Tennessee Valley Authority (TVA), 162, 163, 173
Thabit, Walter, 122
Thomas, Norman, 29
Thurmond, Strom, 172, 196
Timmons, Bill, 173
Tower, John, 169
Townsend, Francis, 41
trade unions, labor-liberal politics in the post–New Deal era, 229–45
Treleavan, Harry, 173, 174
Truman, Harry S., 28, 29, 44, 93, 102, 140, 190
Trumka, Richard, 229

Udall, Stewart, 46
United Auto Workers (UAW), 65, 70, 73, 76, 160, 211, 233, 241
United Electrical, Radio and Machine Workers of America (UE), 160, 206
UNITE-HERE, 241
Unruh, Jesse, 47
Urban League, 70
urban renewal: liberal policy and practice in the postwar era, 135–52; NY projects, 119–24

vagrancy, 119–30
Vera Institute of Justice, 125
Veterans Administration, 118
Vietnam War, 64, 90–93, 95, 97, 98, 100, 159, 167, 171, 176
Voorhis, Jerry, 41, 47
voting rights, 189–97
Voting Rights Act (1965), 160, 167, 181–82, 194–96

Wagner, Robert, 124
Wagner Act (1935), 27, 238
Walker, Scott, 243
Wallace, George, 102, 169, 171, 176, 182
Wallace, Henry, 28, 29, 93
Warren, Earl, 41–42, 45
Warschaw, Carmen, 47
Watson, Albert, 176
Wattenberg, Ben, 64, 105
Webb, Sidney and Beatrice, 21
Welch, Richard, 41

welfare state, 38, 73
West, John, 176
Weyl, Walter, 23
White, John, 75
White, Walter, 190
White, William Allen, 20
White House Office of Urban Affairs, 135
Wilkins, Ray, 183
Williams, William Appleton, 93
Wilson, Edmund, 17
Wilson, James Q., 47
Wilson, Woodrow, 25, 26
Winning the Future (Gingrich), 18
Winpisinger, William, 70, 81
Wolfe, Alan, 135
Women's Equity Action League (WEAL), 211
Woodhouse, Chase Going, 56
Woodward, C. Vann, 176
Works Progress Administration, 118
World War I, 24
World War II, 183, 231
Wright, Jim, 167
Wurth, Jerry, 70, 81

Yarborough, Ralph, 172
Yeager Jr., Wirt, 194, 195
Yorty, Sam, 48
Young, Coleman, 76

Zetterberg, Steve, 47, 48
Ziffren, Paul, 55

The University of Illinois Press
is a founding member of the
Association of American University Presses.

University of Illinois Press
1325 South Oak Street
Champaign, IL 61820-6903
www.press.uillinois.edu